HOME ECONOMICS REVISION
FOR LEAVING CERTIFICATE

HOME ECONOMICS REVISION FOR LEAVING CERTIFICATE

MARY ANNE HALTON

GILL & MACMILLAN

Gill & Macmillan Ltd
Hume Avenue
Park West
Dublin 12
with associated companies throughout the world
www.gillmacmillan.ie

0 7171 3507 1

Print origination in Ireland by Carrigboy Typesetting Services, Co. Cork

The paper used in this book is made from the wood pulp of managed forests. For every tree felled, at least one tree is planted, thereby renewing natural resources.

Contents

FOOD CHOICES

People decide what to eat, when to eat and how to eat, based on a variety of behavioural, social and nutritional awareness factors. Such factors include:

- Age, gender and genetic makeup
- Health status (age, special dietary needs)
- Availability and convenience (types of shops)
- Financial resources (family income, freedom of choice)
- Cultural beliefs and traditions
- Eating patterns and lifestyle (working/school day)
- Personal beliefs or values (religious, environmental)
- Personal preferences (likes and dislikes)
- Advertising and marketing (creating needs and wants)
- Nutritional awareness (making informed choices)
- Food presentation (preparation, cooking and serving)
- Sensory aspects (perception of colour, taste, texture and smell)

PROTEIN

ELEMENTAL COMPOSITION

Protein consists of carbon (C), hydrogen (H), oxygen (O) and nitrogen (N). These combine together to form amino acids.

Basic structure of amino acids
- Made up of carbon, hydrogen, oxygen and nitrogen
- Some contain other elements e.g. sulphur (S), iron (Fe), phosphorus (P)

Basic amino acid

$$\text{(amino group) } NH_2 - \underset{\underset{\text{R (variable)}}{|}}{\overset{\overset{\text{H (hydrogen)}}{|}}{C}} - COOH \text{ (acidic carboxyl group)}$$

Cysteine showing the R (variable) group

$$HSCH_2 - \overset{\overset{\displaystyle H}{|}}{\underset{\underset{\displaystyle NH_2}{|}}{C}} - COOH \quad \text{(carboxyl group)}$$

(amino group)

Essential and non-essential amino acids

The twenty common amino acids are classified as essential and non-essential, eight for adults, ten for children.

Table 1.1 Essential and non-essential amino acids

Essential amino acids	Non-essential amino acids
■ Cannot be made by the body ■ Must be supplied by the diet	■ Can be made by the body ■ Do not need to be supplied by the diet
Isoleucine, leucine, lycine, methionine, phenylanine, threonine, tryptophan, valine *For children:* histidine, arginine	Alanine, asparagine, aspartic acid, cysteine, glutamic acid, glutamine, glycine, proline, serine, tyrosine

Peptides and peptide bonds

Amino acids are linked, end-to-end, by a peptide bond. A carboxyl group (COOH) of one amino acid combines with an amino group (NH_2) of the next amino acid. A molecule of water (H_2O) is released (condensation) during this process.

Figure 1.1 A peptide bond/link

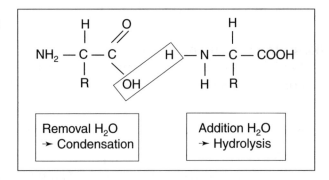

Hydrolysis

During digestion the reverse of the condensation process happens. The peptide bonds are broken by the addition of water molecules producing single amino acids. This is called hydrolysis.

Note: Two amino acids joined together by a peptide bond form a dipeptide, by adding a third amino acid a tripeptide is formed. Ten or more amino acids linked together are called a polypeptide chain.

STRUCTURE OF PROTEIN

The structure of protein can be described in three ways.
1. *Primary structure*: this is the sequence of amino acids in polypeptide chains.

Figure 1.2 Simple polypeptide chain – primary structure

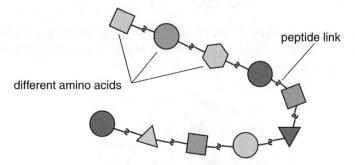

-Ala-Ser-Val-Tyr-Gly-Val-Ser-Cys-Ile-Ala-Val-Ser-

2. *Secondary structure*: this is the coiling or folding of polypeptide chains, which are held together by bonds to form a definite shape. Cross-links are formed by disulphide links or hydrogen bonds.

Figure 1.3 Secondary structure

(a) Disulphide link or bridge

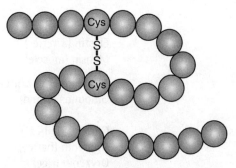

Gly-Ile-Val-Cys-Glu-Gin-Ala-Ser-Leu-Asp-Arg-Cys-Val-Pro-

S ◄── disulphide bridge ──► S

(b) Hydrogen bond

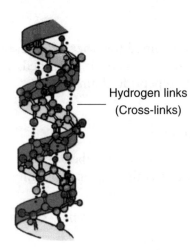

Hydrogen links
(Cross-links)

3. *Tertiary structure*: this refers to the pattern of folding polypeptide chains into a three-dimensional shape. Shapes are held in place by cross-links and may be fibrous (coiled or zigzag) or globular (ball shaped).

Figure 1.4 Tertiary structure

CLASSIFICATION

Simple proteins: consist of combined amino acids
Conjugated proteins: contain amino acids and a non-protein component

Table 1.2 Simple proteins (types, examples and sources)

Type	Examples	Sources
Animal	(a) Fibrous	Collagen (connective tissue) Elastin (arteries) Myosin (muscle)
	(b) Globular	Albumin (egg-white) Globulins (blood)
Plant	(a) Glutelins	Glutenin (wheat) Hordenin (barley) Oryzenin (rice)
	(b) Prolamines	Gliadin (wheat) Zein (maize)

Table 1.3 Conjugated proteins (types, examples and sources)

Type	Examples
Chromoproteins	Haemoglobin (blood)
Glycoproteins	Enzymes, hormones, mucin (egg-white)
Lipoproteins	Blood plasma lipoproteins
Nucleoproteins	DNA with protamines, RNA with ribosomes
Phosphoproteins	Casein (milk)

SOURCE

Table 1.4 Sources of protein

High biological value protein (HBV) Mainly animal	Low biological value protein (LBV) Mainly plant
Cheese, eggs, fish, meat, soya beans	Cereals, pasta, potatoes, pulses, gelatin

Properties of protein
- Denatured by agitation, chemicals, heat or enzymes
- Coagulated by heat and enzymes
- Insoluble in water (exceptions are collagen in warm water and egg white in cold water)
- Forms a foam e.g. whisking egg white, forms air bubbles in the white
- Forms a gel: a gel is a semi-solid viscous solution with a three dimensional network in which molecules of water can become trapped e.g. collagen is converted into gelatine, a soluble protein
- Dry heat causes the Maillard reaction between amino acids and carbohydrates e.g. during baking, grilling and roasting

FUNCTIONS

Structural
- For the development of cells, muscles and skin

Physiological
- Production of enzymes, hormones, blood proteins and nucleoproteins

Nutrient
- Supplies all essential amino acids
- Provides energy (deamination)

Biological value (BV)

The value of the quality of a protein is determined by how many essential amino acids it contains in proportion to the body's requirements. HBV proteins contain all essential amino acids. LBV proteins are lacking in one or more essential amino acids. There are two exceptions, soya beans (HBV) and gelatine (LBV).

Complementation (complementary or supplementary proteins)

If a protein is deficient in one amino acid the deficiency can be overcome by eating a food rich in that amino acid at the same meal e.g. beans on toast.

Energy value

Contribution to total energy value of average diet: 1 gram (g) of protein is required for each 1 kiloogram (kg) of body weight. Children, teenagers and pregnant women have higher protein needs than other groups. One-third of protein intake should be of high biological value.

Role of protein as a supplementary energy source: 1 g of protein provides 4 kCal (17 kJ) of energy. Protein not required for growth and repair may be converted into energy and when other energy sources are inadequate.

Deamination

Excess amino acids are deaminated in the liver. This happens when:
- The amino group (NH_2) is removed from the amino acids, converted into ammonia, then urea and excreted from the body through the kidneys.
- The carboxyl group (COOH) is converted into glucose and used for heat and energy. Excess is stored in the body as glycogen (an energy source).

DIGESTION AND ABSORPTION

Hydrolysis and digestion of protein

Proteins are hydrolysed during digestion to produce amino acids. Food is mixed with saliva and chewed. In the stomach proteins are denatured and broken down into peptones by the action of pepsin. In the small intestine trypsin (enzyme) continues the hydrolysis of proteins. Peptidase completes the digestion of protein to amino acids.

Absorption of amino acids

Amino acids are absorbed by the blood vessels in the villi of the small intestine and transported to the liver via the hepatic portal vein. Amino acids not used by the body are deaminated in the liver.

Utilisation of amino acids

Amino acids are used to repair liver cells, to form new cells, to repair damaged tissues and to make antibodies, enzymes and hormones.

CARBOHYDRATES

PHOTOSYNTHESIS – THE FORMATION OF CARBOHYDRATES IN PLANTS

- Leaves absorb carbon dioxide from the air
- Roots absorb water from the soil
- Chlorophyll in the leaves converts sunlight into energy
- Glucose and oxygen are produced
- Excess glucose is converted into cellulose or starch

Photosynthesis can be represented as follows:

$$6CO_2 \quad + \quad 6H_2O \quad + \text{sunlight} \longrightarrow C_6H_{12}O_6 + 6O_2$$

| carbon dioxide
— from air | water —
from soil | energy | glucose | oxygen |

ELEMENTAL COMPOSITION AND STRUCTURE

Carbohydrates consists of carbon (C), hydrogen (H) and oxygen (O), present in the ratio 1:2:1.

Classification, composition, structure and sources
Classification: monosaccharides, disaccharides and polysaccharides

Monosaccharides
- $C_6H_{12}O_6$
- Simple, single sugar unit
- Single ring structure (glucose)

Table 1.5 Examples of monosaccharides

Examples	Sources
Glucose	Fruit
Fructose	Honey and fruit
Galactose	Milk

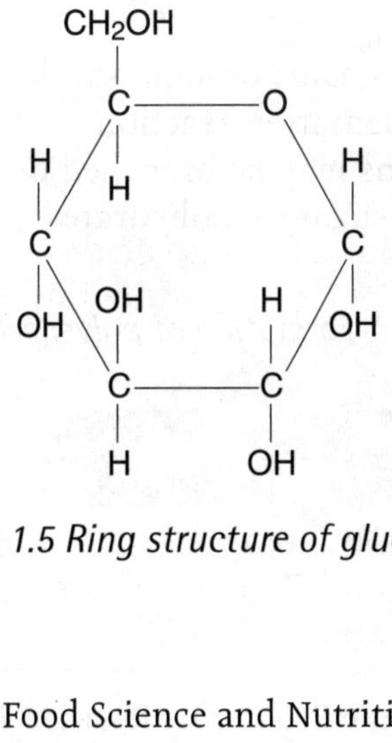

Figure 1.5 Ring structure of glucose

Disaccharides

- $C_{12}H_{22}O_{11}$
- Pairs of monosaccharides joined together
- Condensation reaction (removal of a molecule of water)

$$C_6H_{12}O_6 \; + \; C_6H_{12}O_6 \; = \; C_{12}H_{24}O_{12} \; - \; H_2O \; = \; C_{12}H_{22}O_{11} \; + \; H_2O$$

condensation

Figure 1.6 Formation of a disaccharide

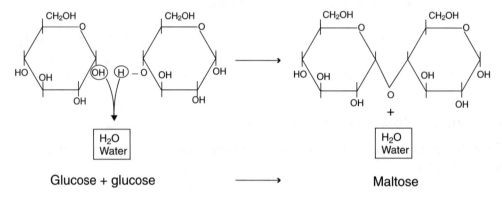

Glucose + glucose   ⟶   Maltose

Table 1.6 Examples of disaccharides

Examples	Composition	Sources
Maltose	Glucose + glucose	Barley, fermentation process
Sucrose	Glucose + fructose	Table sugar
Lactose	Glucose + galactose	Milk (known as milk sugar)

Polysaccharides – complex carbohydrates

- $(C_6H_{10}O_5)_n$
- Long chains of monosaccharides linked together
- Condensation reaction
- Chains may be branched or straight
- Non-sugar carbohydrates

Figure 1.7 Formation of polysaccharides

Table 1.7 Examples of polysaccharides

Examples	Sources
Fibres (NSP)	Outer skins of fruit and vegetables
Glycogen	Animal starch (highly branched chains)
Pectin (NSP)	Fruits
Starch	Cereals, root vegetables, potatoes, two types – amylose (linear chains) and amylopectin (branched chains)

Non-starch polysaccharide (NSP or dietary fibre)
- Soluble fibres (gums, pectins): barley, fruits, oats, legumes
- Insoluble fibres (cellulose, lignins): bran, vegetables, wholegrains

PROPERTIES OF CARBOHYDRATES

Sugars
- Sweet, crystalline solids, soluble in water
- In the presence of water and under slightly acidic conditions sugars split into monosaccharides (invert sugar) e.g. jam-making
- Hydrolysis of sugars also occurs during digestion
- Act as 'reducing agents' by removing oxygen from other substances
- Maillard reaction occurs when sugars and proteins react under heat
- Dissolve in moist heat and form a syrupy liquid, eventually caramelise
- Dry heat causes caramelisation
- Excess sugar, added to a liquid already saturated with sugar, forms crystals on cooling (crystallisation)

Starch
- White, non-crystalline powder
- Insoluble in cold water, starches are hygroscopic e.g. absorb moisture

Gelatinisation
Moist heat causes starch to swell, burst, absorb moisture and thicken liquids e.g. sauce. Gelatinisation happens in stages. Liquid is heated to initial gelatinisation temperatures of 55–70°C and is then absorbed by starch granules e.g. in flour. The starch granules swell and join together to form a sticky paste. On cooking hydrogen bonds form and a gel-like mixture results

Dextrinisation
Dry heat turns starch grains brown and forms short polysaccharide chains called dextrins e.g. toasted bread

Non-starch polysaccharides
Pectin
Gel formation: on boiling the long polysaccharide chains form a network, which on cooling form a gel e.g. jam-making
Pectin extraction: protopectin in under-ripe fruit and vegetables cannot form a gel. It is converted into pectin using an acid or alkali. Pectin forms a gel

Cellulose
- Indigestible complex carbohydrate
- Insoluble in water, absorbs water creating bulk in the diet

BIOLOGICAL FUNCTIONS
Sugars
- Source of heat and energy
- Excess is converted into fat, stored as adipose tissue
- Converted into glycogen, stored in liver and muscles
- Provides insulation in the body
- Act as 'protein sparers'

Starch
- Source of heat and energy
- Excess converted into glycogen and fat

Cellulose (NSP or dietary fibre)
- Provides fibre in the diet, encourages peristalsis
- Prevents constipation and bowel diseases, speeds up waste removal
- Produces a feeling of fullness, prevents over-eating
- Delays absorption of glucose
- Lowers blood cholesterol

CULINARY FUNCTIONS
Sugar
- Acts as a preservative, prevents microbial growth
- Acts as a sweetener in cakes, dessert, drinks and puddings
- Used as a main ingredient and to add colour to foods
- Prevents curdling by raising the coagulation temperature
- Activates yeast, speeds up fermentation when baking bread
- Strengthens whisked egg white proteins (holds air more easily)

Starch
- Thickens gravies, sauce and soups (gelatinisation)
- Extends the shelf-life of cakes (absorbs moisture)

Pectin
- Pectin with sugar and acid forms a gel
- Used as a thickening agent in prepared foods

Energy value
- 1 g carbohydrate = 17 kJ energy

Dietary targets for NSP intake
NSP intake should be approximately 25–35 g per day, drawn from a variety of grains, fruits, legumes and vegetables.

Achieving the targets – increasing fibre in the diet
Replace processed cereals with wholegrain varieties. Eat high-fibre cereals e.g. porridge. Eat whole fruits occasionally rather than juice. Use whole-wheat flour for bread and cakes etc. Eat fruits and vegetables raw with the skins on if possible.

DIGESTION AND ABSORPTION

Digestion
In the mouth salivary amylase (enzyme) breaks down some starch to dextrin and maltose. This process continues in the oesophagus and in the stomach until stopped by gastric juices. In the small intestine pancreatic amylase converts the remaining starch to maltose. Enzymes in the small intestine break down the disaccharides into monosaccharides. Maltase converts maltose to glucose. Lactase converts lactose to glucose and galactose. Sucrase converts sucrose to glucose and fructose.

Absorption
Digested carbohydrates are absorbed through the blood capillaries of the villi of the small intestine. Monosaccharides are transported to the liver by the portal vein where enzymes convert them to glucose.

Utilisation of glucose
From the liver glucose in passed into the bloodstream and is converted to heat and energy. Glucose may be converted into glycogen (energy reserve). When glycogen stores are full in the liver excess glucose is converted to, and stored as, adipose tissue under the skin.

LIPIDS

The *elemental composition* of lipids consists of carbon (C), hydrogen (H) and oxygen (O).

Chemical composition and molecular structure of a triclyceride

Glycerol is a trihydric alcohol with three OH groups. Triglycerides are formed when *one* molecule of glycerol combines with *three* fatty acids. A bond is formed when a series of three condensation reactions (elimination of water) occurs between each OH group of the glycerol and each COOH of the fatty acids. A hydrogen atom (H) from the glycerol combines with an OH from the COOH of the fatty acid and a molecule of water (H_2O) is released.

Figure 1.8 Formation of triglyceride

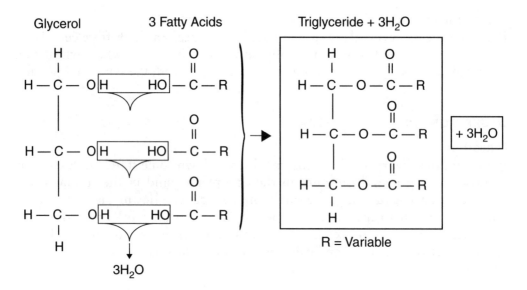

CLASSIFICATION OF FATTY ACIDS

Fatty acids can be grouped according to their degree of saturation with hydrogen atoms and the type of bonds that form between the carbon atoms.

Saturated fatty acids
- Saturated with hydrogen atoms
- No double bonds, carbons linked by single bonds
- Hard (solid) at room temperature
- Do not combine readily with oxygen
- High in cholesterol

$$
\begin{array}{ccccc}
\text{H} & \text{H} & \text{H} & \text{H} & \text{O} \\
| & | & | & | & \| \\
\text{H}-\text{C}-\text{C}-\text{C}-\text{C}-\text{C}-\text{OH} \\
| & | & | & | \\
\text{H} & \text{H} & \text{H} & \text{H}
\end{array}
$$

Saturated fatty acids: $CH_3(CH_2)_nCOOH$

Sources: dairy produce, egg yolk, meat, meat fats, some hard margarines
Examples: stearic acid (meat), butyric acid (butter)

Unsaturated fatty acids (monounsaturated and polyunsaturated)
- Not saturated with hydrogen atoms, (bonds are incomplete)
- One or more double bonds between carbon atoms
- Liquid at room temperature, prone to oxadative rancidity
- Low in cholesterol

Monounsaturates (one double bond)
Example: Oleic acid (olive oil)

Polyunsaturates (two or more double bonds)
Example: linoleic, linolenic, arachidonic (not found in plants)

Methyl end (CH₃)   Carboxyl end (COOH)

Monounsaturated fatty acid with *one* double bond (Oleic acid)

Cis and trans fatty acids
Cis fatty acids
The hydrogen atoms surrounding a double bond are located on the same side of the carbon chain.
Sources: foods with some fat or oil

$$
\begin{array}{cccc}
\text{H} & \text{H} & \text{H} & \text{H} \\
| & | & | & | \\
-\text{C}-\text{C} = \text{C}-\text{C}- \\
| & & & | \\
\text{H} & & & \text{H}
\end{array}
$$

Trans fatty acids
The hydrogen atoms of trans fatty acids are located on opposite sides of the carbon chain.
Sources: hydrogenated fats, and cis changing to trans in fried foods, crisps, snack foods and processed foods

$$
\begin{array}{ccccc}
H & H & & H & \\
| & | & & | & \\
-C - & C & = & C - & C- \\
| & & & | & | \\
H & & & H & H \\
\end{array}
$$

Significance of trans fatty acids in the diet
Trans fatty acids may be involved in the increase in CHD. They raise levels of total cholesterol and LDL (bad cholesterol) in the body. This increases the risk of heart disease. High levels of trans fatty acids may decrease levels of HDL (good cholesterol).

Essential fatty acids
The food we eat must supply the fatty acids that the body cannot make. Linoleic, linolenic and arachidonic acids are essential for building cells. It is thought that essential fatty acids may reduce CHD by counteracting the effects of cholesterol on the arteries.

Omega-3 fatty acids
These polyunsaturated fatty acids, found in oily fish, lower blood fat levels, reducing the risk of blood clots and CHD.
Sources: salmon, fresh water trout, mackerel, tuna

SOURCES OF LIPIDS

Animal
Source: dairy produce (butter, cheese, cream, milk), egg yolk, meat, meat fats
Degree of saturation: mainly saturated except for fish, which has polyunsaturated fatty acids

Vegetable
Source: avocado, cereals, olive oil, vegetable oils, nuts, soya bean, margarine
Degree of saturation: unsaturated except for some margarine

Marine
Source: fish oils (cod, halibut), oily fish (herring, mackerel, salmon and trout), shellfish
Note: shellfish contains cholesterol.
Degree of saturation: mainly unsaturated, fish contain omega-3 polyunsaturated fatty acids (EPA and DHA, *Eicosapentaenoic acid, *Docosahexaneoic acid)

Properties of hard fats
- Solid at room temperature
- Soluble in organic solvents but insoluble in water
- Absorb flavours if left uncovered e.g. onions
- Boil at high temperatures, evaporate on further heating
- Melt when heated to about 165–170°C
- Overheating (200°C fats) causes glycerol to change to acrolein, a blue haze or smoke rises (*smoke point*), vapour can burst into flames (*flash point*)
- Fats deteriorate in the presence of oxygen (oxidative rancidity) and when the bonds between glycerol and the fatty acids are broken (hydrolytic rancidity). Rancidity of lipids can be prevented using antioxidants. They combine with oxygen present and prevent it reacting with the lipid
- Ability of fats to be shaped under pressure is defined as plasticity

Properties of oils
- Liquid at room temperature
- Higher smoke point (250°C) and flash point (300°C) than hard fats
- Hydrogenation: pumping hydrogen gas through the double bonds of unsaturated fatty acids (oils) in the present of a nickel catalyst produces a hard, saturated fat e.g. margarine
- Can form emulsions

Emulsions and stabilisers
Emulsions are formed when two liquids that do not ordinarily mix are forced together to form a solution. Emulsions can be either temporary or permanent.

Permanent emulsions are formed using an emulsifying agent. The hydrophilic end (water-loving) attaches itself to the fat/oil molecule. The hydrophobic end (water-hating) attaches itself to the vinegar/water molecule. *Examples*: lecithin (mayonnaise), casein (butter)

Temporary emulsions are formed when oil and vinegar are shaken together e.g. French dressing. They separate after settling.

Stabilisers maintain the emulsions in cakes, ice creams and salad creams, preventing the ingredients from separating out. *Examples*: agar, gelatin, gums, pectin

BIOLOGICAL FUNCTIONS

- Concentrated source of heat and energy
- Form an energy reserve in the body
- Source of fat-soluble vitamins (A, D, E and K)
- Source of essential fatty acids (linoleic, linolenic and arachidonic)
- Insulates the body, reduce heat loss and protects delicate organs
- Excess lipids stored as adipose tissue (underneath the skin)

Energy value: 1 g yields 9 kCal (37 kJ) energy

Recommended dietary allowance (RDA)

Lipids should provide one-third of the daily energy intake, half from unsaturated and half from saturated sources. It is recommended that people reduce the amount of fat in the diet by:

- Replacing saturated fats with low-fat options
- Removing excess visible fat from meat
- Choosing poultry and fish instead of red meat
- Choosing low-fat products instead of full-fat varieties
- Grilling, poaching, steaming instead of frying
- Avoiding overuse of processed and take-away food (invisible fat content)

DIGESTION AND ABSORPTION

Digestion

Lipids melt in the stomach. Bile salts from the liver emulsify large fat globules. Triglycerides are broken down into glycerol and fatty acids by lipase, an enzyme released from the pancreas.

Absorption

Glycerol and fatty acids are absorbed into the lacteals of the villi from where they are transported to the thoracic duct, emptying into the left subclavian vein. They are then carried in the bloodstream as lipoproteins.

Utilisation of lipids

Some lipids are sent to the muscles and liver for energy production, more are used in cell walls and any excess is stored as adipose tissue or around delicate organs e.g. kidneys.

VITAMINS

CLASSIFICATION

Fat-soluble vitamins: A (retinol, beta-carotene), D (cholecalciferol), E (tocopherol), K (Naphthoquinone)
Water-soluble vitamins: B-group, C

VITAMIN A (RETINOL AND BETA-CAROTENE)

Vitamin A is available in two forms:
1. *Retinol*: pure vitamin A, from animal sources
2. *Beta-carotene*: pro-vitamin A, from plants with chlorophyll

Sources
Retinol: cod liver oil, liver, dairy products, herring, eggs
Beta-carotene: dark green leafy vegetables, broccoli, deep orange fruits and vegetables

Functions
- Formation of bones and teeth
- Essential for healthy skin
- Maintenance of healthy epithelial tissues
- Necessary for the production of rhodopsin

Effects of deficiency
- Retarded growth, malformed bones
- Dry mucous membranes
- Night blindness
- Xerophthalmia, dry eye membranes
- Increased susceptibility to infections

Properties of retinol
- Yellow fat-soluble alcohol, insoluble in water, heat stable, some loss with prolonged heating, reduced by dehydration, powerful as an antioxidant, can be destroyed by exposure to light and air

Properties of beta-carotene
- Bright orange or yellow oil, insoluble in water, soluble in fat solvents, generally heat stable, sensitive to dehydration, powerful anti-oxidant

Vitamin D (Cholecalciferol) – the Sunshine Vitamin

Vitamin D is available in two forms:
1. *Choleciferols*: vitamin D_3, from sunlight
2. *Ergocalciferols*: vitamin D_2, synthetic vitamin D made from plant sources

Sources (the body and food)
- UV rays convert cholesterol in the skin into choleocalciferol
- Dairy produce, oily fish, fish liver oils, margarine

Functions
- Necessary for the absorption of calcium and phosphorus
- Regulates calcium and phosphorus balance in bones and teeth
- Prevents rickets, a bone disease in children
- Reduces the risk of osteomalacia
- Regulates blood-calcium levels

Effects of deficiency
- Rickets in children
- Osteomalacia and osterporosis
- Dental caries
- Muscle and bone weakness

Properties
- A fat-soluble vitamin, insoluble in water
- Stable to heat, unaffected by cooking or food preservation
- Stable to acids, alkalis and oxygen

Dangers of hypervitaminosis – excess vitamins A and D
Vitamin A is stored in the liver. In extreme cases it causes dry skin, enlarged liver, fatigue, hair loss, headaches, loss of appetite, vomiting and death. Risk of birth defects and miscarriage are greater among pregnant women who have higher intakes of vitamin A than is recommended.

Hypervitaminosis D is more common among young children than adults. It results in a high concentration of calcium in the blood (hypercalcemia). Symptoms include nausea, mental confusion, a metallic taste, vomiting and thirst. Excess vitamin D can also result in loss of bone mass as calcium is pulled from the bones into the bloodstream.

Vitamin E (Tocopherols)

Sources
Vitamin E is found in butter, egg yolks, oatmeal, margarine, liver, meat, leafy green vegetable, peaches, avocados, vegetable oils, wheat germ and polyunsaturated plant oils.

Functions
- Powerful antioxidant in the body and in processed food
- May reduce risks of heart disease, stroke, cancer
- Improves the absorption of vitamin A

Effects of deficiency
- Deficiency is rare
- Linked to conditions associated with malabsorption of fat
- Deficiency may be seen in premature infants
- Weakness, difficulty walking, tiredness

Excess vitamin E is rare.

Properties
- Fat-soluble alcohol vitamin, insoluble in water
- Acts as an antioxidant, delays rancidity and oxidation,
- Damaged by alkalis and ultraviolet light,
- Heat stable, unaffected by cooking and food preservation

Vitamin K (Naphthoquinones)

There are three forms of vitamin K:
1. *Phylloquinone* (from plants sources)
2. *Menaquione* (made by bacteria in the intestine)
3. *Menadione* (a synthetic form)

Sources
Vitamin K is found in dark green vegetables, broccoli, liver, eggs and bacteria in the gut.

Functions
Constituent of prothrombin, which is essential for blood clotting.

Effects of deficiency
- Abnormal blood clotting, haemorrhaging may result
- Deficiency is rare but may occur in newborn babies

Properties
- Fat-soluble vitamin, insoluble in water
- Heat stable, unaffected by cooking
- Destroyed by light, strong acids and alkalis

WATER-SOLUBLE VITAMINS – C AND B-GROUP

VITAMIN C (ASCORBIC ACID)

Sources
There is an excellent supply of vitamin C in rosehips, blackcurrants, green peppers, kiwi fruit, citrus fruits (oranges, grapefruit), strawberries, spinach, cabbage, sprouts and broccoli. There is a reasonable supply from peas, bean sprouts and potatoes.

Functions
- Prevents scurvy
- Essential for the formation of collagen (connective tissue)
- Necessary for strong bones and teeth
- Acts as an antioxidant, protects HDL cholesterol
- Supports the immune system
- Promotes the healing of cuts and wounds and healthy blood vessels
- Essential for the absorption of iron

Effects of deficiency
- Scurvy in severe cases (bleeding gums, loosened teeth)
- Poor absorption of iron (leading to anaemia)
- Slow healing of cuts and wounds, increase in infections
- Weakening of connective tissue resulting in bruising

Properties
- White, water-soluble acidic vitamin
- Destroyed by alkalis, dry or moist heat and enzymes
- Acts as an antioxidant (vitamin C is a reducing agent)
- Destroyed by oxygen and light
- Affected by metals e.g. copper, iron

B COMPLEX OR B-GROUP VITAMINS

VITAMIN B$_{12}$ (COBALAMIN)

Sources
Vitamin B$_{12}$ is found in dairy produce, eggs, fish, offal, meats and poultry.

Functions

- Essential for healthy myelin sheath surrounding nerve fibres
- Growth and development of red blood cells
- Helps treat pernicious anaemia

Effects of deficiency

- Fatigue, shortness of breath
- Pernicious anaemia
- Anxiety and irritability
- Degeneration of nerve fibres

Properties

- Vitamin K is a water-soluble vitamin
- Heat stable up to 100°C
- Sensitive to light, strong acids and alkalis

FOLATE (FOLIC ACID)

Sources

Folic acid is found in fortified cornflakes and cereals, green leafy vegetables, potatoes, offal, bread, milk, wheat germ and nutritional supplements.

Functions

- Essential for the synthesis of DNA and RNA
- Reduces the risks of neural tube defects e.g. spina bifida
- Assists the formation of red blood cells
- Supports the immune system
- May play a role in the prevention of cancers, heart attacks and strokes

Effects of deficiency

- Fatigue in mild cases
- Neural tube defects e.g. spina bifida

Properties

- Folic acid is a water-soluble vitamin
- Unaffected by acid environments
- Sensitive to light and oxygen

MORE B-GROUP VITAMINS

Vitamin B₁ (Thiamine)

Sources
Vitamin B_1 is found in breakfast cereals, fortified flour, meats and offal.
Fish. nuts and peas.

Functions
- Required for the metabolism of carbohydrates
- Assists growth in children and good health
- Prevents beriberi

Deficiency
- Beriberi (affects the nervous system and the heart)
- Lack of energy, tiredness, depression, muscle cramps

Properties
- Vitamin B_1 is water-soluble
- Destroyed by high temperatures, dry heat and alkalis
- Some loss occurs during the milling process (70%)

Vitamin B₂ (Riboflavin)

Sources
Vitamin B_2 is found in milk, cheese, eggs, green vegetables, offal, yeast extracts and wheat germ.

Functions
- Involved in the metabolism of nutrients
- Essential for maintenance of eyes, skin and tongue
- General good health, repair and development of tissues

Deficiency
- Sore mouth and tongue, cracked lips
- Lack of energy, tiredness and fatigue
- Sensitivity to light, eye infections
- Checked growth and poor health
- Dermatitis

Properties
- Vitamin B_2 is water-soluble, yellow-orange in colour

- Destroyed by alkalis and ultraviolet light
- Unstable at high temperatures
- Unaffected by acids and oxygen

NIACIN (NICOTINIC ACID)

Sources
Niacin is found in bread, fortified cereals, offal, meat, fish, potatoes, wholegrains, yeast extracts, fortified pulses and peanuts.

Functions
- Assists energy release from carbohydrates and fats
- Necessary for growth and healthy skin
- Prevents pellagra

Deficiency
- Pellagra (symptoms are the five Ds)
- Lack of energy, fatigue and weight loss

Properties
- Niacin is a water-soluble vitamin
- Stable to acids, alkalis and oxygen
- Heat stable
- 80%–90% lost in milling

VITAMIN B$_6$ (PYRIDOXINE)

Sources
Vitamin B$_6$ is found in meats, fish, poultry, legumes, offal, non-citrus fruits, cereals and yeast.

Functions
- Assists metabolism of nutrients
- Formation of red blood cells and antibodies
- Involved in the development of a healthy nervous system

Deficiency
- Tiredness and fatigue
- Pre-menstrual tension, irritability
- Convulsions in infants

Properties
- Vitamin B$_6$ is a water-soluble vitamin,
- Fairly stable at normal temperatures, sensitive to high temperatures, oxygen, processing and milling
- Affected by light

RECOMMENDED DIETARY ALLOWANCES (RDAs) PER DAY

Vitamin A: children 400–500 μg, adolescents 600–700 μg, adult males 700 μg, adult females 600 μg, pregnancy and lactation 950 μg
Vitamin D: children 7–10 μg, adolescents 15 μg, adults 10 μg
Vitamin E: based on polyunsaturated fatty acid intake
Vitamin K: no established recommendations
Vitamin C: infants (under 1 year) 25 μg, children 45 μg, adolescents 50–60 μg, adults 60 mg, during pregnancy or lactation 80 μg
Vitamin B$_{12}$: children 1 mg, adolescents and adults 1.4 μg, during pregnancy and lactation 1.6–1.9 μg
Folate: children 200 μg, adolescents and adults 300 μg, during pregnancy and lactation 500/400 μg

MINERALS

Main minerals
The main minerals are calcium (Ca), chloride (Cl), magnesium (Mg), phosphorous (P), potassium (K), sodium (Na) and sulphur (S).

Trace minerals
The trace minerals are chromium (Cr), cobalt (Co), copper (Cu), fluoride (F), iodine (I), iron (Fe), manganese (Mn), nickel (Ni), selenium (Se) and zinc (Zn).

CALCIUM

Sources
Calcium is found in calcium-fortified foods, dairy products, eggs, hard water, leafy green vegetables, tinned fish and meat.

Functions
- Formation of strong bones (skeleton) and teeth
- Assists clotting of blood and immune defences
- Functioning of nerves (impulses) and muscle (movement)
- Assists regulation of metabolism in cells

Effects of deficiency
- Abnormal clotting of blood
- Poor quality teeth, tooth decay
- Osteomalacia in adults (bone pain and tenderness)
- Osteoporosis in older people (brittle bones)
- Rickets in children (insufficient calcium)
- Nervousness, muscle cramps, pains in joints

Absorption of calcium
The *absorption* of calcium is increased by vitamin D, phosphorus, acid environment, amino acids and parathormone.
It is *inhibited* by fatty acids, fibre, oxalic acid, phytic acid, excess protein, lack of stomach acid, and vitamin D deficiency.

Recommended dietary allowances (RDAs) mg per day
Children 800 mg, adolescents 1200 mg, adults 800 mg, during pregnancy and lactation 1200 mg

IRON

Sources
Iron is available in two forms, haem (ferrous iron, Fe^{2+}, organic) which is soluble and easily absorbed, and non-haem (ferric iron, Fe^{3+}, inorganic) which is insoluble. Non-haem iron must be reduced from ferric state to ferrous state in order to be absorbed.

 Haem iron can be found in chicken, fish, liver, red meat and meat products.

 Non-haem iron is found in broccoli, cereals, eggs, leafy green vegetables and pulses.

Functions
- Essential component of haemoglobin in red blood cells
- Forms part of myoglobin, an oxygen binding protein
- Transports oxygen to cells
- Essential component of enzyme systems
- Essential for the immune system and brain development

Effects of deficiency (can be mild or severe)
- Iron deficiency (haemoglobin levels fall)
- Iron deficiency anaemia
- Breathlessness, fatigue, paleness, loss of appetite

Absorption of iron

Absorption of iron depends on it source, haem or non-haem iron. Haem iron is more absorbable than non-haem iron. Haem iron is independent of meal composition while non-haem iron absorption is strongly influenced by meal composition. The absorption of non-haem is boosted by the presence of vitamin C and meat in a meal, or inhibited by dietary factors.

Absorption is *increased* by:
- Combining haem and non-haem iron sources
- The presence of vitamin C (ascorbic acid)
- Hydrochloric acid in the stomach
- Sugars that assist the absorption of non-haem
- The MFP factor associated with meat, fish and poultry

Absorption is *inhibited* by:
- Oxalic acid
- Phytic acid
- Fibre intake levels above 35 g/d
- Tannin and other polyphenols
- Calcium and phosphorous

Excess iron may result in:
- Iron overload caused by a genetic disorder (hemochromatosis)
- Iron overload associated with nutritional overload (haemosiderosis)
- Accidental poisoning in children (overdose of supplements)

Recommended dietary allowances (RDAs) mg per day

Children 8–10 mg, adolescents 13–14 mg, adults 10–14 mg, during pregnancy and lactation 15 mg

ZINC

Sources

Zinc is found in protein-containing foods (meat, meat products, poultry), oysters, clams and other shellfish, legumes, eggs, bread and whole grains.

Functions
- Critical for functioning of enzymes and hormones
- Essential to the immune system, aids healing of wounds
- Maintains healthy hair, nails and skin
- Involved in nucleic acid metabolism
- Necessary for growth, sexual development and reproduction

Effects of deficiency
- Poor growth and wound healing
- Increased risk of infections
- Dry, flaky skin

Recommended dietary allowances (RDA) mg per day
Children 4–7 mg, adolescents 7–9 mg, adults 7–9 mg, during lactation 9.5–13 mg

IODINE

Sources
Iodine is found in seafood and deep-water fish, seaweed, plant foods grown in soil by the sea, iodised salt, meat, milk and eggs.

Functions
- Component of two thyroid hormones
- Helps regulate growth and repair
- Involved in metabolism

Effects of deficiency
- Reduced thyroid hormone production
- Enlargement of the thyroid gland (goitre)
- Mental and physical retardation (cretinism)

Recommended dietary allowances (RDAs) μg/d
Children 90 μg, adolescents 125 μg, adults 130–140 μg and during pregnancy 130 μg

POTASSIUM

Sources
Potassium is found in all wholefoods, fruits (bananas, melons), vegetables (green leafy, potatoes, spinach, legumes), parsley, whole grains, fresh meat, milk and tea.

Functions
- Formation and functioning of body cells
- Involved in metabolism of carbohydrate and protein
- Regulates nerve impulses and muscle contractions

Effects of deficiency
- Deficiency is unlikely, as most foods contain potassium
- Muscular weakness, loss of appetite and confusion
- Severe depletion can disrupt heart rhythm causing cardiac arrest

Recommended dietary allowances (RDAs) g/d
Children 0.8–2 g and adults 3.5 mg are the RDAs for potassium.

SODIUM

Sources
Sodium is found in breads, cured meats, butter, milk, processed foods, soy sauce and table salt.

Functions
- Regulates fluid and acid balance
- Aids nerve and muscle functioning
- Helps maintain normal heartbeat

Effects of deficiency
- Dehydration, loss of appetite
- Low blood pressure
- Muscle cramps

Recommended dietary allowances (RDAs) per day
Adults 1.6 g is the RDA for sodium.

MINERAL AND VITAMIN INTER-RELATIONSHIP

- Vitamin D is needed for the absorption of calcium
- Vitamin C is needed for the absorption of iron
- Calcium, phosphorus and vitamin D are required for bone formation
- Folic acid, B_6, B_{12} and iron are required for formation of red blood cells
- Absorption of selenium is enhanced by vitamins A, C and E

WATER

Composition
Water consists of 2 hydrogen + 1 oxygen = H_2O (ratio 2:1).

Sources
Water is present in most foods, alcohol, beverages (milk, tea), drinking water, fruit and vegetables. Water is generated during metabolism.

Water loss
Water is lost as sweat, water vapour, urine, in faeces, tears, spit, sneezing, blood and semen. Daily water loss is on average 2.5 litres. Water lost from the body must be replaced. Water makes up about 60% of the body's weight.

General properties
- Found in three states, ice (below 0°C), liquid (0–100°C), steam (over 100°C)
- Boiling point changes with increases or decreases in atmospheric pressure
- Colour, odour and tasteless liquid
- Good as a solvent, substances dissolve readily in water
- Water absorbs and retains heat
- Neutral pH of 7, neither acid nor alkaline

Biological importance
- Component of all body cells and juices
- Assists digestion (hydrolysis) and absorption of food
- Transports nutrients and waste products around the body
- Acts as a solvent for minerals, vitamins, amino acids, etc.
- Source of calcium, fluorine and sometimes magnesium
- Acts as a lubricant around eyes, joints and spinal cord
- Assists the removal of waste from the body
- Regulates body temperature through perspiration
- Refreshing to drink, quenches thirst

Daily water requirements
The daily water requirement is 2 to 2·5 litres per day, with 2 litres coming from beverages and ·5 litres from food.

Effects of dehydration – some examples
- Headaches and thirst
- Fatigue, loss of appetite, poor concentration
- Dry skin and mucous membranes, rapid heartbeat
- Low blood pressure and weakness

CHAPTER 2 – Diet and Health

ENERGY

Definition of energy
Energy is defined as 'the ability or capacity to do work'. Food provides energy and the body converts it to chemical, mechanical, electrical or heat energy.

Role of energy in the body
- Chemical and metabolic reactions (chemical energy), e.g. digestion
- Muscle movement, both voluntary and involuntary (mechanical energy)
- Cell and nerve activity (electrical energy)
- Maintaining body temperature (heat energy)

Sources of energy
The main sources of energy are proteins, lipids and carbohydrates. Of the three, lipids provide the greatest amount of energy.

Proteins	1 g provides 4 kCal (17 kJ) energy
Lipids	1 g provides 9 kCal (37 kJ) energy
Carbohydrates	1 g provides 4 kCal (17 kJ) energy

Respiration
A reaction between glucose and oxygen in the body cells produces carbon dioxide, water and energy. B-group vitamins, iodine and phosphorus are involved in the process.

$$\text{Glucose} + \text{Oxygen} \rightarrow \text{Carbon Dioxide} + \text{Water} + \text{Energy}$$
$$C_6H_{12}O_6 + O_2 \rightarrow CO_2 + H_2O + \text{Energy}$$

Carbon dioxide is breathed out and water is removed via the skin or kidneys.

Energy requirements
The amount of energy needed by each individual depends on:

- Age: younger children need more energy than adults
- Body size and weight: lighter bodies require less energy
- Climate: more energy is needed by the body in cold climates
- Gender: higher energy intakes is required by males than females

- Occupation: sedentary workers require less energy than more active people
- Physical activity: the greater the physical activity, the higher the energy needs
- Pregnancy/lactation: energy is required for the growth of the foetus and to maintain milk supply when breast-feeding
- Illness: reduced energy needs because of reduced physical activity

Energy expenditure (output)

Energy expenditure or output is the amount of energy the body uses. Energy is expended on sleeping, work related activities and non-work related activities. The components of energy expenditure or output are:

- *Basal metabolism*: this is the amount of energy required to maintain life. Basal Metabolic Rate (BMR) is a clinical measure of energy used for metabolism taken when a person is lying at rest, has just woken up from a night's sleep, 10–12 hours after their last meal and no physical activity has taken place. BMR is highest in growing children and decreases as one gets older. BMR varies between individuals due to a variety of factors e.g. climate, after eating a meal, etc.
- *Physical activity*: this refers to the amount of energy needed for performing a variety of activities e.g. working, sporting activities, leisure activities, etc.
- *Growth*: babies and children require more energy as they are growing rapidly
- *Processing of food*: the body uses energy every day when digesting, absorbing and metabolising the nutrients from food. Heat and energy are produced, and the BMR increases. The output is referred to as the thermogenic effect of food or thermogenesis

Energy balance

To maintain a constant *energy balance* energy intake should be equal to energy output. When energy intake is greater than energy output obesity may result.

Total energy expenditure is the energy required for basal metabolism (resting energy expenditure) and the energy required for all other activities (physical activities, processing of foods, minor activities).

Table 2.1 Factors controlling food intake

Physiological factors	Psychological factors	External factors
Hunger (desire to find food)	Appetite (desire to eat)	Cultural preferences
Satiety (fullness)	Dislike of a particular	Stimuli from the food
Hypothalamus (centre of	food or foods	Social occasion
control in the brain)	Stress	Time of day
	Mood	

Table 2.2 Estimated average daily energy requirement

Age profile	Male	Female
Child	1,500 kcal	1,400 kcal
Adolescent	2,800 kcal	2,300 kcal
Sedentary adult	2,400 kcal	2,150 kcal
Moderately active adult	2,800 kcal	2,150 kcal
Very active adult	3,400 kcal	2,500 kcal
Elderly	2,200 kcal	1,800 kcal
Pregnancy		2,400 kcal
Lactation		2,800 kcal

DIETARY GUIDELINES

Dietary surveys carried out in Ireland include:
- National Nutrition Survey 1948
- National Nutrition Survey 1990
- National Nutrition Surveillance Centre Survey 1998

The purpose of surveys is to provide information on the eating habits of the general population within the country.

Purpose of nutritional guidelines
- To encourage people to improve their eating habits
- To encourage people to take more exercise
- To reduce diet-related diseases in Ireland e.g. heart disease

Source of current nutritional guidelines
Guidelines from COMA (Committee on Medical Aspects of Food and Nutritional Policy) are used in Ireland.

Current nutritional guidelines
- Eat a variety of foods, choose servings from different food groups
- Increase intake of dietary fibre to 30–35 g per day
- Increase intake of calcium and iron-rich foods (females)
- Choose vegetable protein as an alternative to animal protein
- Balance energy intake with energy expenditure
- Reduce intake of saturated fats (hard fats) to 10% of total lipid intake
- Avoid processed foods in order to reduce fat, salt and sugar in the diet
- Use foods that are high in fats, salt and sugar sparingly

- Decrease use of salt when cooking and at table
- Drink at least 6–8 glasses of water daily

Measuring nutrient intake

The different terms used to describe the measurements of nutrients include:

(a) Ireland: Recommended Dietary Allowance (RDA)
(b) Britain: Reference Nutrient Intake (RNI)
(c) EU: Population Reference Intake (PRI)

The term *Recommended Dietary Allowance* corresponds to RNI and PRI. The RDA is the recommended daily intake of a nutrient that meets the nutritional needs of almost all the population (97–98% approx.) based on stage of life (age groups) and gender.

Dietary Reference Values (DRV)

DRV may be defined as a set of standards that may be used when:

- Assessing and planning diets for an individual e.g. specific dietary needs
- Assessing and planning diets for the general population
- Planning food supplies for groups of people on the move e.g. on expeditions
- Promoting healthy eating and physical wellbeing across the general population
- Nutritional labelling on food products

Dietary Reference Values (DRV) refers to a range of specific types of values. These are:

Estimated Average Requirement (EAR) refers to the nutrient or energy intake level required by 50% of individuals in a gender and life stage group. Suitable for assessing requirements for groups of people. EAR provides a basis from which the RDA can be calculated.

Recommended Dietary Allowance (RDA) indicates the amount of a nutrient required to meet the dietary needs of 97–98% of people (almost all healthy people) in gender and life stage groups.

Lower Threshold Intake (LTI) refers to the amount of a nutrient that is adequate for individuals with low nutritional needs. Most people will require more than this amount.

Food composition tables

Food composition tables may be described as a database of information about the nutrients found in 100 g portions of different types of foods. Foods are organised into categories e.g. dairy, etc. Individual foods can be analysed and the composition of individual ingredients used in a specific dish can be calculated using the data from the food tables.

DIETARY AND FOOD REQUIREMENTS

Choosing a balanced diet

A well-balanced diet contains all nutrients in the correct proportions for each individual and comes from a wide variety of foods chosen from the food groups. Choose proteins, lipids and carbohydrates in the following amounts:

- One-sixth of protein from equal amounts of animal and vegetable proteins
- One-sixth of lipid/fat from saturated, unsaturated and polyunsaturated lipids
- Two-thirds of carbohydrates to include NSP (non-starch polysaccharides/fibre)
- Vitamins and minerals

Table 2.3 The food groups: servings and dietetic value of groups

Food group	No. of Servings	Single servings	Dietetic Value
Bread, cereals, potatoes, rice, pasta	6 + per day	1 bowl porridge 25 g brown bread 1 potato 2 tbsps rice 2 tbsps pasta	Main energy source NSP (fibre) B group vitamins Low in lipids
Fruit, vegetables	4 + per day	1 piece fresh fruit 1 bowl salad $1/2$ glass fresh fruit juice	NSP (fibre) Minerals Vitamins Water (almost fat free)
Milk, cheese, yoghurt (dairy sources)	3 servings per day	175 ml milk 25 g cheese 1 carton yoghurt	Calcium Protein Lipids Vitamin D (low-fat varieties available)
Meat, poultry, fish, eggs, beans & peas	2 servings per day	50 g cooked meat 75 g cooked fish 2 eggs	Protein Iron (rich supply) B-group vitamins Other minerals
Fats, oils, cakes, snacks, fizzy drinks	Very small amounts		Eat sparingly High in cholesterol, fat, salt & sugar

INDIVIDUAL DIETARY REQUIREMENTS

BABIES

The early stages of life are a period of rapid growth and development. Breast milk or formula milk provides for the dietary needs of infants in the first months of life.

When *breast-feeding* a baby, no preparation is required. Breast-feeding is recommended because:

- Breast milk contains all the nutrients in the correct proportions
- Provides antibodies, enzymes and hormones, protects against infection
- It is at the right temperature and guaranteed to be sterile
- It reduces the risks of respiratory, gastrointestinal and other infections
- It assists the infant and mother relationship (bonding)

Bottle-feeds may be given from birth or at a later stage after a few months. When using formula milk follow the manufacturer's instructions strictly, do not over- or under-dilute. Too much formula can lead to dehydration, too little can lead to under-nutrition.

Dietary guidelines

- When weaning provide a more varied diet, introduce single foods at a time, add soft, sieved/puréed cereals, fruit, vegetables, potatoes and choose foods from the main food groups
- Choose sieved meat, fish or egg yolk for protein, fruit and vegetables for minerals and vitamins, and starchy carbohydrates for energy
- After six months add more chewy, solid foods mashed, grated or in small pieces
- From six months introduce iron-rich and vitamin C rich foods
- Exclude tea, coffee, fatty, fried and spicy foods, sugar and salt

CHILDREN

Food habits are established early in life and 'faddy' eating habits should be discouraged. Regular mealtimes without rushing are recommended. Children should eat healthy nutritious snacks between meals e.g. fresh fruit. Serve small, easy-to-manage, portions to children rather than adult sized meals.

Children need

- Protein for rapid growth and repair
- Carbohydrate rich foods for energy
- Calcium and vitamin D rich foods for bones and teeth
- Iron and vitamin C for general health and to prevent childhood anaemia
- Carbohydrates for fibre or roughage
- Minerals and vitamins to protect against disease

Dietary guidelines

- Choose foods from the four main food groups each day
- Encourage children to eat a breakfast every morning
- Provide a healthy mid-morning snack and a packed lunch for school
- Serve a well-balanced meal to children on their return from school
- Avoid sweets, sugary foods, salty snacks and fizzy drinks

ADOLESCENTS

Adolescence is a time of rapid growth and increased activity. Most of the guidelines for children apply to this age group.

Dietary guidelines
- Adequate protein foods are needed for rapid growth
- Supplies of high-energy foods and high-fibre foods to prevent bowel disease
- Calcium and vitamin D for strong bones and teeth
- Extra calcium for females to prevent osteoporosis later on in life
- Extra iron and vitamin C for females to prevent anaemia
- Minerals and vitamins to protect against disease
- Water and fresh fruit juices for a healthy skin
- Choose healthy snacks instead of bars or crisps
- Avoid eating fast foods and take-aways on a regular basis
- Do not diet unless under medical supervision
- Avoid snacking on 'empty kilocalorie' foods

ADULTS

A well-balanced varied diet provides adults with all their dietary needs. The rate of growth has slowed down and energy needs may have reduced. Body size and activity determine the amount of energy required. Activity and food intake should be balanced. Manual workers require extra energy foods and vitamin B.

Dietary guidelines
- Choose a varied diet to maintain a healthy weight
- Include high-fibre starchy foods
- Eat plenty of mineral and vitamin rich foods
- Ensure adequate supplies of vitamin C and iron
- Include adequate supplies of calcium and vitamin D
- Reduce intake of sugar, salt and saturated fats and cholesterol
- Reduce alcohol consumption

DURING PREGNANCY AND LACTATION

During pregnancy the mother provides for all the nutritional needs of the developing foetus. A well-balanced varied concentrated diet is recommended. During lactation the dietary guidelines are similar to those followed during pregnancy. An adequate supply of folic acid is required prior to conception and for the first 12 weeks of conception to reduce the risk of neural tube defects, e.g. spina bifida.

Dietary guidelines
- Choose concentrated proteins for foetal growth and development
- Include increased supplies of calcium and vitamin D

- Select iron-rich and vitamin C-rich foods for healthy blood
- Choose foods rich in fatty acids for a healthy nervous system
- Ensure adequate supplies of folic acid before and during pregnancy
- Eat plenty of high-fibre foods to prevent constipation
- Reduce high salt intake to prevent high blood pressure
- Eat little and often to relieve morning sickness
- Drink plenty of water and fresh fruit juices
- Avoid fried, spicy or sugary foods, coffee, tea and alcohol
- Eliminate the risk of risk of listeria and salmonella by avoiding eggs just barely cooked or food items containing uncooked eggs, cream cheeses made with unpasteurised milk and cook-chilled products

The Elderly

Dietary problems may develop for elderly people because of:
- Reduced income limits choice and changes priorities, poverty
- Poor general health or physical disabilities e.g. dental problems
- Difficulties when shopping e.g. less mobile, too far from shops
- Difficulties when preparing foods e.g. arthritis in hands
- Loss of interest in buying a varied range of foods
- Loneliness and lack of interest in cooking for one person
- Poor absorption of essential nutrients
- The dietary needs of the elderly include the maintenance of bones, repair of body cells, formation of red blood cells and adequate energy

Dietary guidelines
- Choose a varied well-balanced diet with lower energy intake
- Serve in smaller portions and eat smaller, more frequent meals
- Eat concentrated protein foods for replacement or repair of worn cells
- Reduce intake of high cholesterol foods and saturated fats
- Reduce salt and salty foods to prevent hypertension
- Include dietary fibre to prevent constipation
- Foods rich in minerals and vitamins will help prevent disease
- Eat iron-rich and vitamin-C rich foods to reduce anaemia
- Eat omega-3 fatty acid foods (fish)
- Include foods rich in calcium and vitamin D
- Avoid tea and coffee late at night, may cause insomnia

MODIFIED DIETS

Coeliac Disease

Coeliac disease occurs in individuals who are unable to breakdown the protein, gluten, found in wheat, barley, oats and rye. Symptoms experienced by adults may include anaemia, diarrhoea, reduced body weight and abdominal pain. Children may fail to grow at the normal rate, be irritable and experience loss of weight.

General dietary guidelines
- Follow the doctor's instructions
- Stick to a gluten-free diet, look for the gluten-free symbol
- Read labels on all foods, particularly processed foods

Avoid all hidden sources of gluten e.g. batters, biscuits, bread, cakes, some breakfast cereals, bread, packet sauces and soups, sausages, pasta, pastries, pizza, lasagne, stuffings, foods coated with breadcrumbs or flour mixtures, any product made using wheat, barley, oats and rye.

Suitable foods include dairy products, eggs, unprocessed fresh meat, fish (uncoated), poultry, fruit, vegetables, soya products, rice, breakfast cereals made from maize and rice, cornflour for thickening sauces and soups and gluten-free products.

DIABETES

Diabetes is a disorder of the endocrine system. The body is unable to control glucose levels in the blood because of a deficiency of insulin or inefficiency of the insulin produced. It is more common in older people, children of diabetics and overweight individuals. There are two forms.

Type 1: Insulin-dependent diabetes (juvenile onset)
This occurs when the pancreas does not manufacture insulin. To control blood sugar levels insulin injections are needed every day.

Type 2: Non-insulin dependent diabetes (maturity onset)
This type of diabetes can occur in older people and is associated with overweight. The pancreas produces some insulin but it may not be sufficient or it does not work correctly. Type 2 diabetes can be controlled by diet.

Symptoms include increased thirst, increased urine production, loss of weight, loss of body tissue, wasting and fatigue.

General dietary recommendations
- Follow the dietary and lifestyle programme set out by the doctor
- Balance meals and insulin treatment
- Eat three regular meals with one or more snacks, never miss meals
- Eat fibre-rich carbohydrate foods e.g. vegetables, *most* fresh fruits
- Avoid sugar-rich carbohydrate foods e.g. biscuits, cakes, jams
- Eat high-fibre starches in fixed amounts at regular times each day
- Reduce intake of saturated fats and salt, keep alcohol intake low

CARDIOVASCULAR DISEASE

Examples: aneurisms (blood clots), coronary heart disease, gangrene and strokes
Main cause: atherosclerosis, blood flow is restricted due to hardening of arteries
Locations of atherosclerosis in the body: aorta, cerebral arteries, coronary arteries
and femoral arteries

CHOLESTEROL

Cholesterol is introduced by food and also made in the liver.

Functions of cholesterol
- Involved in the production of hormones
- Essential component of cell walls or membranes
- Necessary component of bile salts

Types of blood cholesterol
- Very Low Density Lipoproteins (VLDL)
- Low Density Lipoproteins (LDL) ('bad')
- High Density Lipoproteins ('good')

LDL carries cholesterol from the liver to body tissues delivering triglycerides.
High levels of LDL are a risk factor for heart disease.
HDL picks up excess cholesterol and transfers it to other lipoproteins, which
return it to the liver for recycling or excretion. High levels of HDL reduce risk of
heart disease.
   Factors that improve the LDL to HDL ratio are antioxidants, polyunsaturated
fats, soluble fibres, weight control and exercise.

CORONARY HEART DISEASE (CHD)

CHD occurs when the coronary arteries become blocked. Blood pressure may rise
and a heart attack could result. It can be mild or fatal. The restriction of blood
flow around the heart muscle could result in angina.

Fixed risk factors
- Age: women over 55 years and men over 45 are most at risk
- Gender: women have less CHD than men, after menopause the rate is the same
- Genetics: individuals likely to develop CHD if parents have CHD

Dietary and lifestyle risk factors
Those dietary and lifestyle risk factors which can be controlled or changed include
cigarette smoking, diabetes mellitus, a diet high in saturated fats and salt, high

blood cholesterol levels (LDL cholesterol only). Also high blood pressure levels, high stress levels, a lack of exercise and weight gain (overweight, obesity).

Dietary measures to reduce CHD
- Reduce saturated fats and cholesterol in the diet
- Replace saturated fats with low-fat alternatives
- Choose foods rich in polyunsaturated fatty acids
- Increase the intake of fibre-rich foods
- Reduce salt in food preparation and cooking, avoid processed foods
- Use cooking methods that do not use fat e.g. grilling, poaching

Lifestyle recommendations
- Exercise, increases levels of HDL cholesterol
- Do not smoke, avoid alcohol, and manage stress
- Reduce weight or maintain correct body weight

VEGETARIANISM

A vegetarian may be defined as a person who does not eat meat or in some cases any animal products. A vegetarian diet is high in fibre and low in saturated fat.

Reasons for vegetarianism
- Cultural: the accepted diet among a family, group or community
- Health: a diet without meat and high in fibre is considered healthier
- Moral/ethical: killing or harming animals is believed to be wrong
- Religious: eating meat may be forbidden by the religion

Different groups/types of vegetarians
Lacto-vegetarians: eat dairy products and plant foods, no animal flesh
Vegans: live completely on vegetable or plant foods, no animal products
Other types: ovo vegetarian, pesco vegetarian, pollo vegetarian

Benefits of a vegetarian diet
- Low in saturated animal fats – reduces risk of obesity
- Low in cholesterol – reduces risk of high blood pressure and CHD
- High in fibre – prevents constipation and other bowel disorders

Main food groups for lacto-vegetarians
Legumes or pulse vegetables, grains and nuts, fruits and vegetables, milk and dairy products.

Nutrient intake

The diet for *lacto-vegetarians* provides sufficient amounts of protein, carbohydrates, dietary fibre, calcium, B-group vitamins, vitamins A, D, E and C, folate, and trace minerals for their dietary needs.

The *vegan diet*, because of the absence of all animal products, may lack HBV protein, vitamins B_{12} and D, calcium and iron.

Dietary guidelines for vegetarians

- Check processed food labels for hidden animal products
- Replace meat with alternatives such as quorn, TVP and tofu
- Include a mix of vegetable proteins to meet protein needs
- Choose soya products as alternatives to dairy products
- Fortified breakfast cereals and fortified soya milk provide vitamin B_{12}
- Use vegetable stocks for casseroles, soups, sauces and stews
- Replace animal fats with vegetable oils and margarine
- Choose high-fibre rich foods e.g. wholemeal breads, fruits, vegetables
- Trace minerals can be supplied by vegetables, pulses and dried fruits
- Choose beans, dried fruit, green vegetables, nuts, whole cereals for iron
- Choose leafy green vegetables, tofu and fortified products for calcium

Selection of ingredients suitable for vegetarian cookery

- Grains: wheat, oats, millet, couscous, bulgar wheat, rice (all varieties), buckwheat, corn (maize), barley, rye
- Pulses: beans (Lima, butter, black, aduki, haricot, kidney, pinto, broad, soya, mung); peas (green, split green, split yellow, chick); lentils (brown, green, red)
- Nuts: almond, Brazil, coconut, cashew, hazelnuts, pecan, peanuts, pine kernels, pistachios, walnuts
- Seeds: linseed, pumpkin, sesame, sunflower
- Dried fruit: apricot, currants, dates, dried figs, prunes, raisins, sultanas
- Sea vegetables: carrageen moss and dulse (Ireland), lavar (Wales)

Suitable vegetarian dishes are vegetarian lasagne, quiche (modify the ingredients), omelette, mixed vegetable or mixed bean curry and vegetable cobbler.
Suitable vegan dishes are vegetarian curry, pasta dishes, rice dishes, vegetable stir-fry, vegetarian risotto and stuffed vegetables (tomatoes, aubergines, peppers).

DIET–RELATED HEALTH PROBLEMS

BOWEL DISORDERS

Bowel disorders associated with low-fibre diets include:
- Bowel cancer: increase the intake of fruit and vegetables in the diet
- Constipation: faeces hard and painful to pass, leads to haemorrhoids

- Diverticulitis: formation of pouches in intestinal walls containing food wastes; bacteria, acids and gases form, which leads to pain
- Irritable bowel syndrome: painful irregular movement of the intestines

Dietary guidelines
- Reduce low-fibre and processed foods in the diet
- Increase intake of whole cereals, fruit and vegetables
- Use fruits and vegetables with skins where possible
- Choose high-fibre breakfast cereals
- Replace white flour with wholemeal varieties
- Replace rice and pasta with wholegrain varieties

OSTEOPOROSIS

Osteoporosis occurs when bones become thinner and less dense. The bones break easily. Osteoporosis is common among women whose peak bone mass is reached on average between 25 and 35 years of age. The main cause is lack of calcium during the bone developmental stage. The effects of osteoporosis cannot be reversed.

Risk factors
- Age: risk increases with age
- Genetic: heredity or family history
- Gender: females are more at risk than males
- Hormonal: menopausal hormonal changes hasten calcium loss
- Dietary: inadequate calcium, vitamin D and phosphorus intake
- Physical activity: exercise is needed to strengthen bones

Dietary and lifestyle guidelines
- Choose vitamin D, calcium-rich, and phosphorus-rich foods
- High intake of calcium creates better bone density
- Get regular exercise
- Avoid smoking, alcohol and caffeine

OBESITY

When an individual's weight is 20% above the recommended weight for their height, they are considered obese or overweight. The main cause of obesity is that energy intake is greater than energy output.

Problems associated with obesity are diabetes, difficulties in childbirth, gallstones, heart disease, high blood cholesterol, infertility, joint problems, respiratory difficulties, strokes and varicose veins.

Factors increasing risk of obesity may be behavioural, environmental or genetic.

Treatments for obesity include dietary changes to reduce weight, changing eating patterns, exercising on a regular basis, surgical procedures and drug treatments.

Dietary guidelines
- Consult a doctor before starting a weight-reducing diet
- Balance a weight-reducing diet with an exercise programme
- Establish a well-balanced meal pattern, three meals a day
- Avoid high-calorie snack foods, avoid snacking between meals
- Eat high-fibre foods e.g. whole cereals, fruits, vegetables
- Increase intake of fruits and vegetables
- Replace saturated fats with low-fat alternatives
- Grill, poach or steam instead of frying
- Drink plenty of water, reduce alcohol intake
- Reduce intake of sugar and sugary foods

DENTAL DISEASE

Dental Caries
Dental caries and periodontal disease are forms of dental diseases. Dental caries results from eating foods containing sugars. These sugars are converted to an acid in the mouth by bacteria. Brushing teeth after meals reduces the risk of build up of sugar and bacteria i.e. plaque.

Preventing dental caries
- Reduce intake of sugary snacks, replace with fresh fruit or nuts
- Avoid fizzy drinks, replace with fruit juices and water
- Drink fluoridated water from the mains
- Use toothpaste which contains fluoride
- Brush regularly, morning, evening and after eating
- Visit the dentist once a year

ANAEMIA

Anaemia may result from a lack of iron and vitamin C in the diet, malabsorption of iron in the body or heavy blood losses.

Dietary guidelines
- Eat iron-rich green leafy vegetables, eggs, red meat, offal and whole cereals
- Include plenty of vitamin C to assist absorption e.g. citrus fruits

Anorexia

Anorexia is a psychological condition where fear of becoming fat is accompanied by some of the following behaviour: abuse of laxatives, over-exercising, self-induced vomiting and starvation. Psychotherapy and special dietary treatment are required to help the sufferer recover. Symptoms include mottling of teeth, weakness, poor concentration, dry skin, increased facial and body hair. Recovery may be short or long-term.

Bulimia

Bulimia is an eating disorder where binge eating is followed by self-induced vomiting in order not to gain weight. Psychotherapy is required to treat the disease.

THE IRISH DIET IN TRANSITION

FOOD AND EATING PATTERNS

Significant events in the 1900s that changed food and eating patterns include:
- Developments in farming, industrialisation and transport
- Changes in retailing of food due to these major developments
- First and Second World Wars

Dietary surveys early in the 1900s reveal that sugar consumption increased ten-fold between 1860 and 1900; fat content of diet increased; consumption of dairy products increased; carbohydrate consumption decreased and consumers considered bought produce superior to home-made varieties.

The twentieth century (1900 to mid–1940s)
- An active lifestyle and manual work were common
- Rural dwellers continued to use home-made produce
- Popular foods were cereals, dairy produce and potatoes
- Home-made bread was a staple food (white and brown)
- Meat was expensive and not eaten on a regular basis
- Poultry (turkey, goose) was served on special occasions
- Iron intake was low resulting in high levels of anaemia in women
- Little knowledge of nutrition; deficiency diseases were common
- Food choices were based on economic status of family
- Fruit and vegetables intake increased between 1930 and 1945

Effects of world wars
Unemployment and high food prices were common. There were insufficient supplies of some basic foods. Diets were limited and deficiency diseases

widespread. Diets were low in iron, vitamins and minerals. The 1930s diet was low in fat and high in carbohydrates.

Post-Second World War (1950–99)

Food supply problems were resolved after the Second World War. Food imports increased and a greater variety of foods became available. Lifestyles became more sedentary and mealtimes were more informal.

New foods and cooking methods were introduced e.g. Chinese, Italian. Meat consumption increased. Diets were higher in fat and lower in carbohydrates. Anaemia continued to be common among females. A dramatic increase in processed foods took place alongside a decrease in fruit and vegetable consumption in the 1980s.

New dietary diseases appeared e.g. obesity, CHD. Knowledge of nutrition and deficiency diseases improved. Low-fat foods, gluten-free foods and other diet specialist foods were developed.

National nutrition surveys

Other changes in the Irish diet have been recorded by two national nutrition surveys:
- National Nutrition Survey 1946–48
- Irish National Nutrition Survey 1990

COMPARISON OF TWO SURVEYS

1946–48 Survey
- High energy and nutrient intake (higher energy needs)
- War food supply problems e.g. sugar, flour
- High intake of complex carbohydrates and dairy produce
- High intake of eggs, potatoes and vegetables
- Greater numbers of farmers supplying food locally
- Greater numbers of people growing vegetables, producing eggs etc.
- Reasonable intake of iron and calcium

1990 Survey
- Energy intake higher for males than females
- Lower consumption of complex carbohydrates
- Reduction in dietary fibre to about 90% of mid-1930s level
- Increase in saturated fats, hidden fats in processed foods
- More convenience processed foods available
- Reduction in intake of dairy produce
- Increase in cheese intake
- Decrease in iron and calcium intake

COMPARISON OF THE IRISH DIET WITH CURRENT DIETARY GUIDELINES

The current Irish diet is low in dietary fibre, iron and calcium, higher than is necessary in fat, protein, salt and sugar. Anaemia, obesity and coronary heart disease are common. Sugar consumption is the highest in Europe.

The main sources of fat are meat and meat products, milk, spreads, biscuits, cakes, chips, savouries, chocolates, etc. Low-fat products are popular. Butter is being replaced by polyunsaturated spreads.

The sources of energy are biscuits, bread, cakes, crisps, meat and meat products. Vitamin C levels are above average while vitamins D and E are below recommended levels. Consumption of fruit is increasing again.

Note: For 'Current Dietary Guidelines' refer to 'Dietary and Food Requirements'.

ASPECTS OF MALNUTRITION

Common malnutrition diseases in Ireland are anaemia, bowel disorders, constipation, coronary heart disease, obesity and osteoporosis.

LOW DIETARY FIBRE INTAKE

The causes of low dietary fibre intake are:
- Eating insufficient fibre e.g. cereals, fruit and vegetables
- Overuse of processed foods e.g. white bread, white flour

The *effects on the body* include the risk of bowel disorders, constipation, CHD, gallstones, inability to control blood-cholesterol levels and blood sugar levels, and varicose veins.

Corrective measures
- Increase fibre intake for all meals and snacks
- Avoid processed foods, use unprocessed foods
- Eat a variety of fruits and vegetables, raw when possible
- Replace white bread with wholewheat varieties
- Replace low-fibre, high-sugar snacks with fruit and vegetables
- Drink more water

HIGH SATURATED FAT INTAKE

The causes of high saturated fat intake are:
- Eating too many foods high in saturated fats e.g. animal foods
- Eating too many processed, take-away foods and fast foods

The *effects on the body* include the increased risk of diabetes, CHD, energy intake exceeding energy output, obesity and raised blood cholesterol.

Corrective measures
- Decrease total saturated fat intake
- Replace cooking fats with vegetable oils
- Trim visible fats on meat, select lean cuts
- Grill, poach or steam instead of frying foods
- Choose low-fat and reduced fat products

LOW IRON INTAKE

The causes of low iron intake are:
- Lack of iron-rich foods in the diet
- Inadequate supply of vitamins C, B_{12} and folic acid
- Lack of variety in type of iron e.g. haem, non-haem
- Presence of inhibiting factors e.g. phytic acid
- Heavy blood loss e.g. menstruation

The *effects on the body* include anaemia, tiredness, fatigue and lack of energy.

Corrective measures
- Eat iron-rich foods
- Include adequate vitamin C for absorption
- Reduce intake of inhibiting factors

LOW CALCIUM INTAKE

The causes of low calcium intake are:
- Insufficient vitamin D in the diet
- Presence of phytates, oxalates and dietary fibre
- Excess saturated fatty acids in the body
- Insufficient calcium-rich foods in the diet

The *effects on the body* include rickets, osteomalacia, osteoporosis, muscle spasm, abnormal blood clotting and poor teeth.

Corrective measures
- Increase amounts of calcium-rich food
- Increase intake of vitamin D for absorption
- Choose products fortified with vitamin D and calcium
- Avoid foods with high levels of inhibiting factors

Part One: The Structure of the Irish Food Industry

The key or main areas of the Irish food industry are divided into sectors:
- Fresh Meat (one of the largest exporters of beef in Europe)
- Dairy products and ingredients. (butter, cheese, casein)
- Prepared consumer foods (ready meals, ready-to-cook foods)
- Beverages (alcoholic and non-alcoholic)
- Horticulture (fruits, vegetables, Ireland supplies 50% of mushrooms sold in the UK)
- Fish/fish products (mariculture, aquaculture)
- Consumer foods (preserves, cereal products, bread, cakes, dressings)
- Speciality foods

Note: Data for exports and imports change. Always check current data.

Major food exports data
The main export sectors of the Irish food and drink industry and distribution by sector are:
- Dairy products and ingredients (31%)
- Meats: beef (22%), lamb (3%), pig meat (2%), poultry (6%)
- Prepared consumer foods (19%), convenience foods in the form of frozen, chilled and dried food products
- Edible horticulture (2%)
- Aquaculture (4%)
- Beverages (12%)

Market distribution of Irish food exports by value include:
- UK 39%, continental Europe 35%, rest of world 26%

Major food import data
Imports represent a variety of foods. Some foods imported cannot be produced in Ireland. Examples of food imports are:
Cereals (17%): barley, rice, maize, cereal products (flour, pasta)
Dairy (7%): milk, milk products, cheese, yoghurt
Drinks (19%): beers, wines, spirits, fruit juices, vegetable juices, soft drinks
Fish (4%): canned, dried, fresh, smoked (many varieties)

Fruit: apples, citrus, dates, figs, grapes, kiwi, melons, pineapples, strawberries
Vegetables: beans, fennel, garlic, lentils, mange tout, onions, peas, peppers
Others: tinned fruit and vegetables, tea, coffee, soya products, sauces, soups

Government departments and agencies

The main *government departments* with responsibility for controlling and regulating the Irish food industry are:
• Department of Agriculture, Food and Rural Development
• Department of Health, community and Children's Affairs
• Department of Communications, Marine and Natural Resources

State agencies with responsibility for supporting the Irish Food Industry are An Bórd Bia, An Bórd Glas, Bord Iascaigh Mhara (BIM), Enterprise Ireland, Food Safety Authority (FSAI) and Teagasc.

Small businesses and home enterprises

Many small businesses and enterprises are family run and involve small numbers of people. EU hygiene and safety standards are implemented. Growth in small businesses and home enterprises has taken place as a result of:
• Innovation, new ideas, desire of individuals to work for themselves
• Reductions in farm incomes and enforcement of farm quotas
• Potential for processing materials using new technology and skills
• Excellent state support for setting up new businesses and enterprises
• Increased demand from consumers for exclusive quality products

The role of small businesses and home enterprises

Small businesses and home enterprises:
• Create new employment, frequently in rural locations
• Provide variety in changing markets to meet consumer demands
• Identify and link into key markets, old and new
• Offer new exclusive ranges of food items
• Promote the use of quality ingredients
• Promote innovation in food production

Irish *speciality foods and drinks* fall into *eight* sectors: bakery, beverages, condiments, confectionery, dairy, prepared foods, preserves, speciality meats and fish.

CAREER OPPORTUNITIES IN FOOD AND RELATED INDUSTRIES

• Gaining a qualification in a chosen area
• Gaining employment directly without a qualification
• Using qualifications and expertise to create new food products
• Manufacturing/preparation in the food industry

- Management and administration
- Food technologists, technicians, biotechnologists, microbiologists
- Non-designated craft: bakers, butchers, confectionery makers
- Designated crafts: fitters, maintenance electricians, instrument mechanics
- Production operators – specific to each area of work
- Marketing and retailing
- Product distribution and transport logistics
- Suppliers of services and raw materials

Careers in the production food industry

Farmer, fisher, horticulturist and miller are careers that can be followed in the food production industry.

Examples of careers in catering and retail food industry

- Chefs, bakers, butchers, confectioners, caterer
- Deli counter staff
- Waitresses, waiters, bar staff (restaurants etc.)
- Hospitality assistant
- Managers (hotel, restaurants, catering)
- Accommodation and housekeeping
- Administrative staff (accountants, receptionists, assistants)

Other food related careers

- Dieticians/nutritionists
- Demonstrators (supermarket promotions, product promotion)
- Environmental Health officers
- Home Economics teachers
- Lecturers in catering colleges
- Public analysts
- Quality controller
- Researchers
- Working in government departments, An Bórd Bia, BIM, FSAI
- Writer (magazines, regional and national papers)
- TV chef (cookery programmes/series, demonstrations)

Part Two: Food Commodities

The main food commodities available to the consumer are: meat and poultry, fish, eggs, meat substitutes (novel protein foods), milk and milk products, vegetables and fruit, cereals, fats and oils.

Note: Check the 'Food Composition Tables' in your *Home Economics* book to find out the composition of each food commodity.

MEAT AND POULTRY

Classification
Carcase meat: cattle, sheep, pig
Game: deer, duck, grouse, hare, rabbit, pheasant
Offal: internal organs of animals that are edible e.g. kidney, liver
Poultry: domesticated or tame birds e.g. duck, goose, turkey

Nutritive significance
Protein: excellent source of HBV protein e.g. actin, collagen, myosin
Carbohydrates: none present
Lipid (fat): saturated fats (visible and invisible)
Minerals: excellent source of iron, source of zinc, phosphorus, potassium and sulphur
Vitamins: B-group vitamins, traces of vitamins A and D in offal
Water: between 50–70%, more in lean meat than in fatty meat
Meat extractives: soluble substances that give meat its flavour

Contribution to the diet
Meat is an excellent supply of HBV proteins, essential for growth in children, adolescents and pregnant women. Good source of essential minerals e.g. iron (meat), zinc (offal). Lacks carbohydrates, vitamins C and A, and calcium. Amount of fat present varies with age, type, size, type and cut of meat.

Figure 3.1 Structure of meat

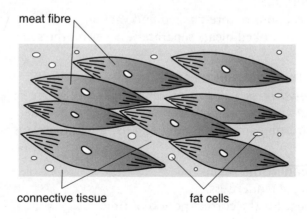

meat fibre

connective tissue   fat cells

Rules for buying meat
Buy meat from a reputable shop with a good turnover where:
- Surfaces and equipment are clean and hygienic
- Assistants do not handle meat and money
- Assistants have hair covered and wear protective clothing
- Raw and cooked meats are stored and handled separately
- Plastic gloves are worn by assistants who handle meat
- The meat supplied is produced under the Board Bia Quality Assured Programme (traceability, quality and safety standards)

Rules for selecting meat
- Buy fresh meat in small quantities unless freezing
- Choose meat that has a good bright colour
- Cuts should be firm and moist, free of slime and of odours
- Choose the correct cut of meat for the dish being cooked
- Cheaper cuts of meat are just as nutritious as leaner cuts

Beef labelling/compulsory labelling, 1 January 2002 (phase 2)
Compulsory labelling provides a minimum of information backed up by an information system, which is certified and monitored. Phase 1 was introduced on 1 January 2001; phase 2, introduced in January 2002, ensured that additional information was included. Fresh, chilled and frozen beef sold as beef cuts or mince, minced meat and beef originating outside the EU must carry specific information.

Storing meat
- Store fresh meat quickly after purchase
- Unwrap, put on a clean plate, cover loosely and store in a refrigerator at 5°C, on the bottom shelf
- Follow instructions on pre-packed and vacuum packed meat labels
- Store raw and cooked meats separately, never on the same plate or shelf

Toughness or tenderness of meat
Activity of animals: less active → more tender, more active → less tender
Age of animals: younger animals are more tender than older animals
Conditioning: resting animals before, and hanging after slaughter

Methods of tenderising meat
- Using chemical tenderisers
- Hanging meat for the correct period of time
- Mechanical methods (beating, mincing, cubing, piercing)

- Selecting long slow moist methods of cooking e.g. stewing
- Marinating meat in order to break down the fibres

Methods of cooking meat

Barbecuing, braising, grilling, roasting, pot-roasting, shallow frying, stir-frying, stewing/casserole are all ways to cook meat.

Effects of cooking on meat

- Colour changes from red to brown
- Micro-organisms are destroyed e.g. bacteria
- Proteins coagulates, meat becomes firmer
- Meat shrinks due to loss of water, fat melts
- Collagen changes to gelatin, meat becomes tenderer
- Some B-group vitamins are destroyed
- Flavour and texture are improved
- Extractives are released

Table 3.1 Methods of preserving and processing meat

Method	Overview of the method
1. Canning	Ingredients are heated to high temperatures, increasing shelf-life of the product. Changes occur in B-group vitamin content, colour, flavour and texture e.g. corned beef, canned stew.
2. Curing	Curing agents used in curing are nitrates, nitrites and salt solution. Curing prevents the growth of Clostridium botulinum.
3. Drying/ dehydration	Small pieces of meat, e.g. mince, are dried for use in packet soups. Freeze dried meat extracts are used in stock cubes. Some loss of B-group vitamins occurs.
4. Freezing	Meat can be frozen at home or commercially. Commercial freezing involves boning, trimming off fat and blast freezing the meat at –30°C. Storing frozen meat incorrectly or for the wrong period of time causes fats to become rancid. A damaged wrapping exposes meat to the air and results in freezer-burn.
5. Smoking	A traditional method of preserving food and preventing bacterial growth. Meat is smoked using chemicals or smoke fumes after the curing process.
6. Vacuum Packing	This involves packing meat into polythene, removing air and heat-sealing the edges e.g. rashers, gammon and sausages. Items must be stored in refrigerators, must be treated like fresh meat when opened.

Examples of meat products

Beef burgers, black and white puddings, cold cooked meats, gelatine, meat extractives, mechanically recovered meat, pate and sausages are all examples of meat products.

Offal

Offal is a term used to describe cheap and nutritious edible internal organs of animals e.g. heart, kidney, liver, sweetbreads and tongue. They are good sources of B-group vitamins, iron and protein.

POULTRY

Classification

Domestic: chicken, duck, goose, turkey
Game: duck, pheasant, snipe

Nutritional significance

Protein: good source of HBV easily digested protein
Carbohydrates: none present, serve with starchy foods
Lipids/fat: varies depending on the type and age of bird
Vitamins: B-group vitamins but less than in red meat
Minerals: less iron than red meat, traces of calcium, phosphorus and zinc
Water: significant amounts, 50–70%

Contribution to the diet

Poultry has a lower fat content than red meat. Poultry is a good alternative to red meat when aiming to reduce saturated fat intake in the diet. It is useful when following low-calorie and low-cholesterol diets, for invalids and the elderly. It is an easily digested food. As poultry has no carbohydrates, it is low in minerals and most vitamins, serve it with foods rich in these nutrients.

Rules for buying poultry

- Buy from a reliable source
- If pre-packed check the 'use by' or 'best before' label
- Check for signs of freshness
- Avoid poultry with a bad smell, poor colour and blemishes on the skin
- Frozen poultry should be frozen solid, with undamaged wrappers

Storing poultry

Frozen poultry should be stored in a freezer as soon as possible after purchase. Do not leave it in the car or lying on the kitchen work surface. Defrost thoroughly before cooking. Incorrect storage can result in salmonella poisoning. Remove giblets when thawed. Never refreeze a thawed chicken.

Fresh poultry should be stored on a clean plate, covered, on a lower shelf in the refrigerator and used as soon as possible.

Rules for cooking poultry

Because salmonella bacteria are associated with poultry it must be prepared and cooked correctly to avoid food poisoning.
- Wash hands thoroughly before and after handling raw poultry
- Wash chopping board and knives to prevent cross-contamination
- Remove wrapper and giblets, thaw frozen poultry thoroughly
- Cook stuffing separately, cook poultry thoroughly to destroy bacteria
- Cool leftover poultry quickly, cover and store in refrigerator
- Use leftovers quickly. Never reheat poultry remaining on the bone

Poultry products: whole (frozen, fresh), boned and rolled, jointed, pre-cooked chicken meals, chicken nuggets, burgers, sausages, Kiev

FISH

Fish may be classified according to (a) nutritive value, (b) shape (flat or round), and (c) habitat (freshwater, saltwater or farmed).

Table 3.2 Nutritional significance (based on fat content)

White fish	Oily fish	Shellfish
Flesh contains little or no fat. Fat stored in liver e.g. cod, haddock, plaice, whiting.	Fat found throughout flesh. Fatty acids present are unsaturated e.g. herring, mackerel, salmon, trout.	Lower in fat than oily fish e.g. crustaceans, molluscs.

Shape
- Flat fish: plaice, sole
- Round fish: salmon, trout

Table 3.3 Habitat or source

Freshwater	Saltwater (two groups)	Farmed
Found in rivers and lakes e.g. eel, perch, pike, salmon, trout.	*Demersal*: fish that swim on seabed e.g. cod, plaice, sole. *Pelagic*: fish that swim in shoals near surface e.g. herring, mackerel.	Fish farming is popular as a method for producing oysters, mussels, salmon and trout.

Nutritional significance

Protein: excellent source of easily digested HBV protein
Carbohydrates: none present
Lipids (fat): high in omega-3 family of polyunsaturated fatty acids, significant amounts of EPA and DHA are present
Minerals: iodine and fluorine (sea fish), phosphorus, potassium, calcium present in shellfish and in bones of tinned salmon
Vitamins: B-group vitamins, oily fish good source of vitamin D
Water: high in white fish, less in shellfish and oily fish (65%)

Contribution to the diet

Fish is a good alternative to meat. It supplies HBV proteins. Its low fat content makes it useful in low-calorie and low-cholesterol diets. The types of fatty acids present are linked with lowering risks of heart disease. Fish is easy to digest (useful in the diets of invalids and elderly). It is a valuable source of iodine (helps prevent goitre), vitamins A and D. As it lacks carbohydrate, vitamin C and adequate amounts of iron, serve fish with foods rich in these nutrients.

Figure 3.2 Structure of fish

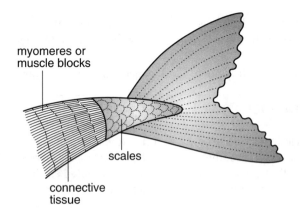

myomeres or muscle blocks

scales

connective tissue

Structure of fish

Fish is composed of bundles of fibres, myomeres, which contain extractives, proteins and water. Myomeres are held together by collagen, which changes to gelatin during cooking. The outer skin of fish is composed of a layer of scales. Fibres in shellfish are coarser, difficult to digest and shellfish is covered with a hard shell.
Cuts of fish: whole, filleted, in cutlets, steaks and tailpieces

Spoilage of fish (staling)

Fish is perishable. Once caught, fish struggle and use up their energy stores of glycogen in the muscles. Lactic acid (which would preserve fish) is not formed, fish stales quickly and begins to 'go off' producing tri-methylamine. Bacteria multiply rapidly. Fish also becomes stale and spoils due to enzymic activity and oxadative rancidity. Polluted waters may contaminate shellfish.

Buying fish
When buying fresh fish (general and shellfish):
- Choose fish when in season, fish should smell fresh
- Eyes should be fresh, bright and bulging
- Flesh should be firm and moist, gills bright red or pink
- Medium-sized fish have a better flavour than large fish
- Colour should be characteristic of species
- Smoked fish should have a glossy skin and smoky smell
- Shellfish should be clean, molluscs should not be open, crustaceans should be active and alive

Frozen and pre-packed fish
Check the sell-by-date when buying frozen or pre-packed fish. Ensure that the fish is frozen solid. Place in the freezer as soon as possible after purchase. Packaging must not be damaged.

Storing fish
- Remove wrapping, and place on bed of ice in a clean dish
- Cover, place in coldest part of fridge, use as soon as possible
- Store away from other foods, other foods will absorb its smell
- Use fresh fish on the same day of purchase
- Place frozen fish into freezer to avoid thawing out
- Cover smoked fish and refrigerate
- Use tinned fish immediately after opening the tin

Methods of cooking fish
Baking, braising, frying (deep-fat, shallow, stir-frying), grilling, microwave cooking, poaching and steaming

Effects of cooking on fish
- Bacteria and parasites are destroyed
- Protein coagulates and sets between 60°C and 70°C
- Fish shrinks slightly
- Collagen changes to gelatin and myomeres separate into flakes
- Colour changes from transparent to opaque
- Overcooking causes flakes to fall apart and the fish to become tough and dry
- Loss of water-soluble vitamins (B-group) and minerals

Effects of cooking on nutritive value
- Baking, poaching and steaming do not change the nutritive value.
- Grilling removes fat, improves flavour, colour and texture
- Braising and all frying methods can increase the saturated fat content

- Coatings, batters and stuffings may increase the fat content or may improve the nutritive value, flavour and texture of fish dishes depending on the ingredients used

Table 3.4 Commercial processing of fish

Methods	Effects of processing	Examples
Canning	Loss of B-group vitamins. Increased calcium because bones are processed and can be eaten.	Crab, herrings, sardines, salmon and tuna in brine, oil or sauces
Freezing	Fish is boned, filleted and blast frozen at −30°C. Action of bacteria and parasites are inhibited. Nutritive value almost the same as fresh fish. A little loss of B-group vitamins.	Fish cutlets, steaks, fish cakes, ready-to-cook fish dishes, fish fingers, fish in batter, breadcrumbs or sauces
Smoking	Can be done naturally in a kiln over oak chips or artificially dyed and flavoured. Bacteria are destroyed, fish changes colour and a smoky flavour develops. Can be cold smoked at 30°C or hot smoked at 110°C.	Cod, haddock, herring, mackerel, salmon

EGGS

Figure 3.3 Structure of an egg

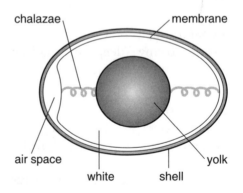

Nutritional significance
Protein: rich source of 100% HBV proteins, especially essential amino acids
Carbohydrates: none present in eggs
Lipids: saturated fat present in yolk, high levels of cholesterol in yolk
Minerals: calcium, iron, phosphorus, sulphur
Vitamins: B-group vitamins in egg white, vitamins A and D in egg yolk
Water: high water content (74% in whole egg), less in the yolk than in the white

Contribution to the diet

Eggs provide 100% high biological value proteins. Eggs are a cheap, versatile food, suitable for savoury and sweet dishes. Eggs provide an alternative to meat, fish and poultry. They are suitable for a lacto-vegetarian diet, are easy to digest and ideal for the elderly and children. They lack carbohydrates and vitamin C. Use with caution because of the saturated fat and cholesterol contents. Restrict intake in low-fat and low-cholesterol diets. Eggs are a good source of iron but need to be served with vitamin-C rich foods.

Shopping for eggs

- Buy from a clean, busy shop with a good turnover of customers
- Choose eggs that are correctly labelled, clean, fresh, free from blemishes
- Check best before date

Labelling of eggs

Information given on egg boxes includes country of origin, name of producer and registration number of packing station, product name and quantity, class, week number (1–52) and expiry date.

Grading of eggs: size 1 (70 + g), size 2 (65–70 g), size 3 (60–65 g), size 4 (55–60 g), size 5 (50–55g), size 6 (45–59 g)

Class

Quality and freshness of eggs: class A (top quality), class B (fair quality), class C (shell may be cracked), extra class (very fresh).

Eggs and the bacteria salmonella

In order to reduce the risk of salmonellosis Ireland has an approved EU salmonella plan.

Quality assurance

Ireland has a quality assurance scheme for egg production in line with EU approved plans or guidelines. Producers and suppliers are inspected and approved. Only heat-treated feed is used. Eggs carry the quality assurance logo, best-before date and house code. Full traceability is guaranteed by the management systems in place. All systems involved are audited before the Quality Assurance mark is awarded.

Storing eggs

- Store in a refrigerator, away from strong smelling foods, with the pointed end down
- Do not wash eggs, this removes the outer coating and causes staling
- Use eggs in rotation

- Egg whites and yolks can be frozen separately
- Remove eggs from the fridge one hour before use

Effects of heat and over-cooking on eggs
- Bacteria are destroyed e.g. salmonella
- Proteins are denatured and coagulate (white at 60°C, yolk at 68°C)
- Egg albumin changes colour and becomes opaque
- On heating, egg albumin becomes insoluble
- Little loss of nutrients except B_1, thiamine
- Overcooking causes curdling and eggs become indigestible
- Formation of sulphide ring if overcooked

Properties of eggs
Ability to entrap air/aeration: egg protein when whisked traps and holds air, and creates foam (foaming)
- Examples of application: meringues, soufflés, sponge cakes

Coagulation: eggs coagulate or set when heated e.g. scrambled egg
- Examples of application: boiled, fried, poached eggs, binding ingredients, coating foods, clarifying soups, glazing and thickening mixtures

Emulsification: lecithin in egg yolk holds two immiscible liquids together as an emulsion
- Examples of application: cakes (fat and sugar), Hollandaise sauces (butter and vinegar), mayonnaise (oil and vinegar)

Preservation of eggs: drying, freezing, picking and pasteurisation

Table 3.5 Culinary uses of eggs

Properties and culinary uses/applications
Aerating (foaming): cakes, desserts, meringues, sponges, soufflés *Clarifying*: soups
Coagulation ■ Binding: burgers, omelettes, potato cakes, potato croquettes, rissoles ■ Coating: batters, coating sweet or savoury fried foods ■ Garnishing: halved, sieved or sliced for salads and other savoury dishes ■ Glazing: pastry flans, pies, scones, tarts ■ On their own: boiled, fried, omelette, poached, scrambled ■ Thickening: custards, quiches, sauces, soups
Emulsifying: cakes (fat and sugar), mayonnaise (oil and vinegar), sauces
Enriching: adding to the nutritional value of dishes, as meat alternative

Novel Protein Foods

Protein alternatives to meat are derived from two non-animal sources:
- Processed plant foods: TVP from soya beans, miso, tempeh, tofu
- New or novel sources: myco-protein (quorn) and micro-organisms

Textured Vegetable Protein (TVP)

TVP is manufactured from soya beans, which consist of HBV proteins. A variety of other products are also made from soya beans e.g. soya milk, tofu, miso and tempeh.

Nutritive value of TVP
Protein: HBV, methionine is added during manufacture
Carbohydrate: removed during processing of bean
Lipid: polyunsaturated fatty acids
Vitamins: B-group vitamins, thiamine and riboflavin added
Minerals: useful for its iron and calcium content

Manufacture of TVP
Oil is removed from the soya bean; beans are ground into a flour-like mixture. Carbohydrate is then removed leaving only protein. Nutritive additives, colour, vegetable oil, flavourings and seasonings are added before the mixture is heated and extruded to create a specific texture and shape (minced, meat cubes, beef or chicken flavour). It is then dried, cooled and packed.

Advantages of TVP
- Less expensive than meat, good substitute for meat
- Makes fresh meat go further (useful as a meat extender)
- Low fat content, nutritive value similar to meat
- Does not shrink during cooking

Disadvantage of TVP
- Inferior flavour to meat, TVP tends to be bland
- Extra flavouring is usually required
- Not as good a texture as in meat and the range of forms available is limited

Uses of TVP in home cooking: burgers, casseroles, curry, lasagne, stews
Use of soya beans: miso, sausage mixes, soya flour, soya milk, soya yoghurt, soya sauce, tempeh, tofu, as a vegetable

Myco-proteins

Protein produced by fungi in a fermenter is called myco-protein. It is low in fat, cholesterol free, high in dietary fibre and a good source of protein.

Quorn

Quorn is made from myco-proteins and is expensive when compared to meat. Sold in chunks or as mince it can be used in a variety of dishes. Quorn is good as a meat substitute or as a meat extender. Its texture is more appetising than TVP. It is not suitable for vegans because of its egg white content. Quorn is added to some commercial food products.

Nutritional value

Quorn is a good source of protein, fibre, B_{12} and zinc. It is low in fat and a poor source of iron and most B-group vitamins. Therefore quorn should be included in dishes high in these nutrients.

Tofu

Tofu is soya bean curd suitable for vegetarian dishes. It requires flavouring.

Milk and Milk Products

Sources: cows, goats, buffalo camel, mares and sheep

Nutritional significance

Protein: HBV protein, caseinogen, lactalbumin and lactoglobulin
Carbohydrate: milk sugar called lactose, a sweet disaccharide
Lipids: mainly saturated fat present, fatty acids oleic and butyric acids
Vitamins: rich source of vitamins A and D, B_1 and B_2, lacks vitamin C
Minerals: excellent source of calcium and phosphorus, traces of other minerals
Water: High water content, almost 87%

Contribution to the diet

Milk is the perfect food for newborn babies and is important in the diet of infants, children, adolescents, pregnant and nursing mothers, invalids and the elderly. It is an easily digested food. Milk provides essential nutrients for growth, development and repair in the form of HBV proteins, calcium, phosphorus, vitamins A and D. It is an important source of B-group vitamins. The fat present is in an easily digested form. Milk and milk products may be fortified with extra nutrients. Low-fat milk is suitable for low-cholesterol or low-kilocalorie diets but not for children.
Culinary uses of milk: in beverages, as a main ingredient, enriching sauces and glazing the surface of scones and tarts

Reasons for processing milk
- Destroys micro-organisms
- Increases shelf-life or keeping qualities
- Develops flavour
- Increasing nutritive value, fortifying with nutrients

Types of milk
- Whole milk: full fat (3.5%) milk, pasteurised, most popular
- Skimmed milk: fat has been removed
- Low-fat or semi-skimmed milk: half the fat is removed
- Supermilk: low-fat fortified with calcium and vitamins A and D
- Buttermilk: liquid leftover after making butter
- Dried milk: water removed from milk
- Evaporated milk: 60% water removed, fortified with vitamins A and D
- Condensed milk: milk is evaporated to reduce volume and sugar is added

Methods of processing milk
There are different methods of processing milk: condensed milk, dehydrated milk (dried or powdered milk), evaporated milk, homogenisation, pasteurisation, semi-skimmed and skimmed milk, sterilisation and ultra-heat treatment.

Note: Refer to 'Food Profiles' – 'Milk in Food Processing and Packaging' for more details on the processing of milk.

Effects of heat/cooking on milk
- Micro-organisms are destroyed (pathogenic bacteria)
- Protein coagulates, a skin forms on the surface
- Flavour changes, lactose caramelises, becomes sweeter in condensed milk,
- Loss of vitamins C and B-group, amount lost varies with type of milk
- Overheating and acids causes curdling
- Shelf-life is increased by processing

Buying and storing milk
- Check 'best before' date
- Store fresh milk in a refrigerator between 2–4°C
- Store milk in its own container in the refrigerator
- Never mix new and old milk, use in rotation
- Store away from strong smelling foods/dishes
- If delivered to the door take indoors quickly

Regulations – preventing disease and spoilage

In Ireland there are laws that prohibit the sale of raw unpasteurised milk. The Milk and Dairy Acts and the Foods and Drugs Acts control the safety of milk to ensure that it is of high quality and fit for human consumption. Animals are regularly tested for diseases e.g. T.B. Farms are registered and milking, transportation and processing of milk are monitored on an ongoing basis.

DAIRY PRODUCTS

Butter

Butter is manufactured from cream that comes from cows' milk. The cream is pasteurised, cooled, heated and then churned. The fat globules separate from the liquid. This liquid, buttermilk, is drained off. The butter is washed, blended, salted, wrapped, weighed and packed for distribution. Regulations control the fat and water content of butter: a minimum of 80% fat must be present and never more than 16% water. Buttermilk is sold for baking.

Nutritional significance

Protein: small amounts of HBV proteins, all the caesin is in buttermilk
Carbohydrates: traces of milk sugar, lactose
Lipids: high percentage of saturated animal fat
Minerals: some calcium, phosphorus, added salt provides sodium chloride
Vitamins: good source of fat-soluble vitamin A, less vitamins D and E
Water: low water content (butter must not contain more than 16%)

Classification of butter – the main types

Salted butter or cream butter, unsalted butter, reduced-fat butter, cream butter and concentrated butter.

Dairy spreads and spreadable butters

Spreadable butter, dairy spreads, reduced-fat or low-calorie spreads.

Culinary uses

Butter and spreads can be used in cake making, fillings for cakes, enriching potatoes, sauce making, sautéing meat or vegetables and spreads for sandwiches.

Cream

Cream is a fat-in-water emulsion, which rises to the top of milk. Milk is heated and the cream separated by centrifugal force in a separator. The skimmed milk is removed. Creams with different fat contents are produced. Fresh cream is heat-treated using pasteurisation, sterilisation or ultra-heat treatments (long life).

Cream is low in protein and carbohydrate, high in saturated fat and has traces of vitamins A and D.

Classification of cream
Half cream (12% fat), single cream (18% fat), whipping cream (36–40% fat), double cream (48% fat), UHT cream (18%), soured cream (18%).
Cream substitutes: crème fraiche, fromage frais, yoghurts (Greek, natural)

Storage
Buy cream that has been stored in a refrigerated unit in the shop. Check 'use-by' date. Store, covered and away from strong smelling foods, in the refrigerator at home, use as soon after purchase as possible.

Ice cream
Ice cream is made from cream, milk, sugar, stabilisers, colourings and flavourings. The ingredients are mixed, pasteurised, homogenised and emulsifiers are added. Air is whipped in as the mixture is partially frozen. The temperature is reduced and the ice cream hardens. Ice creams are stored in a deep freeze and removed a short time before serving.
Types: dairy ice-cream (animal fat), ice-cream (vegetable fat)

YOGHURT

Yoghurt is made from homogenised, pasteurised milk with a bacteria culture added. The lactic acid bacteria incubate and ferment the mixture, lactose is converted to lactic acid, the mixture thickens and is then allowed to cool to form natural yoghurt. At this stage fruit, flavourings and sweeteners may be added to produce fruit yoghurts. Whole milk is used for full-fat yoghurt and skimmed milk is used for low-fat yoghurt.

Nutritional significance
Similar value to milk (whole milk or low-fat milk), good source of HBV protein, calcium, vitamins A and D. Added fruit or/and sugar increases carbohydrate content.

Contribution to the diet
Yoghurt is a nutritious and economical natural food. It provides nutrients, which benefit toddlers, children, adolescents, pregnant and nursing mothers for growth and development. Yoghurt is an excellent source of calcium for healthy bones and teeth. It is easy to digest, suitable for invalids and the elderly, a convenient food for a busy lifestyle, packed lunches, snacks and desserts. Low-fat varieties useful for low-fat diets.

Classification of yoghurt
Full-fat yoghurt, low-fat or diet yoghurt, set yoghurt, live yoghurt and bioyoghurt, Greek yoghurt, drinking yoghurt, frozen yoghurt and fromage frais.

Uses of yoghurt
- On its own as a dessert or snack
- On breakfast cereals instead of milk
- Dips, salad dressings, marinades, smoothies, shakes
- Use in sauces and savoury dishes instead of cream
- As a substitute for cream desserts e.g. cheesecake

Buying and storage
Buy from a shop where yoghurt has been stored in a refrigerator. Check label for 'best before' date. Store in the refrigerator at home below 4°C. Use in advance of the 'best before' date.

CHEESE

Table 3.6 Classification of cheese (according to method of manufacture)

Hard	Semi-hard	Soft	Others
Cheddar	Cashel Blue *	Brie **	■ Processed:
Cheshire	Blarney	Camembert **	Cheese slices
Coolea	Edam	Cooleney	Cheese spreads
Emmenthal	Feta	Cottage	Smoked cheese
Gruyere	Gouda	Ricotta	■ Low-fat cheese
Kilmeadan	Irish Blue	Mozzarella	■ Vegetarian
Parmesan	Port Salut		■ Farmhouse
Wexford	Roquefort *		
	Stilton *		

*   Indicates an internal mould (blue-veined cheese)
** Indicates an external mould (outer coating)

Nutritional significance
Protein: good source of HBV protein, casein
Carbohydrate: none present, lactose is drained away in the whey
Lipids: high percentage of saturated fat, good source of energy
Minerals: hard cheese is an excellent source of calcium and phosphorus
Vitamins: vitamins A and D (whole milk), B-group
Water: hard cheese has less water than soft cheese, it varies with the type of cheese

Contribution to the diet

Cheese is a concentrated source of HBV protein and calcium, which are essential for growth and development. It is a valuable food in the diets of children, teenagers, pregnant and nursing mothers. Cheese is an excellent source of calcium and phosphorus (cottage cheese is low in calcium). Its high saturated fat content makes it a high-energy food (except cottage cheese). As an alternative to meat, fish and poultry it suits a lacto-vegetarian diet. Cheese is suitable for snacks and packed lunches for children, adolescents and adults. It is quick, convenient, and a good value for money food product. It is a versatile food that can be used for a variety of sweet and savoury dishes.

Cheese production

Milk is pasteurised. A starter (lactic acid bacteria) is added to convert lactose to lactic acid. The milk is heated to 30°C. An enzyme, rennet, added to the heated milk, coagulates the milk protein caesinogen producing *curds and whey*. Curd is chopped, whey is drained off, curd is heated again (scalding) to remove more whey and to regulate the consistency of the type of cheese being produced. Curds are allowed to settle and stick together, cut into blocks, salt is added and cheese (curd) is pressed into moulds and pressed for varying lengths of time. Hot water is sprayed onto the moulds to form the rind on cheese. The cheese is removed from moulds, date stamped and left to ripen at 10°C. Cheese is graded and packaged. The different cheeses are created by a variety of techniques e.g. using different starter cultures, moulds, pressing or not pressing the cheese and using skimmed or whole milk.

Buying, storing and using cheese

- Buy in small amounts and use when fresh, check date stamps
- Ensure that wrappers on pre-packed cheese are not damaged
- Store open cheese in a refrigerator, wrapped in greaseproof paper
- Store soft unripened cheese in a covered container in a refrigerator
- Bring cheese to room temperature to develop flavours 30 minutes before use
- Grate leftover hard cheese, store in a jar and use as a garnish

Culinary uses

Eat cheese on its own as a snack or as an accompaniment. Use cheese for fillings, pastry, scones and biscuits. Grated as toppings (au gratin), as a garnish, as a main dish, in dessert and for cheese boards.

Effects of heat on cheese

- Protein coagulates, shrinks and may become denatured
- Fat melts and at high temperatures separates out
- Overcooking causes fat to separate and become stringy
- Dry heat causes cheese to brown

- Add cheese towards the end of the cooking time if possible
- Do not reheat cheese, it becomes tough and indigestible
- Little change in nutritive value

FRUIT

Classification of fruit and examples
Berries: blackcurrants, blueberries, gooseberries, strawberries
Citrus: grapefruits, lemons, limes, oranges, satsumas, tangerines
Dried: currants, dates, figs, raisins, prunes, sultanas
Hard: apples, pears
Stone: avocado, apricots, cherries, nectarines, peaches, plums
Tropical: kumquats, mangoes, melons, passion fruit, pineapples, star-fruit
Others: rhubarb

Nutritional significance
Proteins: traces of LBV protein present, best source are dried fruit
Carbohydrates: fructose, glucose, starch, dietary fibre
Lipids: none in most fruits except avocados and olives
Minerals: calcium, iron and trace elements
Vitamins: rich supply of vitamin C, beta-carotene in some fruits
Water: very high in all fresh fruit, lower amount in dried fruit

Contribution to the diet
- Fresh fruit rich in vitamin C, assists the absorption of iron
- Vitamins and minerals present protect against disease
- Excellent source of non-starch polysaccharide (NSP)
- An ideal food for low-kilocalorie and high-fibre diets
- High water content makes fruit a refreshing food
- Fruit provides a variety of colours, flavours and textures

Buying fruit
- Buy fruits in season when cheapest
- Choose top quality fruits, check the grade
- Choose just ripe fruits, loose rather than pre-packed
- Buy in useable quantities, use as soon as possible

Storing fruit
In the home: remove fruit from plastic wrapping on returning home. Store in a cool area with good dry air circulation to slow down moisture loss and the action of enzymes and moulds. Damp air encourages rapid decay. Wash all fruit before using them to remove traces of sprays.

Commercially: some fruits are treated with sulphur dioxide during storage e.g. apples, peaches, pears. Under-ripe fruit are sprayed with ethylene gas and other fruits are sprayed with a combination of carbon dioxide (CO_2) and oxygen (O_2) to delay the ripening process – referred to as gas storage – promotes longer shelf-life.

Effects of preparation and cooking
- Oxidation occurs during preparation of apples and pears
- Enzymes and micro-organisms are destroyed
- Texture softens, cell-walls break down, becomes digestible
- Colours and flavours change, loss of crispness
- Vitamin C is destroyed, greatest nutrient loss
- Water-soluble vitamins and minerals dissolve into the cooking liquid
- Some metals react with fruit, nutritive value and colour change

Ripening process of fruit – changes that occur
Starch in unripe fruit converts to fructose (sugar) as the fruit ripens. Enzymes promote the ripening, over-ripening and decay of fruit. The sweet smelling ethylene gas is given off during the ripening process.

Culinary uses of fruits
Fruit can be used as garnishes and decorations; for starters, snacks, beverages, in milk shakes and smoothies. Use fruit in main courses and desserts, with a cheese-board and for preserves (jams, jellies, chutneys and pickles).

Effects of processing on fruit
- Canning: texture softens, colour and flavour change, artificial colours are sometimes added, reduces vitamin C, increase in sugar content due to added sugar in syrup
- Drying: reduces water-soluble vitamins B-group and C, increased sugar content due to loss of moisture, iron and calcium are more concentrated
- Freezing: causes little nutritional changes, texture changes

VEGETABLES

Table 3.7 Classification of vegetables

Grown above the ground	Grown below the ground
Leafy greens: cabbage, kale, spinach Flowers: broccoli, cauliflower Pulses: peas, beans, lentils Fungi: mushrooms, truffles Seeds: pulses, sunflowers Stems: celery Fruit: aubergines, courgettes	Bulbs: garlic, leeks, onion, shallot, spring onions Roots: beetroot, carrot, parsnip, turnip Tubers: potatoes, sweet potato

Nutritional significance
Protein: poor source of LBV; pulses provide HBV protein
Carbohydrate: starch, sugar and cellulose (dietary fibre)
Lipids: low except for avocados and olives, polyunsaturated lipids
Minerals: excellent sources of iron and calcium trace elements
Vitamins: excellent supply of beta-carotene, B-group and C
Water: high percentage of water except for dried vegetables

Contribution to the diet
Vegetables are a rich supply of carbohydrates, minerals and vitamins. Cellulose is an important source of dietary fibre, which adds bulk to the diet. Vegetables contain anti-oxidant vitamins A, C and a little E, which protect the body from free radicals. Vegetables lack fat and are useful in a low-kilocalorie and low-cholesterol diets. Pulses are a good alternative to meat for vegetarians. Green vegetables are an excellent source of calcium (bones and teeth) and iron (prevent anaemia), important in the diet of adolescent females, pregnant and nursing women. Vegetables are deficient in vitamin B_{12} and D.

Rules for buying vegetables
* Buy when in season, as they are cheapest, in useable quantities
* Choose clean, fresh, medium-sized vegetables, even in colour
* Choose crisp fresh greens, roots and tubers that appear heavy for their size
* Check grade (quality), 'best before' label and buy in small quantities
* Check pre-packed vegetables for bruising and wilting

Storing vegetables
* Store unwashed, unwrapped in a cool, dry, dark and well-ventilated place
* Store potatoes in a dark place to prevent 'greening' and 'sprouting'
* Store salad vegetables and greens in sealed bags, in the refrigerator
* Place frozen vegetables into the freezer to prevent them thawing out
* Store pulse vegetables in airtight jars
* Discard fruit and vegetables that 'go off' from the storage area

Preparing vegetables
* Use raw whenever possible, or prepare just before cooking
* Avoid early preparation and steeping
* Wash, scrub and peel as appropriate, trim sparingly
* Wash under cold running water to remove all traces of insects and soil
* Prepare according to kind, just before cooking or serving
* Use a sharp knife to prevent nutrient loss, tear leafy green vegetables

Cooking vegetables

Never use bread soda when cooking vegetables as it destroys vitamin C. Cook vegetables *al dente*, never overcook until soggy. Cook in a small amount of water, for the shortest possible time, in a saucepan with a tightly fitting lid. Use leftover cooking liquid for stocks, sauces and soups. Microwaving, pressure-cooking and steaming vegetables retain more nutrients than other methods of cooking.

Effect of cooking on vegetables

- Enzymes and micro-organisms are destroyed
- Cellulose softens, starch cells burst, vegetables become digestible
- Colour, flavour and texture changes
- Water-soluble vitamins and minerals leech into the cooking liquid
- Loss of vitamins C and B_1 due to high temperatures
- Strong flavours of garlic and onions are reduced during cooking

Cooking methods: baking, boiling, frying (deep, shallow), grilling, microwaving, pressure cooking, steaming

Processing vegetables

Home: bottling, crystallisation, dehydration (herbs), freezing, pickling
Commercial: bottling, canning, crystallisation, dehydration, freezing, pickling, irradiation

Effects of processing on vegetables

- Canning: texture changes, loss of vitamins A, C and B-group
- Dehydration: changes in colour, flavour and texture, loss of vitamins
- Freezing: inactivates the actions of enzymes and micro-organisms, nutritive value remains almost unchanged, fruit vegetables lose their shape and texture changes
- Irradiation: stops potatoes sprouting, increases the storage time of vegetables
- Preservatives: sulphur dioxide destroys vitamin B_1

Grading fruit and vegetables

EU regulations state that fruit and vegetables must be labelled and graded correctly. Labels must show the class, country of origin and the variety (name of product).

Table 3.8 Grading of fruit and vegetables

Extra class	Top quality, free from defects in colour, shape and size
Class 1	Good quality, free from bruising and cracking
Class 2	Marketable, some blemishes, defects in colour and shape
Class 3	Inferior quality but marketable, slight blemishes and defects

CEREALS

The *main sources* of cereals are grains of cultivated grasses e.g. barley, oats, maize, millet, rice, rye and wheat.

Figure 3.4 Structure of a wheat grain

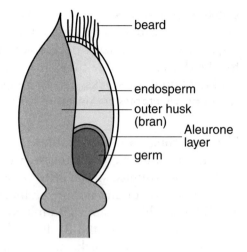

Structure of wheat grain
A wheat grain is composed of three main parts, the outer husk or bran layer (13%), endosperm (85%) and germ (2%).
Bran or husk: contains cellulose, rich in fibre, B-group vitamins (especially niacin), calcium, iron, phosphate
Endosperm: contains the energy store of the grain (mainly starch), some protein and B-group vitamins
Aleurone: the outer layer of the endosperm
Germ or embryo: rich in protein, fat, vitamins E, thiamine, iron and the nutrients for the germination of a new plant, mainly essential fatty acids present
Scutellum: a thin layer between the endosperm and the germ

Nutritional significance
Proteins: small amounts of LBV proteins, mainly gluten, deficient in some essential amino acids (lysine, threonine, tryptophan)
Carbohydrates: high in starch, excellent source of energy, rich in cellulose in the outer husk or bran layer, one of the best sources of fibre in the diet
Lipids: traces in the germ, essential fatty acids in the fat
Minerals: useful amounts of calcium, iron, phosphorus
Vitamins: rich in B-group vitamins (niacin and thiamine)
Water: low water content, about 13%

Contribution to the diet
Cereals are a cheap, nutritious food and are useful in a variety of diets e.g. low-kilocalorie, high fibre.

Coeliacs are unable to absorb gluten. Unprocessed cereals provide roughage in the diet and B-group vitamins, niacin and thiamine. Processing removes outer husk and vitamins, leaving behind high levels of starch. Nutrients are added during processing of some cereals and during the milling of flour.

Dietary problems and diseases associated with cereals
- Absorption of calcium and iron due to the presence of phytic acid
- Coeliac disease sufferers are intolerant to gluten products
- Beriberi occurs in countries where polished rice is the staple food.
- Pellagra is common in countries where maize, which lacks tryptophan, is the staple diet. A lack of niacin results (the human body uses tryptophan to make niacin)

Milling wheat
- Cleaning: wheat is washed to remove dirt, dust and straw
- Conditioning: wheat is dried and conditioned to adjust moisture content
- Blending: mixed wheat is blended to create a 'grist'
- Break rolling: metal rollers are used to split open the grain (wholemeal flour)
- Sieving: germ and bran removed during sieving
- Rolling and sieving: removes the germ and bran completely, produces white flour
- Air classifying: air used to lighten the flour and control the protein quality
- Additives: bleaching agents, improvers and nutrients are added
- Packing: flour is weighed, packed and distributed for sale

Classes of flour
Flour is classed according to its gluten content:
- Strong flour is high in gluten
- Weak flour has lower gluten content
- Plain flour is a mixture of weak and strong flour

Table 3.9 Flour chart – types of flour

Type	Key points
Gluten-free flour	Starch is washed out leaving behind the protein, gluten, used to make products for coeliacs
High-ratio flour	A 'soft' finely milled flour used by commercial bakeries for confectionery, low in gluten, high-quality flour
Self-raising flour	Raising agents, sodium bicarbonate and cream of tartar, are added to flour, which reacts to heat and moisture producing carbon dioxide. Keeps for about two to three months.
Strong flour	High gluten flour from spring wheat, used for yeast cookery and some pastries.
Wheatmeal flour/brown (85% extraction)	Some bran removed, light in texture, brown in colour, less fibre, B-group vitamins, keeps for up to two months. →

Table 3.9 Flour chart – types of flour (cont.)

Wholemeal flour (100% extraction)	None of the grain is removed, light brown in colour, excellent source of B-group vitamins, protein and dietary fibre.
White flour (70–75% extraction) plain or cream	Bran and germ removed, the starchy endosperm and gluten remain, less B-group vitamins, may be fortified with calcium and iron, keeps for up to six months.
Stoneground flour	Two stones replace the metal rollers during milling, 100% extraction.

Gluten
Gluten is a protein found in wheat and rye. When moistened gluten becomes elastic. These elastic properties allow dough to be stretched during the making of bread. Dough rises in the oven, as the gases (CO_2) expand, sets and forms a crust.

Nutritional significance
Protein: LBV proteins, higher in wholemeal flour than in white
Carbohydrate: high levels of starch in white flour, dietary fibre in wholemeal
Lipids: traces present in wholemeal, none in white
Minerals: calcium, iron, some flours fortified with these vitamins
Vitamins: wholemeal contains B-group vitamins
Water: low water content

Fortifying white flour
To replace nutrients lost during milling nutrients are added back in during production. Nutrients added include B_1 (thiamine), niacin, calcium carbonate and iron.

Improvers
Improvers are oxidising agents added to flour to improve the quality of the gluten by making it more elastic, and to whiten flour.

Effects of heat on cereals
- Protein coagulates and in dry heat sets bread or cakes
- Cellulose softens, texture changes and cereals absorb moisture
- Moist heat causes starch grains to burst and thicken liquids (gelatinisation)
- Dry heat causes starch grains to expand, burst and absorb any moisture
- Starch on outer surfaces changes to dextrin in dry heat (dextrinisation)
- Starch becomes more digestible
- Dry heat on surface of cakes causes caramelisation of sugar
- Loss of some B-group vitamins due to heat e.g. thiamine

OTHER CEREALS

Rice

Containing less protein, fat and minerals than other cereals, rice is one of the world's most popular cereals. Many varieties are now available which can be used for a range of sweet and savoury dishes.

Types, varieties and uses

- Short grain rice: short fat grain with a tender, sticky texture when cooked. Sometimes called Carolina rice. *Uses* – sweet dishes, milk puddings
- Medium grain rice: narrow longer grain, between short and long grain rice. Grown in Italy. *Uses* – risotto, rice salads, puddings
- Long grain rice: very long thin grain with a light fluffy texture. *Uses* – savoury dishes e.g. serve with curry, sweet and sour, casseroles
- Brown rice: some of the outer bran layer removed, takes longer to cook, rich in dietary fibre, minerals and vitamins. *Uses* – casseroles, curries, rice salads
- White rice: germ and bran removed. *Uses* – savoury dishes
- Aborio rice: plump rice with a soft moist texture when cooked. *Uses* – risotto
- Basmati rice: long grain rice grown in India, good aroma, flavour and texture. *Uses* – Indian and Middle Eastern dishes
- Jasmine rice: long grain rice with nice aroma and flavour. *Uses* – savoury dishes
- Easy cook rice: long grain rice is steam treated so that it cooks quickly

Rice products: breakfast cereals, canned rice puddings, cartons of creamed rice, ground rice, rice flour, rice paper and rice starch

Pasta

Pasta is made from durum wheat (high in gluten). The wheat is milled into semolina and mixed with eggs, salt, vegetable oil and water to produce strong stiff dough, which is made into different shapes. Pasta is a good alternative to potatoes or rice. It is available in many shapes and colours, fresh or dried; it is a nutritious healthy carbohydrate food that may be used in a variety of ways. It can be cooked in boiling, salted water until *al dente*, drained well, tossed and served immediately. Rinsing in hot water removes starch.

Other cereals and uses

- Barley: pearl barley, used in soups and stews
- Oats: rolled for use in oatmeal and porridge
- Maize: cornflakes, cornflour, corn on the cob and sweetcorn
- Rye: biscuits and breads

FATS AND OILS

Main characteristics
Fats, mainly saturated, are solid at room temperature and oils, mainly poly-unsaturated, are liquid at room temperature.

Sources of fats and oils
- Animal fat: milk fat (butter, cheese, cream), meat and meat fat (dripping, lard, suet)
- Marine oils: fish liver oils (anchovy, cod, halibut), oily fish (herring, mackerel)
- Vegetable oils: nuts, seeds, vegetables, margarine

Nutritional significance
Protein: low levels of protein
Carbohydrates: traces
Lipids: excellent source of essential fatty acids
Minerals: traces of calcium
Vitamins: fat-soluble vitamins A, D, E and K, traces of B-group
Water: depends on the amount of fat present

Value in cooking
Fats and oils act as preservatives, prevent foods sticking together and prevent foods drying out. They improve the flavour and appearance of foods, improve the texture of pastry and delay feelings of hunger.

Culinary uses of fats and oils
- Creaming, flavouring, frying, shortening and spreading
- As an emulsifying agent in a variety of sweet and savoury dishes
- As anti-staling agents, help keep baked products fresher for longer
- In emulsions, e.g. mayonnaise, salad dressings and sauces
- For basting food, sautéing, frying and other cooking methods
- Greasing baking tins
- Preventing food drying out
- Glazing breads, scones, pastries, meats and vegetables

Production of vegetable oils
Seeds, nuts or grains are cleaned, crushed in break rollers and heated. Oil is extracted either physically or using a solvent. Refining removes the impurities in several stages – degumming, neutralising, bleaching, filtration, deodorising and packing. Oil is blended and antioxidants, anti-spattering agents, colours and flavours may be added. Oil is packed for use.

Production of margarine

Margarine is manufactured from vegetable oils by:

- Extracting and refining oils from vegetable sources
- Forcing hydrogen gas through oil, in the presence of a catalyst, to harden the mixture
- Adding and blending colourings, emulsifiers, flavourings, nutrients, other oils, salt, skimmed milk and vitamins
- Churning these ingredients to regulate consistency using a rotator machine and adding stabilisers
- Lowering the temperature, kneading, moulding, shaping, weighing, wrapping and packing

Types of margarine/spreads: block margarine, soft margarine, low-fat spreads, functional spreads

Storing fats and oils

To prevent rancidity store fats, covered and away from strong smelling foods in a refrigerator. Store oils in cool, dark, dry, well-ventilated place. Keep covered and do not leave on the kitchen work surface when not being used.

Part Three: Food Preparation and Food Processing

MEAL PLANNING AND MANAGEMENT

When planning meals consider:

Current dietary guidelines: balancing the nutritional content of the meal, reducing fat, salt and sugar, and increasing fibre

Individual dietary requirements: coeliacs, high-fibre diet, vegetarian diet, low-kilocalorie diet and individuals recovering from illness

Dietary needs through the 'life cycle': babies, toddlers, school-going children, adolescent girls and young women, adolescent boys and young men, pregnant and nursing women, mature adults, elderly people

Resources available: time, skills, money, equipment and technology

Other factors

There are also other factors to consider such as the time of year or season, availability of fresh foods, the occasion, number of people, lifestyle, balance of colours, flavours and textures, variety of ingredients and dishes, presentation and garnishes.

Guidelines for meal planning
- Plan ahead, make a shopping list based on a week's menus
- Choose foods in season (cheaper than out-of-season foods)
- Avoid repetition, vary cooking methods, plan to use all leftovers
- Serve hot dishes in winter, chilled dishes in summer
- Choose fast methods of cooking if time is limited
- Use equipment that speeds up preparation and cooking time
- Plan accompaniments, garnishes/decorations to suit the food

FOOD PREPARATION AND COOKING PROCESSES

Reasons for cooking food
- Micro-organisms and enzymes are destroyed
- Foods look more appetising, colour develops
- Foods taste better, flavour develops
- Cooking aromas stimulate the appetite
- Food becomes more digestible (rice, potatoes)
- Cooking preserves some foods (chutney, jam)

Physical changes in food
- Colour changes e.g. meat looks more appetising on cooking
- Texture becomes softer and more digestible, dried foods become bulkier
- Flavour changes, new flavours can be developed
- Release of extractives or flavourings from meat
- Cooking destroys micro-organisms
- Overcooking changes colour, flavour and texture

Chemical changes in food
- Water-soluble vitamins leech into the cooking liquid
- High heat and a long cooking time destroy vitamins and minerals
- Enzymic browning occurs (enzymes react with oxygen in air)
- Non-enzymic browning (protein and carbohydrates react on heating)

Preventing loss of nutrients
Prepare food just before cooking. Use a sharp knife when cutting fruit and vegetables. Use the minimum amount of cooking liquid. Never steep in water or overnight. Cook vegetables for the shortest possible time. Cook vegetables in the smallest amount of boiling liquid. Use cooking liquids for soups, stocks and gravies.

Principles underlying cooking methods

Cooking causes physical and chemical changes in the food. Heat produced during cooking passes into the food, causing the food to cook. Heat is transferred in three ways:

1. *Conduction*: heat passes from an area of high temperature to an area of lower temperature. It passes from one molecule to the next molecule.

Cooker Hob → frying pan or wok → food

   Example: frying

2. *Convection*: gases or liquids expand and rise when heated. When they cool they become denser and fall. Convection currents are set up which circulate heat.

Cooker hob → saucepan with liquid → food
Oven → convection air currents → food

   Examples: boiling, stewing, roasting

3. *Radiation*: heat travels in straight lines in the form of rays.

Grill → heat rays → food

   Examples: grilling, toasting, barbecuing

Applying the principles of cooking methods

Cooking methods and times are influenced by:
- Composition of food: light or dense
- Shape and size of food: joint, thin slices or pieces, cake
- Type of food: dense meat, spongy cake mixture, fish
- Personal taste: raw, medium or well done

Methods of cooking

Table 3.10 Methods of cooking

Methods	Examples
Dry heat	Grilling, barbecuing, baking
Moist heat	Boiling, braising, poaching, simmering, roasting, steaming, stewing
Using fat	Roasting, frying (deep-fat, dry, shallow, stir-frying)
Microwave	Cooking food using electromagnetic waves

DRY HEAT

Dry heat is the application of heat directly on to the surface of food.

Grilling

Grilling uses intense heat at high temperatures to cook food in a short time under the cooker grill or on the barbecue, sealing in the flavour, moisture and nutrients.
Foods to grill: rashers, sausages, burgers, steaks, chops, cutlets, fish, au gratin dishes, tomatoes, mushrooms, small thin pieces of fruit and vegetables, toast, sandwiches

Rules for application of principle
- Choose food which can be cooked quickly
- Season food with pepper, avoid salt which draws out the juices
- Always pre-heat the grill before cooking
- Brush the grill grid with oil to prevent food sticking
- Seal both sides of the food quickly, so that juice cannot escape
- Turn food frequently using tongs (do not use a fork)

Baking

Baking uses dry radiant heat in an oven to cook food. Heat is transferred by convection. Baked foods have a crisp outer surface. Fan ovens keep the temperature even throughout the oven.
Foods to bake: bread, cakes, pastries, biscuits, pies (sweet and savoury), puddings, fish, vegetables, potatoes

Rules for application of principle
- Pre-heat the oven to the correct temperature (important for breads and cakes)
- Do not overfill the oven, allow space for air currents to circulate
- Avoid opening the oven door frequently, sponges will fall
- To keep some foods moist use foil during the cooking process
- Use oven gloves when removing hot dishes from the oven

MOIST HEAT

Moist heat is the application of heat through a liquid.

Poaching

Poaching means cooking food in gently moving liquid between 80°C and 90°C in an open saucepan or poaching pan. Cooking is by conduction. Poaching is not a fast method of cooking, but it is not as slow as boiling or stewing.
Foods to poach: eggs, fish, fruit

Rules for application of principle
- Read recipe carefully. Some foods need to be poached starting with cold liquid others can be put into warm liquid
- Choose a suitable saucepan or poaching pan
- Suitable poaching liquids include water, stock, milk, syrup, fruit juice, wine
- Barely cover the food with liquid
- Do not leave unattended, food can overcook and fall apart e.g. fish
- Drain food on kitchen paper

Boiling
Boiling means cooking food in a fast-moving liquid at 100°C in an open or covered saucepan. Heat is transferred by conduction. When food reaches boiling, the heat is turned down and the food is left to simmer. Boiling is used when making sauce, jam, chutney, marmalade, stock and syrup.
Foods to boil: vegetables, fresh and salted meat, fish, eggs, cereals

Rules for application of principle
- Choose a saucepan with a well-fitted lid
- Some foods need to be put into fast boiling water (green leafy vegetables)
- Other foods are placed in cold water, brought to the boil and then simmered
- Meat is usually covered with liquid
- Use minimum amount of liquid for vegetables, cook in shallow water
- Develop flavours by adding herbs and other flavourings
- Watch carefully as food can fall apart easily
- Use leftover cooking liquid for soups and sauces
- Remove the food using a slotted spoon, drain before serving

Stewing and casseroling
Stewing is a long, slow method of cooking even-sized pieces of food in liquid in a saucepan with a well-fitting lid. It can be done on the hob (simmered at 90°C) or in the oven (casseroling). Stewing tenderises tough foods and is an economical method of cooking. Collagen changes to gelatine in meat. The cooking liquid is generally served as part of the dish. There is little loss of nutrients.
Foods to stew: tough, cheap cuts of meat (neck, shin, rib beef), poultry, fish, fruit, root and pulse vegetables

Rules for application of principle
- Remove excess fat from meat and poultry
- All food should be cut into even-sized pieces
- Bring liquid to boiling point, reduce and simmer
- Barely cover the food with the liquid cook slowly
- Cover saucepan or dish with tightly fitting lid

- Check from time to time
- Use oven gloves to remove casserole dish from oven

Steaming

Steaming is a slow method of cooking food over steam rising from a saucepan of boiling water on the hob. The food may or may not come into contact with the steam. The liquid does not come into contact with the food. Steaming can be done using two plates over a saucepan, a steamer, bamboo baskets, a pressure cooker, or in a pudding bowl.

Foods to steam: thin pieces of meat, poultry and fish, savoury and sweet puddings, egg custards, potatoes, root vegetables, rice

Rules for application of principle
- Rapidly boiling water is essential
- Bring the water to boiling point before cooking begins
- Never allow the water and the food to come into contact with each other
- Pay attention if using a pressure cooker for steaming, do not leave unattended
- Never allow the saucepan to boil dry
- Season food to make up for the lack of flavour

Pressure cooking.

Similar to steaming, temperatures are higher in the saucepan because of the pressure that builds up. Water boils at a higher temperature in a pressure cooker, steam cannot escape and food cooks more quickly.

Foods for pressure cooking: meat, poultry, preserves, vegetables, rice, complete meals layered in perforated trays

Rules for application of principle
- Never fill more than half full with liquids or two-thirds with solids
- Place the indicator type weight over the air vent to increase pressure and temperature, put the pressure cooker on the hob
- Put the screw type weight in position once a steady stream of steam is coming out of the control valve
- Lower the heat when pressure has been reached, time the cooking of the food from this point and time carefully to avoid overcooking
- Turn off the heat source, lift the pressure cooker off the hob and allow the pressure to reduce to normal
- Remove the lid carefully to avoid a burst of steam hitting the face

HOT OIL OR FAT

Heat can be applied to food by using oil and fat.

Roasting

Roasting is a method of cooking food in a small amount of hot fat or oil at high temperatures, in an oven or on a roasting spit. Food is placed on a roasting tin, rotisserie, in a casserole dish or in roasting bags.

Foods to roast: joints of meat, poultry, game, potatoes, onions, peppers, root vegetables, nuts

Rules for application of principle

- Pre-heat the oven to the recommended temperature
- Do not place food directly from the refrigerator into the oven. Allow food to reach room temperature. Defrost frozen food fully before cooking
- Prepare food and calculate cooking time
- Baste food with hot fat and continue basting during cooking
- If meat is tender quick roast it, if tough slow roast it
- Remove roasting dish from the oven using oven gloves
- Allow to 'stand' for 10 minutes, drain, carve and serve

Frying

Frying is a quick method of cooking food in hot fat or oil. Extra fat is absorbed by the food during frying, as the food is directly in contact with the fat or oil. Heat is conducted from the hob through the frying pan to the food.

Methods of frying

Table 3.11 Methods of frying

Deep-fat frying	Food is immersed in hot oil or fat in a saucepan or deep-fat fryer e.g. chips, fish, fritters, onion rings.
Dry frying	Food is cooked in a shallow pan without fat or oil e.g. rashers, sausages.
Shallow frying	Thin pieces of food are fried in a small amount of fat or oil in a shallow pan e.g. burgers, cutlets, fish cakes, rashers, sausages, steak.
Stir-frying	Small pieces of food are cooked very quickly in hot oil in a wok e.g. vegetables, thinly sliced chicken, beef, lamb.

Rules for application of principle

- Never leave frying pans, deep-fat fryers or woks unattended
- Prepare all ingredients before heating the oil
- Dry food with kitchen paper to remove moisture
- Pre-heat fat or oil before adding the food for cooking
- Seal both sides of food to keep in juices

- Turn food carefully in the wok
- Turn off cooker or deep-fat fryer
- Remove food with a slotted spoon, drain and keep warm
- Allow oils and fats to cool, strain and put into suitable containers

SOUPS

Stock
Good soups are made using stock. Home-made stock is made by simmering a combination of the following fresh ingredients in a liquid until soft: bones from fish, meat or poultry, vegetables such as onions, carrots, celery, leek and/or fish, giblets, meat or poultry and herbs. Once made stocks should be cooled quickly, covered and stored in the fridge or frozen for future use. Use within a few days. Commercial stock cubes are available but tend to be salty in flavour.

CLASSIFICATION OF SOUPS

Thin soups
Broths: thin, unclarified soups with pieces of chicken, meat or vegetables, thickened with barley, rice or pasta.
- Example: chicken broth

Consommé or clear soup: a concentrated clear rich stock that has been clarified using egg white, garnished with strips of root vegetables e.g. carrots
- Example: consommé à la Julienne

Thick soups
Pureés: ingredients are blended or sieved together to create a smooth consistency and texture
- Examples: potato and leek

Thickened or cream: thickened soup using starchy ingredients e.g. flour, cornflour
- Examples: bisque, chowder, white (cream of vegetable)

Cold soups: raw ingredients are blended and chilled
- Example: gazpacho

Thickening soups using liaisons
Soups may be thickened with arrowroot, cornflour, flour, beurre manié, cereal products (barley, rice, pasta), roux or eggs. Roux is equal quantities of fat and flour, fat is melted, flour added, cooked for 1 minute and stock or liquid added.

Characteristics of a good soup
Soups should be free of grease on the surface, have a good flavour, colour, texture and consistency, be well-seasoned (never too salty), serve chilled or piping hot.

Serving soups – garnishes
Garnish according to soup e.g. chopped chives, finely chopped parsley, julienne of carrot, swirl of cream, grated cheese, swirl of yoghurt, chopped bacon, croutons.

Serving soups – accompaniments
Suitable accompaniments include garlic bread, slices of wholemeal bread, toast Melba, yeast dinner buns or rolls, tomato or herb rolls or bread.

SAUCES

Sauces are well-flavoured liquids containing a liaison or thickening agent, used in the preparation of dishes or as accompaniments to dishes in order to enhance the food. Sauces should never overpower the main flavour of the dish. Sauces may be sweet or savoury.

Advantages of sauces
Sauces aid digestion, add variety and interest, enhance the flavour of bland ingredients, counteract the high-fat richness of some dishes, introduce new flavours, textures, colour and improve the nutritive value of the dish.

Culinary uses of sauces
Sauces may be used as an accompaniment, a main part of the dish, to coat fish, meat or vegetables, to bind ingredients and to add colour.

Classification of sauces
Sauces may be classified according to consistency or type.

Sauces according to type
- Simple sauces: apple sauce
- Roux-based sauces: (a) white or (b) brown, and variations
- Cooked egg sauces: custard sauces, cornflour custard sauce
- Cold sauces and dressings: (a) mayonnaise, (b) salad dressings
- Unclassified sauces: simple blended e.g. thickened with cornflour
- Butter sauces: garlic butter sauce, herb butter sauces
- Sweet sauces: chocolate sauce, lemon sauce, cranberry sauce

According to consistency of roux

Consistency of roux sauces is referred to as pouring, stewing, coating and binding. *Variations of roux sauces*: cheese, parsley, onion and mushroom sauces

Thickening a sauce

Sauces may be thickened by puréeing, using a roux base (starch thickens the sauce), addition of eggs (coagulation of protein or emulsification of fat) or adding blended cornflour to the liquid.

Serving sauces

- Serve savoury or sweet sauces separately in a sauce boat
- Do not mask the food with sauce
- Serve hot or cold, depending on the dish
- With desserts serve on plate around the food
- Use a mix of sauces to create interesting effects
- Dredge sweet sauces with icing sugar

PASTRY

Pastry is a mixture of fat, flour and water. Richer pastries contain whole eggs, egg yolk, caster or icing sugar or extra fat.

Classification of pastry

The main types include:

- Shortcrust: basic, flan, biscuit, cheese, all-in-one shortcrust
- Suet: raised pie crust, hot water crust
- Rich or layered pastry: flaky, puff, rough puff
- Hot pastry: choux, hot water crust
- Filo pastry

Table 3.12 Uses of Pastry

Type	Uses
Shortcrust	Apple tarts, bakewell tart, fruit flans, savoury pies
Rich shortcrust	Mince pies, sweet and savoury flans, quiche lorraine
Wholemeal	Sweet and savoury tarts and pies, quiches
Cheese	Cheese straws, quiche, cheese biscuits
Suet crust	Dumplings, puddings, steak and kidney pie
Flaky and rough puff	Sausage rolls, cream horns, mince pies, savoury pies
Puff	Cream horns, cream slices, vol-au-vents, bouchée
Choux	Eclairs, profiteroles, gougère
Filo	Apple strudel, spring rolls, millefeuille

Characteristics of pastry
Well-made pastry has a light golden colour (not too dark or pale), it is not greasy, tough, soggy or brittle, has a fully cooked, crisp texture, a good flavour, not shrunken or uneven.

General guidelines for making pastry
- Weigh and measure ingredients accurately (fat, flour, water)
- Keep utensils and ingredients cold
- Preheat the oven to the correct temperature
- Handle ingredients as lightly and as little as possible
- Lift fingers above the bowl to introduce as much air as possible
- Add water gradually, watch out do not add all of it in at once
- Use a knife to mix in the water, never use your fingers or hands
- Sprinkle flour onto a clean surface
- Knead lightly with the tips of the fingers
- Roll out the pastry evenly without stretching it
- Put it on a plate, cover and rest in refrigerator for 20 minutes
- Make up dish, decorate with pieces of pastry
- Cook in a preheated hot oven

Serving pastry
- Hot or cold depending on time of year, type of meal and dish
- Choose oval dishes for savoury pastry dishes and round for sweet dishes
- Decorate sweet dishes with icing sugar, piped cream on the side of the plate, pastry flowers (cooked as part of the dish)
- Garnish savoury dishes with finely chopped parsley, sprig of parsley, chopped chives, savoury cream
- Serve with appropriate accompaniments (depends on the dish)

RAISING AGENTS AND YEAST COOKERY

Raising agents ensure that gas is produced in the dough. On heating, gas expands, the dough rises and sets. Gluten (protein in flour) becomes sticky when moistened, enabling the dough to stretch until the crust sets. Gas may be produced because of a chemical reaction, a biological reaction or by the introduction of air.

Natural raising agents (air)
Air is introduced by beating, creaming, folding, rolling, rubbing-in, sieving and whisking, or steam is introduced during cooking in batters, cakes and choux pastry.

Chemical raising agents (baking powder, bread soda and sour milk)
Baking powder contains an acid and an alkali. Bread soda is the alkali and sour milk is the acid and the liquid.

Biological raising agents (yeast)

Yeast reacts with flour and sugar (food) in the presence of moisture (eggs, milk, water) and warmth. This biological reaction in home baking is called fermentation.

$$\text{yeast} + C_6H_{12}O_6 + \text{moisture} + \text{warmth} \rightarrow 2C_2H_5OH + CO_2 + \text{energy}$$

glucose   alcohol   carbon dioxide

During the fermentation process the enzymes present in flour and yeast react in the presence of sugar, moisture and warmth. The enzyme in flour is diastase, and in yeast are maltase, sucrase and zymase. The actions involved in fermentation are:
- Diastase in flour changes starch to maltose
- Maltase in yeast changes maltose to glucose
- Invertase in yeast changes sucrose to invert sugar (glucose and fructose)
- Zymase in yeast ferments glucose and fructose and produces carbon dioxide and alcohol

Gluten in the flour becomes elastic and holds the carbon dioxide produced during fermentation. When proving (outside the oven) CO_2 in the dough expands and raises the dough until double in size. When placed in a preheated hot oven yeast is killed, the dough crust is set and the dough stops rising. Any alcohol produced evaporates, gluten sets, starch is converted to dextrin, forming a crust on the bread.

FOOD PREPARATION AND COOKING EQUIPMENT

A variety of factors influence a person's choice of food preparation and cooking equipment. Frequency of use, quality and budget will be key factors in the final selection.

Selection of food preparation and cooking equipment

Refer to 'Household Technology' for points to consider.

Safe use of food preparation and cooking equipment – general points
- Follow the manufacturer's instructions carefully
- Choose equipment/appliances that are of good design
- Use the equipment/appliance for what it was intended
- Store sharp kitchen items safely out of reach of children
- Do not use electrical equipment with wet hands
- Check that all knobs and handles on saucepans are heat-resistant
- Turn off or unplug electrical appliances after use

Saucepans and frying pans

Examples: selection of saucepans with lids, stockpot, stewing pan, steamer, double boiler, milk pan, 'lipped' saucepan, fish kettle, sauté pan, frying pan, omelette pan
Materials used: aluminium, cast iron, ceramic, copper, earthenware, stainless steel, vitreous enamel

Choosing cooking equipment

- Choose pots and pans that can perform two or three functions
- Choose pans of various makes, materials and types – different needs
- Choose pots and pans that will suit different size hotplates
- Bases should be flat, thick and well grounded
- Cheap thin, light pots and pans wear out quickly and develop 'hot spots'
- Choose handles with a comfortable grip, angled away from heat source
- Handles should be heat-resistant and well attached to pot or pan
- Lids should fit well, easy to remove and replace
- Pots and pans should be easy to clean

Safe use

- Avoid heavy pots and pans if suffering from arthritis or back problems
- Use both hands to lift heavy pots and pans, choose models with two handles
- Ensure that handles of pots and pans are turned inwards when using the hob
- Handles should be made of heat-resistant materials, use oven gloves if handles are made from stainless steel or other metals

Care

- Fill with cold water to steep once contents have been removed
- Wash in hot, soapy water, use a brush to remove any attached food, rinse and dry thoroughly

Non-stick finishes

PTFE (polytetrafluoroethylene) is applied as an inside coating to baking tins, roasting tins, frying pans, saucepans and woks to create a non-stick finish. Remove burnt-on food by soaking in warm water. Wash in hot soapy water, rinse well and dry thoroughly. Never use metal cooking spoons, fish slices or abrasives on non-stick pans. Always coat non-stick pans before applying heat.

Knives

Examples: selection of knives for a variety of food preparation, cook's knife, bread knife, carving knife, sharpening steel, filleting knife, cleaver, freezer knife, small vegetable knife, paring knife
Materials: carbon steel, high-carbon stainless steel, stainless steel

Choosing knives
- Handles should have a comfortable secure grip
- Knife should feel balanced and heavy
- Choose knives with handles riveted into the blade
- Stainless steel are best for food preparation
- Blades should be easy to sharpen, easy to maintain a good edge
- Choose strong knives that do not rust and that cut acid foods without discolouring

Safe use
- Hold the knife firmly away from the body
- Do not handle with wet or damp hands, it might slip
- Keep knives and similar cutting equipment out of reach of children
- To avoid risk of accidents never put knives into a basin filled with soapy water

Care
- Wash, rinse, dry and put away in a safe place
- Keep knives in a knife block, prevents damage to each other
- Sharpen knives, as required, to maintain a good edge

Other basic kitchen utensils
Examples: balloon whisk, basting spoon, can-opener, chopping board, colander, fish slice, flour dredger, flexible spatula, garlic press, grater, ladle, meat thermometer, measuring jugs/cups, melon scoop, mixing bowls, perforated spoon, pastry brush, pastry cutters, pallet knife, pot stands, potato masher, pudding bowls, sieve, soufflé dishes, spatula, tongs, vegetable peeler, weighing scales, whisk, wooden spoons

Care of basic kitchen utensils
- Wash according to the materials used in the utensil
- Rinse and dry thoroughly to avoid rusting

Bakeware
Examples: baking sheet, bun/muffin/tin, cooling rack, deep cake tin, éclair tin, flan ring/tins (a variety), deep flan dish, icing bag and nozzle, loaf pan, pastry brush, pie dishes (various sizes), roasting tin, sandwich tins, springform cake tin, Swiss roll tin

Care of bakeware
- Wash non-stick bakeware in hot soapy water, rinse and dry with a clean cloth
- Items made from other materials should be washed in hot soapy water, rinsed, dried thoroughly with a cloth and aired fully before being stored away

Cutlery (knives, forks, spoons)
Materials: EPNS (electroplated nickel silver), silver, stainless steel

Safe use of cutlery
Keep sharp knives out of reach of small children. Handles should be heat-resistant and fixed securely to the blade. Cutlery should be comfortable to use and not feel too heavy.

Care of cutlery
Wash in warm soapy water, rinse and dry thoroughly. Make sure to get all food particles from between the prongs of forks. Avoid using harsh abrasives or acids. Never soak cutlery. Always care for EPNS and silver as directed by manufacturer using the recommended cleaning cream. It is recommended that silver and stainless steel cutlery are not washed together in a dishwasher. Hard water may leave stains on stainless steel cutlery.

SMALL APPLIANCES

Blenders (hand), food mixers, food processors and liquidisers are examples of small appliances.

Choosing small appliances
Ensure that appliances are well balanced on a flat surface. Apart from the basic functions consider what attachments are available with the appliance. Decide which extra functions are required. Attachments should be easy to clean and safe to use.

Safe use of small appliances
- Read the manufacturer's instruction booklet before use
- Ensure hands are dry before operating appliance
- Attachments should be easy to use
- Small appliances with blades should have a safety lock
- Do not overfill small attachments, take note of recommended levels

Care of small appliances
- Disconnect appliance from electricity before cleaning
- Wash according to the manufacturer's instruction
- Never wash the motor part, never immerse it in water
- Wipe outer casing with a cloth wrung out in hot soapy water
- Dry well before storing away
- Be careful when cleaning blades, graters and slicker discs
- Store appliance unplugged in a safe place with its attachments
- Wind flexes loosely to avoid damage

RECIPE BALANCE AND ADAPTATION

Reasons for adapting or modifying recipes
- To improve the nutritive value
- To alter a dish to suit special dietary requirements
- To alter the number of portions, increase or decrease
- To introduce variety of colour, flavour and texture
- To use up leftovers

Example of modifications
Improve the nutritive value by increasing fibre, reducing fat, reducing salt and reducing sugar. When examining the list of ingredients consider modern substitutes that could be used e.g. sugar alternatives, new dairy spreads, reduced fat products, unsweetened products.

Balancing menus – examples
- Keep in mind the latest dietary guidelines
- Avoid repetition of ingredients across the courses
- Choose a variety of dishes that compliment each other
- Avoid over seasoning dishes, e.g. use garlic only in one dish
- Use fresh herbs rather than dried varieties
- Use a variety of colours to make the menu interesting
- Textures should be varied e.g. soft to crunching textures
- Add variety and interest with sauces, do not 'hide' food with sauces

Aesthetic awareness in the choice of food
The main aesthetic factors to be considered when choosing food are its colour, flavour, aroma, texture and 'sound'. Other factors to consider include:
- Season of the year – determines availability of fresh foods
- Current dietary guidelines for a balanced diet
- Nutritional needs of the family and personal tastes
- Knowledge of nutrition and meal planning
- Availability of perishable foods and convenience foods
- Skills and ability of the cook to make food aesthetically pleasing
- Budget and lifestyle of family

AESTHETIC AWARENESS IN THE PREPARATION OF FOOD

Appreciation of food is linked with the senses. Appearance and colour are key indications of the freshness and quality of foods. When preparing foods consider how each of the following factors can enhance people's appreciation of the meal.

Colour

- Choose natural brightly coloured foods
- Add a variety of colours across the different courses
- Prepare simple garnishes e.g. sprig of parsley, twist of lemon
- Choose methods of cooking that suit the ingredients and the dishes
- Watch cooking times as overcooking can destroy the colour
- Enhance food by roasting, grilling, stewing, etc.

Flavour

Flavour involves a combination of taste and aroma. Aromas from foods stimulate the taste buds. Words describing tastes are sweet, salty, sour and bitter. To enhance flavour during food preparation:

- Choose a variety of flavours for each course
- Arrange flavours to suit the meal, from savoury to sweet
- Avoid strong overpowering flavours in every course e.g. garlic
- Use only one strong flavour in the meal e.g. onion or orange
- Introduce combinations of contrasting flavours
- Use temperatures to intensify flavours
- Garnish or decorate dishes to add to the flavour

Aroma

Each individual food has its own variation. The smell of food is an indication of quality and freshness. To enhance the aroma of foods during preparation and cooking:

- Add herbs and spices that improve the aroma of bland ingredients
- Cook foods with appetising smells that stimulate the taste buds
- Avoid overcooking foods which produce unpleasant 'burnt' aromas
- Prevent cross-flavours developing during preparation
- Avoid undercooking as food remains bland and uninteresting

Texture

Texture can be hard, soft, soggy, creamy, crumbly, crunchy, crispy, nutty, smooth, etc. In food preparation:

- Introduce a variety of textures to add interest to menus
- Individual foods produce expectations of what the textures will be
- Texture of foods change during cooking e.g. roast potatoes
- Lumpy white sauces and curdled custard sauces look unappetising

Sound

The sounds made by food during preparation enhance our appreciation of individual foods e.g. rashers frying, fizzy drinks, breaking a biscuit in two.

AESTHETIC AWARENESS IN THE PRESENTATION OF FOOD

The sight of food well presented, is pleasing to the eye and stimulates digestive juices and taste buds. Good food presentation requires an understanding of arrangement, balance and garnish or decoration. Balance refers to colour, flavours, textures and shapes or form.
- Foods should look attractive and be arranged neatly on plates
- Serve cold or chilled food on cold plates
- Serve hot food piping hot on warmed plates
- Use plain plates and dishes for serving savoury foods
- Choose fancy plates and dishes for sweet foods
- Serve meat towards the centre or to the side of the plate
- Serve sauces in a sauce-boat or around the meat
- Garnish and decorate food lightly, in keeping with the food
- Choose hot garnishes for hot food, except for lemon and fresh herbs

Garnishes: chives, croutons, cucumber, carrots, lemon, mint, radishes, parsley, spring onions, tomatoes

Decorations: almonds (flakes, toasted), cherries, cream (piped, swirl), chocolate (grated, leaves, swirls, melted), icing (feathering, writing, piping)

SENSORY EVALUATION AND SENSORY ANALYSIS

Sensory analysis is used to determine the acceptability of a new food product to consumers by measuring, analysing and explaining reactions to a food. It is dependent on the five senses, the person tasting the food and the food itself. A data bank of sensory descriptors (words) is used when implementing a sensory evaluation of a food product. Sensory analysis involves implementing specific tests.

SENSORY EVALUATION

Taste
- Taste evaluates the sweetness, sourness, saltiness or bitterness of food
- Taste buds on tongue sense different tastes (sweet, sour, salt, bitter)

Example of descriptors: acid, bitter, bland, burnt, creamy, pungent, salty, sharp, sour, tasteless

Mouth
- The mouth evaluates the results of thermal or chemical reactions
- Thermal or chemical reactions stimulate nerves in the skin of the mouth
- Mouth feel is how the food feels as it is moved around the mouth

Example of descriptors: cold, creamy or smooth, crisp, crumbly, dry, flaky, hard, juicy, lumpy, tough, warm, hot

Smell
- Smell evaluates the aroma of food
- Acceptable aromas make foods appetising to consumers

Example of descriptors: baked, burnt, coffee, floral, fruity, roasted, sour, spicy, sweet

Texture
- Texture evaluates food consistency
- Texture is evaluated by the eyes, senses of the skin and muscles in the mouth

Examples of descriptors:
(a) Less desirable textures – chewy, coarse, greasy, lumpy, mushy, rubbery, slimy, sticky, tough
(b) Acceptable textures – creamy, crisp crumbly, juicy, moist, nutty, smooth, soft, tender

Sight
- Sight evaluates appearance and colours of food
- Sight influences initial food choices, judgements are made based on colour, shape, size and surface appearance (acceptable, freshness, quality)

Example of descriptors: appetising, bright, clear, cloudy, colourful, dull, dry, fresh, greasy, mouth-watering, soggy, wilted, medium-sized, uneven

Sound
- Sound/hearing evaluates sounds made by food during preparation and eating
- Consumers associate particular sounds with individual foods

Examples of descriptors: bubbling (soups), crunchy (salads), percolating (coffee), popping (drinks)

SENSORY ANALYSIS

Using our senses to evaluated food is referred to as Organoleptic Assessment. It involves measuring, analysing and interpretation of properties such as appearance, aroma, flavour, aftertaste and texture. Tests are carried out on foods products prepared in a specific way under controlled conditions and the results are analysed to determine the acceptability of the products.

TYPES OF SENSORY ANALYSIS TESTS

Preference tests
The purpose of preference tests is to determine the acceptability of a food or food products.

Techniques
- *Paired preference tests* (two food samples are evaluated)
- *Hedonic test* (one or more samples are ranked on a five-point or nine-point verbal or facial scale)

Difference tests
The purpose is to identify differences in taste between two food samples or to evaluate consumer preferences and acceptability of a food sample.

Techniques
- *Simple paired test* (two food samples are evaluated)
- *Paired comparison test* (pairs of samples are presented for evaluation)
- *Triangle test* (three food samples are evaluated, one of which is different)

Grading or quality tests
The purpose is to rank specific organoleptic characteristics of food product samples e.g. intensity of colour, flavour or texture, consumer preferences (likes, dislikes).

Techniques
- *Ranking test* (sorting foods in order of preference, hedonic ranking, or according to a particular characteristic)
- *Rating test* (useful for finding out people's likes and dislikes or comparing two or more food samples for aspects of quality. Five, seven or nine-point scales are used)

Controlling test conditions
- Timing of tests – avoid strong foods for 30 minutes before test, mid-morning or mid-afternoon is best
- Temperature of food samples
- Quantities of food in each sample
- Rinsing water for taster/s
- Containers in same size, shape and colour, white or colourless
- Coding of samples
- Sequence of samples (random, balanced or a combination)

Presenting results

Analyse and present results using pie charts, histograms or star diagrams, in order to determine the changes required to the food product.

FOOD PROCESSING AND PACKAGING

Reasons for processing
- To extend shelf-life, provide variety and choice
- To improve nutritive value by fortifying food
- To create new food products and flavours
- To provide variety and choice all year round
- To make food safe to eat

Categories of processing
Primary: processing of basic foods e.g. milling of wheat, oil extraction
Secondary: using processed basic foods to create new products e.g. margarine

Range and categories of processed foods
- Bottled and canned foods (sweet and savoury)
- Cook-chill products (meat, poultry, sauces, soups)
- Dehydrated foods (bread mixes, coffee, custard, soup, TVP)
- Frozen foods (individual foods, prepared meals, cooked meals)
- Fortified foods (additions of nutrients e.g. vitamins)
- Functional foods (health benefits above nutritive value)
- Instant foods and ready prepared meals (fresh or frozen)
- Novel protein foods (TVP, quorn)

FOOD PROFILE 1

A food that undergoes extensive processing – cereal
Flour may be made from wheat, barley, rice, rye, soya and maize.
Uses: baking, thickening soups and sauces, coating food

Milling Process
- Preparing grains: weighing and drying
- Cleaning: cleaning, washing, drying and conditioning
- Blending: a mixture of wheat is blended to create a 'grist'
- Break rolling: high-speed metal rollers are used to split open the grain
- Wholemeal flour is produced at this stage
- Sieving: flour is separated into 'first break flour', 'middlings' and 'coarse bran'
- Rolling and sieving: removes the germ and bran completely (white flour)

- Air-classifying: addition of air to lighten the flour
- Additives: bleaches, improvers and nutrients are added
- Packaging: weighing and packing of different products

Note: Refer to 'Cereals' in 'Food Commodities' for more information.

FOOD PROFILE 2

A food that undergoes processing to extend shelf-life – milk
Milk is a perfect medium for microbial growth. Processing delays spoilage and extends shelf-life. Processing of milk is carried out in two stages:
- Homogenisation develops a uniform consistency
- Heat treatments destroys pathogenic bacteria and increase shelf-life

Homogenisation
This process distributes fat globules evenly throughout the milk. Milk is heated to 60°C, forced through holes to make the fat globules smaller and to suspend them evenly in the milk. Homogenised milk then undergoes a heat treatment.

Heat treatments to extend shelf-life
Pasteurisation: milk is heated to 72°C for 25 seconds, cooled rapidly and sealed in sterilised containers. All Pathogenic and some souring bacteria are destroyed.
Sterilisation: homogenised milk is bottled and sealed, heat-treated to 110°C for 30 minutes. Milk will keep for months as all bacteria are destroyed.
Ultra heat treated (UHT): milk is heated to 132°C for 1 second, cooled rapidly, packed and sealed. UHT milk keeps for months because all bacteria and their spores are destroyed. The flavour changes and vitamins C and B_1 are lost.
Dehydration: homogenised milk is evaporated to 60% of its volume, spray or roller dried and packed. Moisture is not present to support the growth of microbes.
Evaporation: pasteurised milk is evaporated to half its volume, homogenised, sealed and sterilised at 115°C for 20 minutes in sealed cans. It keeps indefinitely.
Condensed: milk is homogenised, pasteurised, 15% sugar added, its volume reduced to one-third, canned, sealed and sterilised. All bacteria, vitamin C and B-group are destroyed. The low moisture content and increased levels of sugar create an unsuitable environment for microbial growth.

Note: Refer to 'Milk' in 'Food Commodities' for more information.

FOOD PROFILE 3

Processing food to add value – cook-chill foodstuffs
These foods are categorised into two groups, cook-chill and cook-pasteurise-chill foods. Foods prepared using these methods extend shelf-life, save time and energy.

There is some loss of vitamin C. Low storage temperatures prevent microbial growth. Foods carry 'best before' date, instructions for storage and use.

General cook-chill method
- Ingredients are prepared and cooked at source
- Food is divided into portion size
- Portions are chilled to 3°C within 30 minutes of cooking
- Chilling is completed within 90 minutes
- Food is stored between −1°C and 3°C
- Food is transported in cold conditions
- Food is stored in a refrigerated cabinet in the supermarket
- Shelf-life is up to five days

General cook-pasteurise-chill method
- Food is prepared, cooked and divided into portions
- Hot food is put into flexible containers
- A partial vacuum is formed and the container is heat sealed
- Container with food is pasteurised to 80°C for 10 minutes
- Container is rapidly chilled to 3°C and stored from −1°C to 3°C
- Food is transported in cold conditions
- Shelf-life varies between two to three weeks

PACKAGING AND MATERIALS

Packaging is used on foods for the following reasons:
- To prevent dehydration, oxidation and contamination
- To prevent the transfer of flavours, to extend shelf-life
- To prevent damage during storage and transport
- To inform consumers e.g. nutritional information
- To attract consumer interest in existing and new products

Properties of good packaging
- Quality in design (colour, image, shape and similarity)
- Economical, environmentally friendly, functional in shape and size
- Durable, strong, odourless, moisture/vapour proof
- Free of reactions between container and food
- Controls movement of micro-organisms

TYPES OF PACKAGING

Glass
Glass is useful, clean, hygienic, rigid and transparent (displays contents). It provides total protection for foods, suited to heat treatments, easily moulded, easy to stack and transport, it is fragile as glass breaks easily.
Uses: preserves, pickles, mayonnaise, sauces

Metal (aerosols, cans, aluminium foil)
Aluminium, stainless steel and tin used. Internal and external lacquers may be applied. Convenient, easy to store, provides total protection. Unsuitable for microwaves.
Uses: *tin* for fish, meat, fruit and vegetables, *aluminium cans* for beer and soft drinks, *aluminium foil* for wrapping food, foil trays for take-aways and frozen foods

Paper
Paper comes in a variety of forms and weights (plain, parchment, cardboard, waxed, laminated, ovenable containers).
Uses: *waxed paper* – lining cake, tins; *greaseproof paper* – wrapping produce, fish and meats; *paper bags* – bread, cakes, scones, flour and sugar; *cardboard* – an outer covering for dry foods; *waxed cartons* – chilled fresh soup, cream, milk

Flexible packaging
Flexible packaging comes in a variety of forms, shapes (cellulose films, polyethylene wrapping, polystyrene, PET bottles) and properties e.g. heat sealing, resists low temperatures, moisture-proof, strong. Low production costs, easy to handle, convenient, unbreakable.
Uses: to cover food, bottles, food trays, freezer containers, containers for custard, rice, margarine, spreads and yoghurt, freezer bags, boil-in-the-bag foods, vacuum packing

ENVIRONMENTAL IMPACT
- Glass is reusable, recyclable, broken glass is dangerous
- Metals have high production/transport costs, are non-biodegradable
- Aerosols with CFCs damage the environment (ozone layer)
- Paper is biodegradable, cheap to produce/transport, easy to use
- Plastics (from crude oil), cause litter and pollution, recycling is limited
- Lack of recycling facilities for PET bottles, useful for other products

Problems created by packaging
- Use of non-renewable valuable resources
- High energy-costs e.g. production and transport
- Waste disposal and collection e.g. landfill sites
- Non-biodegradable nature of some materials
- Litter in urban and rural areas

Reducing the environmental impact
- Recycle, reuse, refuse excessive packaging
- Examine products and packaging
- Watch out for the EU Eco-label
- Compost organic materials

FOOD LABELLING

The Labelling Regulations state that *pre-packed foods* provide the following information:
- Name of the food, net quantity, list of ingredients in descending order, 'use by date' or 'best before date', country of origin, if alcohol is present, if food has been irradiated or contains genetically modified ingredients, instructions for use and storage, manufacturer's name and address
- Name of flavourings
- Indication if 'packaged in a protective atmosphere'
- With sweetener or with sugar(s) and sweeteners

For *non-packaged or loose foodstuffs* the following information must be displayed at the point of sale:
- Name of food
- Origin, class and variety (displayed at point of sale)
- Metric unit price e.g. price per kilo

Nutritional labelling
- Provides consumer with information
- Compulsory only if a nutritional claim is made
- Nutritional labels must comply with regulations
- Regulations specify the format
- Content must be given for 100 g or 100 ml
- Nutrients may be given per portion or per serving
- Declaration of min/max must be given where special emphasis is given to a particular ingredient e.g. low-fat

Price and labels
- Selling price must be displayed
- Unit price and selling price are required for pre-packaged foodstuffs
- Unit price per kilo/per litre must be displayed beside loose foodstuffs

Note: Refer To 'Contaminants' in 'Food Additives'.

Part Four: Food Additives and Food Legislation

FOOD ADDITIVES

Additives must fulfil acceptable and useful functions. An additive is not normally consumed as a food but added to food intentionally or by accident.

Direct additives are added to foods for specific beneficial reasons.

Indirect additives are part of a product due to handling, packaging or storage. Additives may be described as:
- Natural: obtained directly from plants and animals
- Nature identical: identical to a natural substance but synthetically made
- Artificial: synthetically made

Advantages of additives
- To enhance colour, flavour and texture
- To facilitate processing and transportation of foods
- To improve or increase shelf-life of food
- To inhibit action of enzymes and micro-organisms and prevent waste
- To increase the variety of foods available throughout the year
- To maintain or supplement nutritional value
- To prevent food poisoning by preserving foods

Disadvantages of additives
Side effects of additives are allergies, hyperactivity and toxin build up.

CLASSIFICATION AND EXAMPLES OF ADDITIVES (DIRECT)

Antioxidants (E300–E399)
Antioxidants are used to prevent oxidative rancidity of fats and oils, and to prevent oxidative discolouring of fruits and vegetables.

Types of antioxidants:
- Natural antioxidants: vitamins C and E
- Synthetic antioxidants: BHA, BHT

Colourings (E100–E199)
Colourings are used to improve the natural colour of food, to improve the colour of preserved foods (jams, jellies), to replace colours lost during processing and to respond to consumer demand for foods with good colours.

Types of colourings
- Natural: annatto, caramel, carotene, chlorophyll, cochineal, paprika, saffron, tumeric
- Artificial: amaranth, green S, ponceau 4R, tartrazine, yellow 2g, sunset yellow

Examples of uses
- Natural: baked foods, butter, canned vegetables, cheese, cooking oils, confectionery, ice cream, jams, jellies, margarine, savoury rice, soft drinks, soups, whiskey
- Artificial: biscuits, cheese sauces, custards, jams, sausages, soft drinks, soups, sweets

Flavourings
The types of flavourings are:
- Natural: alcohol, citric acid, essential oils, herbs, salt, spices, sugar
- Artificial and nature identical: aldehydes, esters, maltol
- Flavour enhancers: monosodium glutamate

Examples of uses: bread, cakes, crisps, essences, synthetic flavourings, soups, Chinese foods

Sweeteners
The types of sweeteners are:
- Natural: fructose in fruit, table sugar (beet or cane)
- Intense sweetener: aspartame, saccharin (low-calorie products)
- Bulk sweeteners: glucose syrup, sorbitol (useful for diabetic products)

Examples of uses: low-calorie products, diabetic products, diet drinks

Nutritive additives or supplements
Nutritive additives are used to enhance the nutritive value of food (added-value), to replace nutrients lost during processing and to satisfy consumer demand for enriched products. Specific foods are fortified with nutrients e.g. calcium (flour), iron and vitamin B-group (white flour, breakfast cereals), vitamins A and D (margarine) and vitamin C (fruit drinks).

Table 3.13 Physical conditioning agents (E400–E499)

Main agents	What they do
Anti-caking agents	Prevent lumps forming in foods *Uses*: cake mixes, icing sugar, powdered milk, salt
Anti-foaming	Prevents foaming and a scum forming *Uses*: packet soups
Anti-spattering	Keep water droplets apart in oils and fats
Antioxidants	Prevent oxidation and rancidity *Uses*: biscuits, cooking oils, crisps, packaged foods
Buffers	Used to keep a specific pH in a food
Bulking agents	Add to the bulk of food but not to energy value *Uses*: slimming foods
Emulsifiers	Stabilise the consistency of foods *Uses*: desserts, ice cream, salad dressings, mayonnaise
Glazing agents	Give a shiny appearance, seal and prevent food drying out *Uses*: fruits, salads, vegetables
Packaging gas	Used to prevents oxidation
Stabilisers	Prevent droplets clumping together in emulsions *Uses*: baked goods, ice cream, sweets
Thickeners	Adds to viscosity of food

Preservatives (E200–E299)

Preservatives are used to:
- Inhibit growth of enzymes and micro-organisms
- Increase shelf-life and variety of foods available out of season
- Reduce waste by preserving foods for use out of season

Preservatives are not allowed in baby foods. Examples of preservatives are:
Natural: alcohol, salt, spices, sugar, vinegar
Chemical: benzoic acid (coffee), potassium and sodium nitrate (cured meats), sorbic acid (cakes, flour, yoghurt), sulphur dioxide (cider, dried fruits, sausages, wines)

Legal control of food additives

Approved substances may only be used as additives. Approval is granted only if a substance performs a useful purpose, is safe and does not mislead the consumer. An additive list with designated E numbers (from E100 to E1518) has been developed. Additives awarded an E number are considered safe (GRAS) and those without an E number are in the proposal stage. The EU controls the use and amounts of additives. Reviews are carried out to determine maximum residue levels (MRLs) and acceptable daily intake (ADI). The Department of Agriculture, Food and Rural Development in Ireland implement the EU regulations in Ireland.

INDIRECT ADDITIVES – CONTAMINANTS

Classification
Endogenous plant toxins
These natural toxins are produced by plants. Endogenous plant toxins include:
- Caffeine: chocolate, coffee, cocoa, tea
- Cyanide: traces in fruit kernels, beans, peas
- Protease inhibitors: beans (kidney, soya), chick peas

Endogenous animal toxins
These are natural toxins produced by animals. They include:
- Fish poisoning: fish with poisonous tissues
- Paralytic shellfish poisoning: shellfish contaminated with toxic algae

Microbial toxins
These include bacterial toxins and mycotoxins from moulds.

Toxic residues
- Metal residues: aluminium, cadmium, lead, tin
- Industrial residues: dioxins
- Agricultural residues: antibiotics, growth promoter, pesticides
- Radioactive residues: fallout, radioactive waste

Chemicals from food processing
- Carcinogens: smoked food products, by-product of cooking methods
- Fumigants: used in the sterilisation of food

FOOD LEGISLATION

Food legislation aims to protect human health, inform the consumer, prevent fraud, provide information and facilitate trade.

Food hygiene regulations (1950–89)
These regulations set out statutory requirements for food hygiene and food premises and are enforced by the Health Boards. These regulations:
- Prohibit the sale of food that is diseased, contaminated or unfit for human consumption

- Require that adequate precautions are taken to prevent food contamination at all stages of production and distribution
- Allow the seizure and destruction of food unfit for human consumption
- Require specific food businesses to be registered e.g. butchers
- Require that mobile food stalls are licensed annually

Failure to comply with the regulations may result in court action, fines and closure. The Chief Environmental Officer of the Health Board may initiate action.

European Communities (Hygiene of Foodstuffs) Regulations 2000

These EU regulations require owners of food businesses to operate and maintain hygienic conditions, to observe hygienic practices in food, to ensure that staff are trained in hygiene practices and that HACCP is implemented at all stages of the operation. European countries must have sampling and inspection programmes in place.

Labelling regulations (1982 and 1991)

These regulations state that labels should be clear, legible and indelible, written in a language understood by consumers, must not mislead the consumer and should not be covered or hidden by pictures or written information.

Note: Refer to 'Food Processing and Packaging' for (a) labelling pre-packaged foodstuffs, (b) non-packaged or loose foodstuffs and (c) nutritional labelling of foods.

Sale of Food and Drugs Acts (1875, 1879, 1899, 1936)

These acts were amended between 1875 and 1936. They protect consumers against fraud and adulteration of foodstuffs, which may be damaging to human health. It is illegal to mix, colour, stain or powder any article of food with an ingredient which would make it injurious to health. Under the acts of 1935 and 1936 compositional criteria were set down for milk and associated products. Irish and European legislation provide for the analysis and inspection of food products.

Health (Official Control of Foodstuffs) Regulations (1991)

These regulations set out rules regarding general food hygiene from production to retail sale, to prevent danger to public health, the importance of HACCP as part of quality assurance, the setting of food compositional standards and details of penalties for breaking the regulations. The act allows for inspection of food premises by Enforcement Officers who may prescribe the penalties.

Part Five: Food Spoilage – Microbiology

Microbiology is the study of micro-organisms i.e. bacteria, fungi, moulds, yeasts and viruses. Food spoilage may be caused by natural decay or by contamination by micro-organisms (moulds, yeast and bacteria).

Environmental factors affecting the growth of micro-organisms are: food/nutrients, light/darkness, moisture/water, oxygen, specific pH levels, time and warmth/temperature.

Food/nutrients
Micro-organisms get their food for energy and growth from other sources, living and dead matter because they do not contain chlorophyll.

- Parasites survive on living matter (pathogenic bacteria are parasites)
- Saprophytes (also called decomposers) live on dead or decaying matter

Competitive effects occur where bacteria compete with each other for food, oxygen and moisture, only some bacteria survive. *Mutualism* occurs where both organisms benefit from growing near each other. In *parasitism*, the host or food source is damaged by the parasite.

Foods particularly useful for micro-organisms are protein foods (meat and fish). Some bacteria use complex carbohydrates, others use only sugars. The nutrients supplied by the foods are absorbed through the cell walls and use by the micro-organisms.

Light/darkness
Most micro-organisms grow best without light and are destroyed by strong ultra-violet sunlight.

Moisture/water
Micro-organisms require water to transport nutrients and to remove waste. Food sources with a high water and a high nutrient content provide the water for bacterial growth. Micro-organisms cannot use ice, frozen or dried foods. They grow best in foods with a 'water activity' above 0.61.

Oxygen
Micro-organisms can be grouped according to their oxygen requirements.
- Aerobic: need oxygen for growth
- Anaerobic: do not need oxygen

- Facultative: can grow with or without oxygen
- Microaerophilic: grow in reduced oxygen environment

Specific pH levels

Most micro-organisms prefer a neutral pH level i.e. pH7. Bacteria prefer a neutral pH, moulds and yeasts prefer an acidic pH. Some micro-organisms prefer slightly acidic or alkaline environments, just either side of pH7. Strong acids or alkalis destroy them. There are exceptions to the rules.

Time

The growth and reproduction rate of micro-organisms varies depending on the type and environmental conditions. If conditions are favourable bacteria will multiply every 20 minutes, but rapid growth is limited by the extent of the food sources available.

Warmth/temperature

Micro-organisms have a preferred temperature range for growth and reproduction.

Table 3.14 Temperature ranges

Group	Temperature range for growth
Mesophiles	+10°C to +45°C (flourish best between 25°C and 24°C), the majority of micro-organisms fall into this group
Psychrophiles	–5°C to +20°C (low temperatures)
Thermophiles	35°C to 70°C (ideal temperature is above 45°C)

Table 3.15 Reactions at different temperatures

–5°C to –25°C	Growth inhibited, micro-organisms inactivated, freezing makes them dormant
+30°C to +45°C	Optimum for growth, micro-organisms flourish
70°C+	Most are destroyed, except some bacteria
100°C+	All bacteria destroyed except heat-resistant spores
121°C	Heat resistant spores destroyed by maintaining temperature for 15 minutes

FUNGI

Like bacteria fungi lack chlorophyll, cannot make their own food and are dependent on ready-made sources of food to survive. Fungi can be parasites or saprophytes.
Types of fungi: moulds, yeasts, large fungi (mushrooms)

Moulds

Basic structure
Moulds develop from a single cell or spore. When a single cell or spore lands on a ready made food source, and conditions are favourable, it develops a thread-like filament (hypha) that grows into the food. Multiple hyphae develop, form branches and an interlocking network of filaments, called a mycelium, extends over the food source. Hyphae excrete enzymes to break down the food source. Nutrients and moisture are absorbed. After a time hyphae grow upwards and form branches where spores will grow.

Reproduction of moulds
Asexual reproduction
Hyphae grow vertically out of well-established mycelium and a spore-forming head develops at its tip called a sporangium (round shape) or conidia (branched shape). When mature the sporangium or conidia releases the spores to be spread by water or air to a medium where they reproduce if conditions are favourable.

Figure 3.5 Asexual reproduction

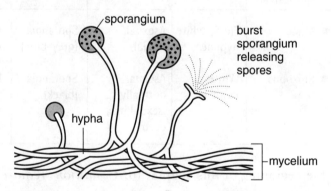

Sexual reproduction
Sexual reproduction occurs when two hyphae, growing side by side, come into contact with each other and fuse together forming a zygospore. Spores form within the zygospore. Under suitable conditions zygospores germinate, hyphae develop, sporangium form and eventually spores are released. The zygospore has a thick wall, which allows it to remain dormant for long periods of time if conditions for germination are unfavourable.

Figure 3.6 Sexual reproduction

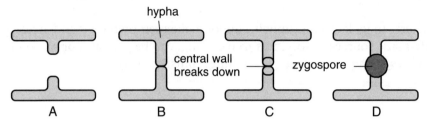

Classification of moulds
- Ascomycetes: aspergillus, penicillium
- Phycomycetes: mucor, rhizopus
- Basidiomycetes: mushrooms
- Saccharomycetes: yeast

Table 3.16 Common food spoilage moulds

Classification	Mould	Colour	Method of reproduction	Shape of spore head	Food sources
Ascomycetes (saprophytic moulds) 20°C to 25°C most septate	▪ Aspergillus	green-grey (green/ black)	Asexual	Sporangia	Cereals, dried fruit
	▪ Penicillium (several species)	greenish-blue	Asexual	Conidia	Cheese, citrus fruit, bread
Phycomycetes (saprophytic moulds) 30°C non-septate	▪ Mucor	Fluffy white hyphae	Asexual/ sexual	Sporangia (grey-blue)	Bread, cakes
	▪ Rhizopus	White hyphae	Asexual normally, sexual may occur	Sporangia (black)	Bread, rot on fruits and vegetables

Note: Refer to the beginning of this chapter for *Conditions required for growth of moulds.*

Mycotoxins
Mycotoxins, produced by moulds, are toxic to both animals and humans. Mycotoxins cause illness in humans. Production of toxins is associated with poor hygiene during food processing, poor-quality fruit and inadequate storage for cereal crops.

LARGE FUNGI – BASIDIOMYCETES

Some large fungi are edible others are poisonous. Large fungi include edible mushrooms, truffles and poisonous fungi. More varieties of mushrooms have become available in the last few years.

Examples: commercially produced button mushrooms, chanterelles, oyster mushrooms, morels and wild truffles

Development of a mushroom
- Mushrooms spores develop a network of tightly packed hyphae, forming a mycelium; organic material underneath the soil provide food
- A stalk develops and pushes out of the ground with a closed cap
- Cap swells, bursts open and pink gills become visible underneath
- Gills darken, basidia form and spores are released from between gills onto the ground and into the air

YEAST – SACCHAROMYCETES
- Unicellular facultative, saphrophytic fungi, destroyed by high temperatures
- Found in the air, on skins of fruits, survive in slightly sweet and acidic foods
- Important source of B-group vitamins, used in health products, food supplements
- Used in bread-making, wine-making and brewing

Structure of yeast
Yeasts have thin, single outer cell walls, filled with cytoplasm containing a nucleus, one vacuole and food storage granules.

Reproduction of yeast
- Reproduces asexually by the process called *budding*
- Requires a suitable medium, moisture, acid environment and warmth
- Small swelling forms and develops on the side of a single cell
- Cell nucleus divides, a wall forms, dividing the two cells
- The new cell eventually separates from the main or parent cell
- New cell begins to bud or reproduce into chains of yeast cells
- In unfavourable conditions spores develop

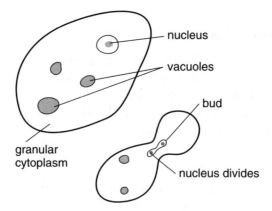

Figure 3.7 Yeast cell

Note: For *conditions for growth of yeast* refer to the beginning of this chapter.

Fermentation

This is the process by which yeast breaks down sugar to produce carbon dioxide and alcohol. The by-products of fermentation are used at home and commercially in baking and making alcohol e.g. beer, wine.

BACTERIA

Bacteria are small, single-celled micro-organisms. Bacteria can be parasites or saprophytes, pathogenic or non-pathogenic and are found in air, animals, foods, plants, soil and water.

Structure of bacterial cells

A bacterial cell consists of an outer, rigid cell wall which gives bacteria its shape, a semi-permeable cell membrane and cytoplasm, which contains nuclear material, food stores and ribosomes. Some bacterial cells have flagella to help them move and a capsule for protection. Flagella may be polar, bi-polar or tufted.

Figure 3.8 Structure of a bacterial cell

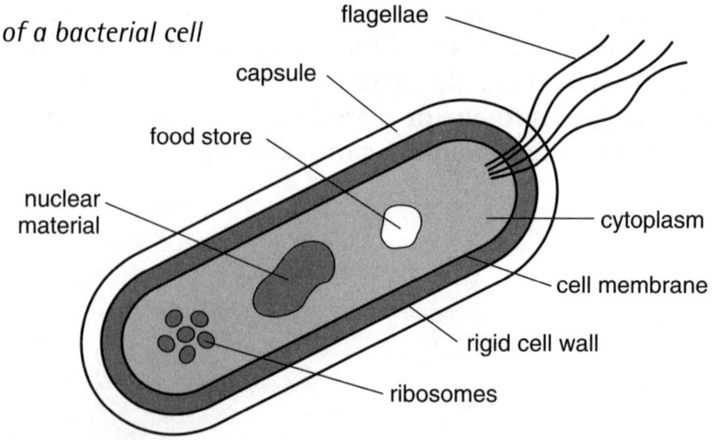

flagellae

capsule

food store

nuclear material

cytoplasm

cell membrane

rigid cell wall

ribosomes

Reproduction of bacteria

Bacteria reproduce rapidly by binary fission. The bacterial cell increases in length and the nuclear material reproduces itself by dividing into two separate parts separated by a membrane. A cell wall is formed. Two separate cells, equal in size, develop and then separate. The time between each division is referred to as *generation time* (about 20 minutes). Bacteria can produce a million bacteria in a short space of time. Overcrowding results in bacteria competing for food, oxygen and moisture and death eventually results.

The growth curve of bacteria is divided into four phases:

1. *Lag phase*: 'settling in' phase, bacteria get used to environment, slow growth
2. *Log phase*: rapid reproduction
3. *Stationary phase*: no increase in bacteria numbers, nutrient supply, oxygen, moisture and space reducing, bacteria competing, toxic waste produced
4. *Decline phase*: rapid decrease in number, same reasons as for stationary phase

Figure 3.9 Growth curve of micro-organisms

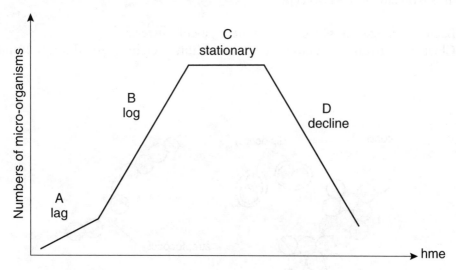

Endospores

These are tough dormant cells produced by bacilli and clostridia when conditions are unsuitable for reproduction, lack of food, oxygen and moisture. Such spores are resistant to cold, heat and some chemicals. Endospores can be destroyed by dry heat (150°C for 1 hour) or steam (121°C for 15 minutes).

Conditions for growth of bacteria – summary

Suitable foods are dead, decaying or living matter from animal or plant sources. Most bacteria prefer a near neutral pH range. Each bacterium has a maximum, minimum and ideal range, either psychrophile, mesophile or thermophiles. Oxygen needs vary (aerobic, anaerobic or facultative). They thrive in darkness and are destroyed by ultra-violet rays of the sun. A good supply of moisture is required for the rapid growth of spores in dry conditions.

Classification of bacteria

Bacteria can be classified according to shape or gram staining.

Figure 3.10 Classification of bacteria by shape

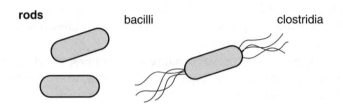

Bacillus (rod shaped) – two types

(a) Bacilli, arranged singly, e.g. salmonella, e-coli, listeria
(b) Clostridia, arranged in chains e.g. clostridium welchi, clostridium botulinum

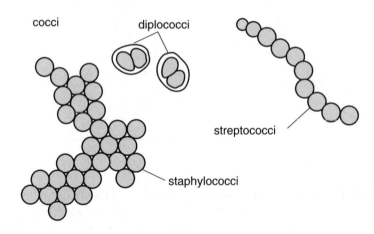

Coccus (round) – four types/arrangements

(a) Coccus, (singly)
(b) Diplococci, (pairs) e.g. pneumonia
(c) Streptococci (chains) e.g. scarlet fever, throat infections
(d) Staphylocci (clusters) e.g. boils, food poisoning

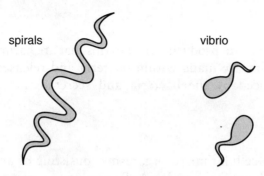

spirals   vibrio

Vibrio and spirillum – two types

(a) Spirals/vibrio – short, curved, rod-shaped e.g. cholera
(b) Spirillum – long, coiled, comma shaped e.g. syphilis

Classification of bacteria by gram-staining

The steps involved in staining bacteria are:
1. Smear an agar filled place with a cult
2. Incubate in a suitable place
3. Pour crystal violet dye over the sample to locate the bacteria
4. Using distilled water, wash off the dye
5. Pour solution of iodine over the culture to fix colour
6. Add acetone to remove colour

GRAM-STAINING RESULTS

Gram-positive bacteria
- Blue-black, the colour of the crystal violet dye
- Thick single cell wall
- 2% lipid in cell wall
- Generally aerobic
- Non-mobile
- Spore producing
- Little resistance to antibiotics

Examples: clostridium, lactobacillus, streptococci

Gram-negative bacteria
- Reddish, the colour of iodine
- Two thin layers in cell wall
- 20% lipid in cell wall
- Aerobic and anaerobic
- Mobile – have flagella
- Do not produce spores
- More resistant to antibiotics

Examples: e-coli, salmonella

Toxins

Some bacteria produce waste products called toxins that are harmful and poisonous to humans. Endotoxins are made within bacteria and released when they die. Exotoxins are produced by the bacteria and secreted into the surrounding environment.

Viruses

Viruses are small non-cellular micro-organisms consisting of an outer protective protein coat that encloses DNA or RNA. Reproduction occurs within the host cell. Viral diseases that affect humans include AIDS, cold sores, common cold, flu, hepatitis, measles, mumps, polio, rabies and warts.

Examples of viruses from food sources
- *SRV* (Small round structured viruses): from shellfish
- *BSE* (Bovine Spongiform Encephalopathy): affects cattle
- *NvCJD* (New Variant Creutzfeldt-Jacob Disease): human form of BSE

FOOD POISONING

Food poisoning is an illness caused by eating foods contaminated by chemicals, bacteria or toxins. Bacterial food poisoning results from pathogenic bacteria that are transmitted by dust, foods, pets, people, pests, foods, soil and water.

Symptoms of food poisoning include abdominal cramps, diarrhoea, fever, nausea and vomiting. Some or all of the symptoms may be present depending on the type of food poisoning.

TYPES OF FOOD POISONING

Bacterial – toxic or infectious
Infectious: eating food contaminated by pathogens
- Examples: salmonella, e-coli, clostridia welchi

Toxic: eating foods containing toxins produced by bacteria
- Examples: staphylococci, clostridia botulinum

Chemical
Chemical poisoning can occur in antibiotics, chemical contamination of the water supply, accumulation of metals, insecticides, pesticides and residues from farming and horticulture.

Natural

Food poisoning can occur in natural toxins produced by foods: traces of cyanide, solanine (potatoes), oxalic acid (rhubarb).

High-risk foods

Milk and dairy products, eggs and egg products, cooked meats and cooked meat products, poultry and reheated dishes are all high-risk foods.

COMMON PATHOGENIC OR FOOD POISONING BACTERIA

Clostridium botulinum

Characteristics
- Exotoxin food poisoning bacteria, one of the most serious forms
- Produces a deadly toxin that causes botulism
- Rod-shaped, anaerobic, gram-positive, produces gas, forms spores and toxins
- Optimum temperature is 30–37°C, pH range is 4.6 to 4.8 inhibited by nitrates

Illness/symptoms
- Toxic illness, incubation period 12–36 hours
- Blurred vision, diarrhoea, dizziness, headache, slurred speech, paralysis
- Mortality rate is 5–15%
- Recovery takes months

Sources: decaying matter, contaminated soil, low acid canned food, vacuum packed foods, meats, cheese, smoked foods e.g. fish
Prevention: dispose of damaged canned protein foods, cook food correctly, destroyed by cooking temperatures of 121°C if maintained for 15 minutes

Listeria monocytogenes

Characteristics
- Infectious toxic food poisoning bacillus causing listeriosis
- Rod-shaped, anaerobic, gram-positive, produces heat-resistant spores, salt-tolerant, toxin produced after eating contaminated food
- Multiplies at low temperatures, can survive heat treatments

Illness/symptoms
- Infectious illness, incubation period 1–70 days
- Flu-like fever, septicaemia, meningitis in babies and the elderly
- Can cause serious illness in unborn babies, children and the elderly
- For pregnant women may cause miscarriage or premature birth

Sources: survives in soil, animal and human waste, raw meat, unpasteurised milk, soft cheese, prepared salads, paté, cook/chill products, raw vegetables
Prevention: store food below 4°C, cook chilled products thoroughly, never reheat cooked chilled products, avoid eating high-risk foods

Escherichia-coli 0157:H7

Characteristics
- Different forms, but e-coli 0157:H7 is the dangerous type
- Rod-shaped, aerobic or facultative, gram-negative

Illness/symptoms
- Infective illness, incubation period 12–24 hours, duration 1–5 days
- Abdominal cramps, bloody diarrhoea, fever, nausea, vomiting
- Serious cases can lead to death, kidney failure

Sources: unpasteurised milk, cheese, undercooked beef and beef products (mince, burgers, salami), survives in the intestines of animals and humans
Prevention: correct cooking and storage temperatures, chlorinating of water, high standards of hygiene, avoid cross-contamination

Salmonella

Characteristics
- Different types of this bacilli, over 2,000 types
- Rod-shaped, facultative, gram-negative, non-spore forming, mobile
- Optimum temperature is 37°C, pH range is 6.5–7.5
- Inhibited by salt, destroyed by high temperatures

Illness/symptoms
- Infectious food poisoning bacteria, incubation 12–36 hours, duration 1–2 days
- Abdominal pain, diarrhoea, fever, headache, nausea and vomiting
- Very young, elderly and ill people most at risk

Sources: survives in human and animal intestines (farm animals, pets and vermin), contaminated eggs and poultry, raw foods, sausages, raw milk, untreated water and incorrectly cooked meat
Prevention: avoid unpasteurised milk, chlorinating of water, correct sewage disposal. High-risk foods should be refrigerated below 4°C and separated from other foods. Maintain high standards of hygiene in supermarkets, slaughter houses, food outlets and homes

Factors favouring food poisoning bacteria
- Contamination by food handlers
- Poor food, kitchen and personal hygiene
- Cross-contamination between raw and cooked foods
- Incorrect cooking and storage of foods
- Using high-risk foods

CONTROLLING THE MICROBIAL SPOILAGE OF FOOD

Preventing food contamination will help control microbial spoilage of food. Areas to focus on are personal, kitchen and food hygiene, cooking and chilling of food.

Personal hygiene
- Do not work with food if suffering from illness
- Wash hands before handling food and after handling pets, using the toilet, smoking
- Cover cuts and abrasions with waterproof dressings
- Keep nails short and clean, tie up or cover hair
- Wear a clean apron or coat
- Do not cough, sneeze or spit over food

Kitchen hygiene
- Keep kitchen ventilated, open windows daily
- Keep all pets out of the kitchen
- Check refrigerator daily, clean regularly, dispose of unused leftovers
- Disinfect food preparation, serving and eating surfaces
- Wash all knives used to prepare raw meat and fish before using them again
- Use separate chopping boards for raw and cooked foods
- Wipe spills as they occur, wash up as you go along
- Wash kitchen cloths, tea towels and hand towels daily
- Empty, disinfect and wash kitchen bin daily
- Sweep, wash and disinfect kitchen floor daily

Food hygiene, cooking and chilling
- Store food in the correct place and at the correct temperature
- Put chilled and frozen food away as soon as possible after shopping
- Label home prepared frozen foods, name, quantity and date
- To prevent cross-contamination store raw and cooked meats separately.
- Handle all food as little as possible, use tongs or forks
- Cook all foods to a core temperature of 70°C for 2 minutes
- Store leftovers in the refrigerator and reheat only once until piping hot
- For pre-prepared chilled foods follow instructions on package
- Cook meat until juices run clear, use a meat thermometer

Principles underlying control of microbial spoilage of foods

Remove the factors that contribute to food poisoning. Follow good hygiene practices. Store foods at low temperatures and in the correct place. Avoid cross-contamination. Cover foods when not in use.

Role of micro-organisms in food production

- Moulds used in the manufacture of some cheese
- Edible fungi (mushrooms) used as main ingredient
- Provide starter cultures for cheese, yoghurt and vinegar
- Necessary for bread-making and brewing
- Food supplements and tonics – vitamin B
- Some produce vitamins B and K in the human gut
- Production of vegan foods e.g. quorn

Role of micro-organisms in food spoilage

- Souring of foods (cream, milk, yoghurt)
- Spoilage of food (breads, cheese, fruits and jams)
- Produce slime and 'rotten' smells

ENZYMES

Enzymes are organic catalysts that speed up or control a chemical reaction without changing themselves. Each enzyme is involved in one reaction. Examples of enzymic activities include fermentation, food spoilage and cellular respiration. They require specific temperatures and pH levels to function.

Role of enzymes in food spoilage

- Spoilage in fruit and vegetables: enzymic browning, oxidation and discolouration, maturation, decay
- Spoilage in fish: fish enzymes work at low temperatures, cause rapid deterioration
- Spoilage in meat: proteolytic enzymes act on meat 'hung' for too long, enzymes cause lipids to go rancid

Controlling enzymic spoilage of food

Enzymic spoilage of food can be controlled by the additions of acids (lemon juice on apples or bananas), blanching vegetables for freezing, correct storage and low temperatures in freezer/refrigerator.

Part Six: Food Preservation, Safety and Hygiene

PRESERVATION

Spoilage of food is caused by loss of moisture, enzymes and micro-organism. To flourish enzymes and micro-organisms need warmth, moisture, food and oxygen.

Enzymes cause browning of some foods on exposure to air, ripening as part of the natural life-cycle of fruits and vegetables, and a reduction in the nutritive value of some foods as a result of oxidation caused by enzymes.

Micro-organisms contaminate food with toxins produced by bacteria, or by moulds and yeasts growing on the food.

HOME PRESERVATION

Reasons for preserving foods
- To keep food longer, extend shelf-life, to have food out of season
- To destroy micro-organisms e.g. pathogenic bacteria and toxins
- To maintain colour, flavour, texture and nutritive value
- To avoid waste by preserving garden produce
- To save money by using foods in season when they are cheapest
- To provide food for emergencies, convenience

Aims of preservation – underlying scientific principles
- To destroy micro-organisms
- To prevent their re-entry into food by sealing food correctly
- To inhibit the activity of enzymes
- To control conditions that encourage microbial growth

Table 3.17 Methods, application and underlying principles

Methods – controlling growth conditions	Application	Underlying principle
Heat treatments, increasing temperatures	Canning, bottling, jam-making, pasteurisation, sterilisation	High temperatures destroy enzymes and micro-organisms.
Removing warmth – lowering temperatures	Freezing, refrigeration	Low temperatures inactivate enzymes and micro-organisms.
Chemical treatments	Jam-making, chutney, pickles, curing, smoking	Using sugar, salt, alcohol, nitrates, nitrites, sulphur dioxide and acids (pH).

→

Table 3.17 Methods, application and underlying principles (cont.)

Methods – controlling growth conditions	Application	Underlying principle
Removing moisture	Dehydration, accelerated freeze-drying	Without moisture, bacteria will not survive.
Removing air	Vacuum packing, controlled-atmosphere packaging	Some bacteria need oxygen to survive, sealing prevents their re-entry.

HOME FREEZING

Underlying principle

Freezing involves the removal of warmth and moisture to inactivate enzymes and micro-organisms. The formation of ice-crystals removes the source of liquid used by bacteria. On thawing, the temperature rises, moisture becomes available and bacteria begin to grow again. Blanching vegetables before freezing inactivates enzymes.

Quick freezing: converts water into small ice crystals at –25°C, causes little damage to cell walls, little loss of liquid on thawing, good colour and texture

Slow freezing: converts water into large ice crystals at 0°C to –25°C, extensive damage to cell walls, loss of nutrients and increased loss of liquid on thawing

Advantages of freezing
- Great variety of foods available
- Bulk freezing saves fuel, time and money
- Foods are available out of season
- Food can be frozen in useable quantities
- Leftover foods can be frozen
- Minimum loss of flavour, colour and nutritive value

Disadvantages of freezing
- Freezers are expensive – initial outlay, running costs
- Bulk cooking and freezing requires a lot of time and work
- Danger of buying too many prepared foods/meals for the freezer
- Danger of 'freezer burn'
- Packaging and running costs may be high
- Keeping the freezer filled requires constant restocking

General guidelines for freezing

Preparation
- Choose fresh, high quality foods
- Turn freezer to coldest setting 2–3 hours before freezing fresh food
- Divide food into useable quantities
- Freeze only one-tenth of the capacity of the freezer in 24 hours

Packaging
Use suitable packaging material. Pack food in small quantities; remove as much air as possible. Allow headspace for expansion of liquids, seal food correctly. Use extra foil over sharp bones on meat. Label food with name of product, number of portions or weight and date.

Freezing
- Freeze in fast freeze section, allow circulation space
- Open freeze foods that would stick together e.g. soft fruits
- Freeze food according to type for example:
    - Fruit: open freezing, in dry sugar, in syrup, purée, juices;
    - Meat: joints, steaks, minced, cubed
    - Poultry: whole, sections, fillets, in a sauce or casserole
    - Fish: whole, fillets, cutlets, steaks
    - Bread, cakes, pastry: cooked, uncooked.

Never refreeze thawed out food. Return the fast freeze button to normal within 24 hours.

Storing
Keep a list of what is in the freezer – use a notebook. Store similar foods together, and for the recommended time. Use in rotation. Keep freezer filled to reduce running costs.

Rules for thawing food
- Thaw foods slowly and completely in the refrigerator or in a microwave oven
- Thoroughly cook all thawed foods, some dishes do not require thawing but require thorough cooking e.g. stews, fish, commercial ready-prepared meals
- Never re-freeze frozen foods, use thawed foods quickly
- Cook vegetables from frozen to retain colour, flavour and texture
- Never allow other foods to come in contact with 'thaw drip' from meat/poultry

Freezer burn
freezer burn results when protein foods, exposed in the freezer to the cold air toughen, dry out and discolour (oxidation).

Blanching

Before freezing, vegetables are immersed in boiling water for a specified time to destroy enzymes which would cause deterioration of colour, flavour and texture, and to destroy food spoilage bacteria. On removal from the boiling water vegetables are dipped into ice cold water for the same length of time as blanching.

Foods suitable for freezing

Foods suitable for freezing are cooked and fresh meats and meat dishes, poultry, fish, sauces, soups, fresh fruits and vegetables, uncooked cakes, bread and pastries, breadcrumbs, breads, cakes, pastries, cooked sweet and savoury dishes. Also commercial products e.g. pizza, fruit yoghurt and whipped cream.

Foods unsuitable for freezing

Foods unsuitable for freezing are those with a high water content (salad vegetables) and whole eggs (yolk and white can be frozen separately). Foods containing gelatine and dairy produce should not be frozen. Bananas blacken due to the action of enzymes, strawberries lose their texture and 'collapse' on thawing.

Packaging materials

Good materials include aluminium foil, polythene sheeting, freezer papers, polythene freezer bags, containers in aluminium, ceramics and rigid plastic, and waxed cartons. Packaging materials should be durable, easy-to-use, greaseproof, non-perishable at low temperatures, vapour-proof and waterproof.

HEAT TREATMENTS

Bottling

Bottling is the process of preserving fruit by sterilisation at a high temperature in order to destroy enzymes and micro-organisms. A vacuum is formed by the lid preventing re-entry of air and micro-organisms into the jar.

JAM-MAKING

Underlying principle

Fruits are boiled to 100°C, in the presence of sugar, to soften the fruit and to destroy enzymes and micro-organisms. Sugar inhibits the growth of micro-organisms by surrounding the bacterial cells and drawing out the water from the cells by a process called osmosis. Jam needs 65% sugar content to inhibit microbial growth.

Pectin, acid and sugar

Pectin is a polysaccharide present in cell walls of fruit. The use of an acid helps draw out the pectin from the cell walls. The proportions of *pectin, sugar* and *acid* determine the setting quality of jams and jellies. The stage of maturity of the fruit influences the amount of pectin present.

Table 3.18 Pectin

Fruit	Contains	Setting quality
Unripe fruits	→ Pectose	→ Poor
Ripe fruits	→ **Pectin**	→ Good
Over-ripe fruits	→ Pectic acid	→ Poor

Test for pectin

Take a small sample of the fruit, boil and remove one teaspoon of the fruit juice. Mix with three teaspoons of methylated spirits and cool slightly. Check after 1 minute. The fruit juice will react with the methylated spirits.

Table 3.19 Results

High in pectin	→	large single clot
Medium pectin	→	two or three soft clots
Low pection	→	several small soft clots

Pectin content of fruit – some examples

- Rich in pectin: cooking apples, blackcurrants, green gooseberries
- Medium pectin: apricots, blackberries, plums, raspberries
- Low in pectin: late blackberries, pears, rhubarb, strawberries

Fruits with a medium or low pectin content must have pectin added in the form of fruits rich in pectin, commercial liquid pectin or use a preserving sugar such as 'Sure-set'.

Guidelines for jam-making (general stages involved)

- Choose a large stainless steel saucepan
- Check that jars are perfect without chips or flaws
- Clean jars thoroughly, sterilise in oven for 15 minutes
- Select top quality sound fruit
- Prepare fruit according to kind, remove dust, dirt, etc.
- Soften the fruit, depending on fruit type add a little water
- Test for pectin

- Warm sugar, add to softened fruit and dissolve without boiling
- Bring to the boil, test for setting point, boil rapidly until setting point has been reached, remove scum by skimming jam, do not stir
- Remove from heat, pour into preheated sterilised jars, filling close to the top, wipe rims and cover with a dampened cellophane disc
- Label, cool and store in a dark, dry, well-ventilated cupboard

Three setting tests

1. *Temperature test*: using a warmed sugar thermometer, check the jam until it reaches the setting point of 104°C.
2. *Cold plate test*: remove a small quantity of jam with a spoon, pour onto a cold plate and cool. If the surface of the jam sample wrinkles when the plate is tilted, setting point has been reached.
3. *Flake test*: using a wooden spoon take a spoon of jam, cool slightly and pour the jam off the spoon. Setting point has been reached if the jam falls off in one flake. Jam pouring off the spoon (like a custard sauce) indicates that it needs more cooking.

Jam-making problems

Crystallisation: too much sugar (over 65%), sugar not dissolved before boiling, insufficient boiling, insufficient acid, overcooking
Fermentation: too little sugar (less than 65%), poor quality fruit, insufficient boiling
Mould growth: too little sugar, over-ripe fruit, damp storage conditions
Poor set: incorrect ratio of pectin, sugar and acid, insufficient boiling
Shrinkage: cellophane loose on jar, warm storage conditions

Marmalades and jellies

Marmalade is made from citrus fruits e.g. oranges, lemons, grapefruits. *Jellies* are made from fruit pulp which has been strained to produce a clear set jelly. Marmalades and jellies are made using the same stages as for jam-making.

Chutney and pickles

Chutneys and pickles are made from a mixture of quality fruits, vegetables, salt, sugar (brown), spices (whole in a muslin bag) and vinegars (5% acetic acid). Ingredients are cooked in a saucepan without a lid to allow evaporation to occur. Chutney has a consistency similar to jam. Once the chutney has cooked, pot, label and store in a dark, dry well-ventilated place. The flavour of chutneys and pickles improves with storage. Leave for about three months before use.

Underlying principles
Chutneys are sweet pickles cooked to 100°C with vinegar, sugar, spices and salt. This destroys the micro-organisms and enzymes. Vinegar produces an acid pH level which is not favoured by the micro-organisms. Concentrations of salt or sugar kill bacterial cells by osmosis.

Pickles are preserved in vinegar with salt, spices and sugar added. The high temperatures, vinegar, salt, spices and sugar destroy the enzymes and bacteria.

COMMERCIAL PRESERVATION

Commercial preservation includes bottling, canning, chemical preservation, dehydration, freezing, irradiation, pasteurisation and sterilization.

Bottling and canning
Commercial bottling and canning are similar to home methods except for the scale of production, the ultra-high temperatures involved and the fact that all types of foods can be processed e.g. fish, meat, vegetables, milk products, soups and prepared meals.

Underlying principle
Bottling and canning involve using ultra-high temperatures which destroy enzymes and micro-organisms, and keeping food in air-tight containers. Canning also involves (a) treating high acid foods at 100°C for a few minutes (having a pH less than 4.5 is adequate to destroy pathogenic bacteria); (b) destroying possible spores in low acid foods by raising temperatures to 115°C and maintaining the temperature for several minutes; and (c) using the principles of pressure cooking in aseptic canning (HTST).

Aseptic canning involves sterilising the cans and the foods separately. Food is sterilised at ultra-high temperatures of 120°C to 150°C for a short time and cooled. Pre-sterilised cans are filled with food under sterile conditions to produce a hermetic seal.

Spoilage of canned foods
Cans with bulges should be disposed of and never eaten as bulge may be an indication that gas has been produced by bacteria inside the can. Rusted or dented cans must never be used, dispose of safely.

Effects of canning
Loss of heat-sensitive, water-soluble vitamins B-group and C, changes in colour, flavour and texture.

COMMERCIAL DEHYDRATION

Underlying principle
Enzymes and micro-organisms require moisture to survive. In dehydration moisture is removed from the food, the salt and sugar concentration increases. Micro-organisms cannot multiply as moisture is removed from their cells during the drying process.

Methods of dehydration
- *Sun drying* is a traditional practice in hot, dry countries for fruits, vegetables, fish and meat. Food dried in this way is more prone to contamination and attacks from animals, birds and insects.
- During *accelerated freeze drying (AFD)* food undergoes quick freezing at –30°C, and water is converted to ice crystals. Food is then passed through a heated vacuum cabinet. The ice crystals are changed to a vapour by the process of sublimation. Foods rehydrate quickly.

Examples: coffee, dried fruits and vegetables, meat

The *effects of AFD* are loss of heat-sensitive, water-soluble vitamins, shape and colour of food changes, foods with fats are prone to oxidative rancidity.

- In *fluidised bed-drying* foods are prepared, blanched and passed through a tunnel where warm air is circulated around the food to prevent sticking, and the temperature, humidity and air flow are monitored until the moisture level is reduced to 5–10%. The food is also agitated to prevent sticking.

Example: vegetables

When *roller drying* prepared food is poured over revolving heated drums or rollers, dries and is scraped off in powder or flakes. Moisture is reduced to 10–14%.

Examples: baby foods, breakfast cereals, milk, potato flakes

During *spray drying* liquid or semi-liquid food is sprayed through fine nozzles into a heated chamber with currents of hot air, and dehydrated as droplets or powder as it falls to the bottom of the chamber.

Examples: eggs, milk

Commercial freezing
Commercial freezing is carried out at very low temperatures, –30°C, resulting in small ice crystals forming. The product produced is as near as is possible to the nutritive value, colour, flavour and texture of the fresh food.

Table 3.20 Commercial freezing

Technique	Method
Air blast freezing or tunnel freezing	Cold air at –30°C blown over food on a conveyor belt as it passes through a refrigerated tunnel.
Contact or plate freezing	Food is arranged between two refrigerated metal surfaces. Food freezes in a short time due to contact with the shelves and a circulating refrigerant e.g. burgers, thin pieces of fish or meat.
Cyrogenic freezing	Liquid nitrogen is used to freeze foods in a short time through spraying or immersion e.g. prawns.
Flow freezing or fluidised freezing	Cold air at –30°C is blown under foods to prevent them sticking together and to freeze them in the process e.g. berries, peas, sweet corn.
Spray freezing	Prepared food is sprayed with freezing liquid brine or syrup before it is packed.
Immersion freezing	Large foods are immersed in freezing brine and then packed. All traces of the brine is removed before packing e.g. poultry.

Pasteurisation

Pasteurisation is an effective commercial method of destroying enzymes and micro-organisms including disease-causing (pathogenic) bacteria. Foods pasturised include fruit juices, eggs, milk and milk products.

Sterilisation

Food is packed in sealed containers and is heated to temperatures higher than boiling point in order to destroy disease-causing and food-spoliage micro-organisms. *Example*: milk

CHEMICAL PRESERVATION

Natural and chemical preservatives are used to prevent the action of enzymes and to destroy or inactivate micro-organisms. Preservatives added to commercially produced or manufactured foods are strictly controlled. Chemical preservation involves the use of salt, sugar, alcohol, vinegar, a variety of acids, sulphur dioxide, nitrate and nitrite.

Underlying principle

Chemical preservatives change the concentration of the food as liquid passes from the microbial cell to the food. It causes the cell to become dehydrated and unable to reproduce itself. Some chemical preservatives create unfavourable conditions for growth of micro-organisms. The most commonly used preservatives are:

Alcohol: denatures proteins and destroys micro-organisms
Antioxidants: used to inhibit enzymic action, to prevent rancidity
Acids: acetic, beznoic, propionic, sorbic
Nitrates and nitrites: used in curing meats
Salt: prevents decay, improves flavour
Smoking: produces aldehydes and phenols
Sugar: onhibits microbial growth
Sulphur dioxide: forms sulphuric acid which acts as a preservative

FERMENTATION

In the fermentation of food specific micro-organisms are used to create new textures, new foods and to preserve foods. By-products of fermentation are in themselves preservatives e.g. alcohol, vinegar. These fermented ingredients are combined with other methods of preservation (chilling, heat treatments, pasteurisation) in order to preserve other foods. Carbohydrates in food are converted into acid (lactic acid), ethanol and carbon dioxide, or acid, ethanol and carbon dioxide.

Methods of fermentation
- Yeast fermentation with CO_2 as the end product in baking
- Yeast fermentation with alcohol as the end product in brewing and vinegar
- Acid fermentation produces yoghurt, and pickles (fermented vegetables)

Examples
The production of *vinegar* involves two fermentations; (a) yeast converts sugars into alcohol; and (b) alcohol is converted into acetic acid.
The production of *alcohol* involves three-stage fermentation; (a) starch changes to maltose and dextrins by the enzyme diastase present in the starch source; (b) maltose changes to glucose by the enzyme maltose present in yeast; and (c) glucose changes to alcohol by the enzyme zymare.

Irradiation
Irradiation involves passing ionising gamma radiation through food to sterilise it, to delay ripening, to inhibit or destroy food poisoning bacteria, to kill insects and prevent sprouting. Three levels of radiation treatment are used (low, moderate and high). Irradiated foods may carry an internationally-recognised label.

Advantages of irradiation
- Increases shelf-life of products, prevents sprouting, delays ripening

- Increases the potential range of foods available e.g. tropical fruits
- Destroys food poisoning bacteria, reduces damage by insects/pests
- Little change in colour, flavour and texture

Disadvantages of irradiation

Consumers are not convinced that irradiation is a safe method of preservation because of their concerns regarding radioactivity, the potential for micro-organisms and insects to develop resistance to radiation, its unsuitability for foods with high fat content, the loss of nutritional value, concerns over the abuse of using irradiation on inferior products.

Figure 3.11 Radura symbol on irradiated food

Vacuum packing

Prevents the growth of aerobic micro-organisms, food wrapped in polythene has the edges sealed by heat to prevent re-entry of microbes into food.
Examples: bacon, rashers, joints of meat e.g. beef, lamb

COMPARATIVE EVALUATION OF THREE METHODS OF PRESERVATION

When carrying out comparative evaluation of foods preserved by different methods investigate the following:
- Ingredients used
- Nutritional information
- Consumer information
- Shelf-life
- Cost
- Packaging
- Effects of cooking on nutritional content, colour, flavour and texture
- Risk of spoilage

FOOD SAFETY AND HYGIENE

SAFE FOOD PREPARATION

Inadequate food handling and storage practices may lead to cross-contamination in fresh and cooked foods. Temperature control during storage, preparation and cooking is important in preventing the multiplication of bacteria. Food poisoning can occur if there are high levels of bacteria present in food, in the food environment or in humans. Areas within the food environment to be considered for specific attention include, food storage, re-heating procedures, personal hygiene practices and kitchen hygiene.

Note: For sources and conditions for growth refer to section 'Food Poisoning' in 'Food Spoilage – Microbiology'.

Aims of good food hygiene practices/systems
- To destroy any micro-organisms
- To prevent their re-entry into the food
- To prevent contamination and cross-contamination
- To prevent carriers of food poisoning bacteria (humans) causing an outbreak of food poisoning

Food storage – guidelines
- Store food at the right temperatures for each food type
- Storage cupboards should be clean, dry and well-ventilated
- Clean out and wash exterior surfaces weekly including edges of doors
- Ensure that cupboards are free of mice and insects e.g. ants, mites
- Use food in rotation, check stocks and replace as required
- Store perishable foods in the refrigerator until required, use quickly
- Never mix raw and cooked foods, store separately
- Place bought frozen food in the freezer on returning home
- Never leave perishables at room temperature
- Store dry goods (non-perishables) in a clean dry cupboard
- Store opened dry foods in airtight containers
- Refrigerators must not be warmer than 4°C, allow for circulation of air
- Store foods in the recommended areas within the refrigerator

Note: For preparation and handling of food refer to section 'Food Poisoning' in 'Food Spoilage – Microbiology'.

Reheating procedures – guidelines
- Use leftover foods within two days, handle as little as possible
- Reheat food in a microwave or conventional oven
- Heat protein foods to temperatures of 100°C
- Serve fresh foods/dishes at once piping hot or cool quickly
- Never place warm food in a refrigerator, it raises the temperature

Personal hygiene
(Refer to 'Controlling the Microbial Spoilage of Food' in 'Food Spoilage – Microbiology'.)

- Wash hands using liquid soap, hot water and a nail brush
- Never wash hands in the sink used for food preparation

Note: For kitchen hygiene refer to 'Microbial Spoilage of Food' in 'Food Spoilage – Microbiology'.

HAZARD ANALYSIS AND CRITICAL CONTROL POINTS (HACCP)

Definitions

The HACCP System
HACCP is a system of analysis that identifies potential food hygiene and safety hazards that might occur at specific points in food production. These 'danger' points can be identified, monitored and controlled in order to prevent contamination.

HACCP can be applied to all areas of food production from seed to the kitchen table.

The hazards
Hazards in a food product can be described as anything that may cause harm to consumers. It can occur at any stage of production. The three main hazards are *biological*, *chemical* and *physical contamination*.

The risk
A risk refers to the probability of a hazard occurring during food production. The risks present can be categorised into three main types: high, medium and low.

Hazard analysis
The particular hazard is analysed and the implications for consumer safety are examined. Hazard analysis in food production investigates each of the steps involved from purchase of raw materials to point of sale for any hazard that might cause harm to the consumer.

Critical control point (CCP)
A 'critical control point' can be defined as a step in the food production process where hazards must be controlled. Controls can be applied in order to eliminate, prevent or minimise hazards. The critical control point is the final opportunity to correct a hazard.

Identification of steps in the production of food – a practical example
For each step consider the potential hazard, the controls that could be put in place and the arrangements for monitoring the steps from start to finish of the food production process.
- Purchase of raw materials (supplier, deliveries, records, sampling)

- Delivery of raw materials (delivery vehicles, temperatures, unloading)
- Storage of raw materials (chilled, frozen, dry)
- Preparation of food product (cleaning, monitoring, equipment, environment)
- Application of baking, cooking or heating methods (times, temperatures)
- Cooling food product (times, temperatures, storage)
- Assembly of food product (equipment, monitoring, staff)
- Storage (temperatures, containers, time)
- Display (temperatures, dates)
- Reheating (core temperatures)
- Delivery/ sale (vehicles, temperatures, unloading, records, date stamps)

Setting up a HACCP system – an overview
- Set up a HACCP team (representing all areas of production)
- Develop a flow chart of all aspects of food production
- Identify potential hazards at all stages of food production
- Carry out a risk assessment of hazards happening
- Decide on steps needed to eliminate or reduce the risk at CCPs
- Recommend the action to be taken for each control point
- Implement monitoring and control strategies
- Record the HACCP process and the monitoring of the CCPs
- Implement further action at control points if necessary
- Evaluate the HACCP system regularly

Advantages of HACCP
- HACCP involves forward planning
- Prevention can eliminate or reduce potential hazards
- Identification of hazards is key to producing a safe product
- All individuals working in the food production plant are focussed on safety
- Legal requirements for safety are fulfilled
- Records provide evidence of efforts made to produce safe food products
- Food products are safer
- Evaluation of HACCP system provides an accurate snapshot of the overall operation and can influence future planning in terms of safety, time and money

ISO 9000
ISO is the International Organisation for Standardisation, a global federation of national standard bodies that sets standards of quality to ensure that consumer needs are met. The ISO 9000 standard indicates that a company has attained standards of quality that are acceptable internationally. The standards are general and not specific. Schemes are operated by the National Standards Authority of Ireland (NSAI). Food companies who have been accredited by the NSAI and awarded this quality mark will have achieved a high standard of food hygiene.

ROLE OF NATIONAL AGENCIES IN FOOD SAFETY

Control, monitoring and enforcement of food safety regulation involves government departments, local authorities, Health Boards and specialised agencies.

FUNCTIONS OF GOVERNMENT DEPARTMENTS AND LOCAL AUTHORITIES

Department of Agriculture, Food and Rural Development
- To provide food safety monitoring and inspection for a variety of operations
- To monitor and control animal health, to eliminate TB and brucellosis
- To monitor and eliminate the use of illegal substances in animals
- To monitor slaughtering plants, meat processing and milk processing
- To provide a system for animal identification and tracing
- To monitor horticultural production

Department of Communication, Marine and Natural Resources
This department allocates licences to fishing and passenger vessels, monitors fish processing, transportation and fish products, licences and monitors aquaculture production.

Department of Health and Children
- To formulate, develop and evaluate health policy
- To protect and promote good health (Health Promotion Unit)
- To provide information to educate consumers (Food Unit)
- To issue guidelines for the food and catering industry (Environmental Health)
- To inspect, monitor and issue licences to premises serving food
- To monitor general food safety and hygiene, baby food, nutritional labelling, food additives and food contamination

Department of Enterprise, Trade and Employment
This department is involved in the monitoring of food labelling and the formulation of consumer protection legislation.

Department of the Environment and Local Government
This department legislates for public drinking water supplies (main and group schemes).

Local Authorities
- To licence dairies and milk retail outlets
- To monitor retail butchers and abattoirs
- To inspect milk quality at processing plants
- To inspect and monitor drinking water supplies
- To supply good quality drinking water for the local area

Functions of Regional Health Boards

The regional Health Boards implement the Department of Health and Children regulations governing food hygiene and safety in their local areas. Some premises may need to register with the local Health Board e.g. butcher shops, food manufacturers. Following registration Environmental Health Officers carry out routine inspections. The EHO has the power to enforce regulations, resulting in improvements or closure of the premises for non-compliance.

SPECIALISED AGENCIES

Public Analyst Laboratories

These laboratories test drugs, food and water. Food samples can be tested for bacteria, foreign bodies or chemical substances. EHO carry out routine food sampling and send it to these laboratories for testing. Individuals can have samples tested for a fee.

Food Safety Authority of Ireland (FSAI)

The Food Safety Authority of Ireland Act, 1998, established the FSAI. Its key functions are to enforce and co-ordinate all food safety programmes, to consult with caterers, consumers, distributors, manufacturers, producers and retailers with regard to food safety. To engage in research, advice, co-ordination of services and certification of food.

Director of Consumer Affairs

The Office of the Director of Consumer Affairs has responsibility for ensuring that food labelling provides the consumer with the legally required information as demanded under European and national legislation. The general food labelling regulations are enforced by the Director of Consumer Affairs on behalf of the Food Safety Authority. Food producers who ignore this legislation are likely to be prosecuted.

Other agencies

An Bord Bia, Bord Iascaigh Mhara, Enterprise Ireland, Teagasc.

CHAPTER 4 – Resource Management and Consumer Studies

FAMILY RESOURCE MANAGEMENT

Management involves the choice, use and control of resources to achieve goals that will improve the quality of life. Management allows people to take charge of their lives and to determine, in so far as is possible, desired outcomes.

Resource management means using resources wisely to achieve goals e.g. time, human resources, technology and money.

Home management involves planning, controlling and evaluating the use of family resources in order to fulfil goals and improve the quality of family life.

Purpose of resource management
- To use resources to achieve goals
- To help people take control by creating order
- To improve the quality of family life
- To assist individuals achieve goals

Management systems – two basic types
An open system means dependence on and interactions with systems outside the family e.g. school, health service, social welfare system, places of work, etc.
A closed system means all activities occur within the family or community.

The family as a managerial unit
A family is an open system. Household operations are completed in an efficient manner (budgeting, childminding, meal planning, shopping, cleaning, laundry) using an effective management system. Family management or home management involves the choice, use and management of resources to set goals, gather information, identify and solve problems, to make decisions, budget, resolve conflict, manage time and evaluate the outcomes based on the decisions made.

COMPONENTS OF MANAGEMENT

Management plans consist of three components, inputs, throughputs and outputs.

1. *Inputs* are made up of demands and resources needed to fulfil these demands.
   - Examples of demands: needs, values, goals, events, family commitments
   - Example of resources: human resources, material environment, finance

Needs are the essentials required for survival (not a luxury or a want).
Values are personal to individuals, family and cultures (visible through behaviour).
Goals are the end results that individuals plan and work for.
Resources are tools available to us to achieve our goals.
2. *Throughputs* involve processing the inputs, making a plan, implementing and adjusting the plan as necessary. Throughputs link inputs and outputs.
Planning involves clarifying the goals identified at the input stage, setting standards and sequencing activities.
   • Examples: contingency, directional or strategic plans
   Organising a plan involves using all relevant information to design the plan, which may be task-centred or person-centred.
Decision-making aids the design, implementation and evaluation of the plan.
3. *Outputs* are the end results of the inputs and throughputs. They are visible in a variety of ways e.g. goals achieved, changes in values and goals due to change in circumstances, satisfaction that the plan has worked and evaluation of the plan provides feedback useful for planning new tasks or setting new goals.

Figure 4.1 A basic management framework

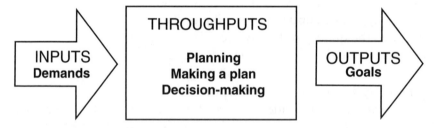

DECISION-MAKING

Decision-making may be described as the process of examining two or more alternatives and making a choice between them based on personal values and goals.

Basic steps in decision-making – summary
• Define the decision
• Examine the alternatives or possible solutions
• Consider the consequences of each solution
• Make a decision. Develop an action plan
• Implement the plan
• Evaluate the outcome/decision

The decision-making process may be influenced by advice or guidance provided by primary or secondary reference groups (different people). Within the family decisions may be reached through accommodation, consensual or *de facto* agreement.

COMMUNICATION

Communication is the process of exchanging information between people. It may be verbal or non-verbal. Management systems use communication as a tool to persuade people to co-operate in the management process.

Characteristics of effective communication
The message sent is clear. The receiver hears and understands the full message. The receiver understands the verbal and non-verbal aspects of the message. The receiver relates to the message and responds to the sender of the message.

Attributes affecting management
Stages in life: families with children, retired or elderly people, newly-weds, pre-retirement stage, retirement stage (different resources needed at different times)
Size and composition of family: adults and children, gender, relationships, family members with special needs
Employment pattern: number employed determines household income
Gender roles: equal division of tasks, equality of participation
Culture: socially accepted and transmitted patterns of management
Values/standards: influence what we want to achieve, priorities
Socio-economic status: opportunities, lifestyle, employment, resources

MANAGEMENT OF HOUSEHOLD FINANCIAL RESOURCES

THE HOUSEHOLD AS A FINANCIAL UNIT
- Families are small financial units
- Important units within the national economy
- Income provides the family's financial resources
- Money management skills are essential
- Income provides for needs, wants and luxuries
- Income varies from family to family

Factors affecting family income
- Age: income increases as people get older, reduces in retirement
- Culture: different emphasis placed on the value of money
- Gender: equality of pay (Anti-Discrimination Pay Act 1974)
- Socio-economic status: determined by occupation/employment
- Wage-earners in the home: one/two parents, teenagers, adult children
- Increase in number of women at work: dual income families

Sources of household income
Household incomes come from different sources: wages and salaries, pensions, social insurance allowances and benefits, investment (bonds, saving schemes, etc.).

FINANCIAL TERMS

Terms associated with income include wages, salaries, net income and irregular income.

Examples of deductions from wages/salary
Compulsory (statutory): income tax (PAYE), government levies, (PRSI)
Voluntary (non-statutory): health insurance, saving schemes, superannuation, union subscription

Statutory, compulsory deductions
PAYE (income tax)
- Tax deductions from each employee's salary/wages
- Tax deduction sent directly to government by employer
- Citizen has a Personal Public Service number (PPS)
- Tax return to be filled in at end of year
- Self-employed responsible for assessing and paying tax
- Tax liability calculated according to an individual's tax credits
- Tax is paid at the standard rate on first part of income and at a higher rate on the remaining amount

Overview of tax credits
- Personal tax credits: single person, two-income married couples
- Widowed person: without dependent children, one-parent family tax credit
- One-parent family: widowed person, other person
- Child credit: in respect of an incapacitated child
- Dependent relative credit
- Bereaved in 2001: other years listed with different credits
- Home carer's credit maximum
- Age tax credit: single/widowed, married
- Blind tax credit: one spouse blind, both blind

Other tax credits – some examples
- Incapacitated child credit maximum
- Dependent relative credit maximum
- Carer for incapacitated child
- Medical expenses
- Pension contributions
- Mortgage interest relief
- Rent relief
- Job expenses
- Installation of home alarms (people over 65 years)

Low income exemption limits

People with incomes below a certain level are removed from the income tax net.

Note:
- Check current rates, credits, benefits and allowance for recent changes
- Small income exemptions: if an individual's income does not exceed particular limits no income tax has to be paid
- Documents related to PPS number include P60 and P45

PRSI (Social Insurance) deductions
- PRSI is Pay Related Social Insurance contribution
- Pays for social welfare benefits, pensions, health services, employment and training schemes
- Workers aged 16 and over are liable for PRSI
- Benefits include unemployment benefit, contributory old-age pension, survivors contributory pension, dental benefit, optical benefit, maternity benefit

Pensions

Types of pensions available include contributory old-age pension (state), non-contributory old-age pension (state), occupational pensions and personal pensions.

Social welfare payments

The social welfare system provides payments to some members of society who find that they are in need of/dependent on state assistance.

There are *three categories of social welfare payments*:
- Social Insurance Payments (based on PRSI contributions)
- Social Assistance Payments (paid subject to a means test)
- Universal Payments (do not depend on PRSI contributions or a means test)

Main social welfare payments – examples

Unemployment payments, employment supports, payments for retired or elderly people – pensions, occupational injuries benefit payment, family income support payments, supplementary welfare allowance.

Examples of other payments

Universal payments: child benefit, free travel for old-age pensioners
Other benefits: fuel allowance, smokeless fuel allowance, free electricity allowance, free natural gas allowance, free television licence, free telephone rental allowance, bereavement grant

HOUSEHOLD EXPENDITURE

Essential expenditure: money used for essentials, food, clothing and shelter (fixed and irregular)
Discretionary expenditure: disposable income, money spent by individuals according to personal choices

BUDGET PLANNING

A budget is a plan for spending money over a specific period of time in a balanced way. Personal budgets and family budgets can be calculated using the same method.

Reasons for budgeting
- To develop good money management habits
- To control spending, including credit spending
- To reduce financial worry and stress, create security
- To balance expenditure and income
- To plan for irregular and regular bills
- To reduce unnecessary, impulse spending
- To identify areas where economies can be made
- To make short- and long-term saving goals

Budgets need to be
- Re-organised as family needs/priorities change
- Examined as income changes e.g. employment/unemployment
- Checked annually or more regularly if necessary

Table 4.1 Planning a budget: general guidelines

Area of expenditure	Suggested	Examples
Housing/shelter	25–30%	Rent/mortgage, insurance, repairs, maintenance
Food	25%	A healthy balanced diet to prevent disease
Household	15–20%	Heating, cooking, lighting, telephone, furniture
Clothing	5–10%	Clothes, footwear, dry cleaning
Transport	5–10%	Depends where you live/work, petrol, bus, train
Health	5%	Medical insurance, dentist, doctor, pharmacy
Personal/leisure	5–8%	Entertainment, sports, holidays, gifts, hobbies
Savings	5%	Long-term, short-term for emergencies or goals

Preparing a household budget
- List all expected regular net income (omit irregular income)
- List planned expenditure – fixed, irregular and discretionary

- Add up the totals, divide by fifty-two to calculate weekly expenditure
- Set aside money on a regular basis to cover the planned spending
- Allow for discretionary spending e.g. Christmas, birthdays, etc.
- Make provision for personal spending
- Make provisions for savings in the budget

CREDIT 'BUYING NOW, PAYING LATER'

Credit allows consumers to buy goods or services and to repay the money along with interest and other charges on a regular basis.

Types of credit
Personal and term loans, overdrafts, credit unions, charge cards, credit cards, store cards, hire purchase, licensed moneylenders.

Advantages of credit
- Use of goods while paying for them
- Help to meet costs of emergencies
- Can buy large expensive items e.g. home, car
- Can buy luxury items e.g. holiday
- Do not need to save, low initial cost
- Little need to carry large sums of cash
- Credit-free period on budget accounts and credit cards

Disadvantages of credit
- Goods can be repossessed if repayments are not made
- Goods not owned by consumer until final instalment is paid
- Expensive as interest rates are high
- Easy to overspend when buying on credit
- Encourages impulse buying and overspending
- Borrowers might not be able to maintain the repayments

CONSUMER LEGISLATION

Hire Purchase Act (1946, revised 1960)
Hire purchase agreements must identify the agreement as 'hire purchase'. The act states that hire purchase agreements must give names and addresses of the parties, a description of the goods, cash price of goods, details of hire purchase price, APR – rate of interest being charged. Instalment arrangements, information on termination of agreement, recovery of goods (repossession) and details of penalty clauses and cooling off period.

Consumer Credit Act 1995

The Consumer Credit Act, implemented by the Office of the Director of Consumer Affairs, deals specifically with credit. It provides protection for consumers (the borrowers) in relation to consumer loans and credit agreements, hire purchase and leasing agreements, housing loans and moneylenders.

All *credit advertisements* must give the following information:

- Rates of APR and how it is calculated, amount needed for deposit and instalments, current restrictions in place (if any), security requirements e.g. deposit, cash price, total cost of credit, instalment information

All *credit agreements* must:

- Be in writing, show the names and addresses of all parties, be signed by all parties involved, outline costs and penalties that apply, contain the ten-day 'cooling-off' period arrangements

A copy of the agreement must be given to the consumer on completion or within ten days of that date. Consumers may withdraw from the agreement within ten days of receiving a copy of it by providing written notice to the creditor.

HOUSING FINANCE AND CHOICE

In Ireland most people finance house purchase by taking out a mortgage from a lending institution and repaying it over a set term. To get a mortgage a person must be over 18 years of age, be employed and have a regular income. The size of mortgage depends on the value of the property, borrower's earnings and the size of deposit available.

Sources of mortgages: banks, building societies, local authorities

Types of mortgages
- Low-start mortgage
- Annuity mortgage
- Endowment mortgage
- Pension mortgage

General terms and conditions that apply
- *Amount borrowed*: general guideline is two and a half times the principal salary and half of the secondary
- *Deposit*: lending institutions expect borrowers to have 10% of cost price
- *Credit record*: borrowers must have good credit and savings records
- *Proof of income*: PAYE balancing statement or P60, self-employed must show audited accounts for three years and a statement that tax liabilities are paid up
- *Mortgage indemnity bond*: required if more than 75% of cost is borrowed
- *Term of repayment*: varies from 5 to 35 years

- *Title deeds*: lending institution holds title deeds until final repayments are made
- *Mortgage agreement*: states the amounts of each payment, interest payable, date due, term of mortgage
- *Life assurance*: legal requirement when a mortgage is taken out
- *House insurance*: must be organised before mortgage cheque is released
- *Cost of surveyor*: borrower must pay this cost
- *Legal fees*: solicitor's fees, legal searches, registration of title
- *Stamp duty*: government tax to be paid by borrower at specific rates

Methods of payment for goods and services (cash and credit)
A variety of options are available:
- ATM, bank overdraft, bill pay (post office), cash, cheque with matching bankers' card, credit card, credit transfer/giro, hire purchase, laser, leasing, smart cards, store cards, internet, 24-hour banking

SAVINGS

Methods of saving
When considering saving schemes check out the following: rate of interest, ease of withdrawal, saving terms, confidentiality, security arrangements, tax payable (dirt), other benefits.

Advantages of saving
Saving provides security, encourages planned spending for future goals and reduces stress associated with debts. It is easier to get a loan with a good savings record.

Summary of saving options/schemes
Many options are available to savers but the terms involved for each option are liable to change from time to time.

Banks and building societies
Deposit accounts/savings accounts, fixed-notice accounts, fixed-term accounts, special savings accounts (SSAs), guaranteed bonds, personal investment, portfolio, direct equity investment.

An Post (state guaranteed)
Regular deposit account, deposit account plus, childcare savings account, pension save, savings bonds, savings certificates, instalment savings scheme, savings account.

Credit Unions

Deposit account, savings account/shares.

Insurance

Insurance provides financial protection against a risk and sharing that risk with an insurance company by paying annual premiums.

- Insurance: protects against something that might happen e.g. car crash
- Assurance: protects against something that will happen e.g. death
- Broker: an agent who provides advice and receives commission upon a sale
- Policy: the name given to the scheme into which money is paid
- Premium: the money paid in instalments or annually to the company
- Claim: request/demand for compensation

Categories of insurance

Obligatory insurance: Pay Related Social Insurance, car insurance, home insurance
Optional/voluntary insurance: health insurance, travel insurance, life assurance

Examples of insurance/assurance options

Life assurance

Life assurance is taken out on an individual's life, provides financial security for family and provides income support. There are three basic types:

- Term: taken out for 10–20 years, cheapest type of insurance
- Whole life: more expensive, no time limit, covers person for entire life
- Endowment: combines higher savings element and whole-life cover

A *Mortgage Protection Policy*: this is a life insurance policy taken out on the value of the mortgage. The insurance company repays the loan to the lending institution if the borrower dies.

Property insurance: a fixed sum is paid monthly with mortgage repayments or annually to the insurance company. It covers the house (buildings) against damage caused by fire, storms, burst pipes and in some cases floods and the contents.

Car insurance: monthly or annual payments are paid to an insurance company, premiums vary depending on age, gender, type of licence held and size of engine.

Travel insurance: policy taken out when travelling abroad to protect the traveller against cancellations, accidents, medical expenses and lost luggage.

Private health insurance: there are two types available, VHI and BUPA Ireland. Covers a range of medical expenses in the case of illness.

Salary protection insurance: if a person has to retire from work due to illness or injury an income representing 75% of original salary is paid until the person retires.

HOUSING

FACTORS AFFECTING HOUSING CHOICES

- Socio-economic factors
- Life circumstances, income, age, life-cycle
- Buying, renting, sharing with others
- Money available, cost of homes on market
- Type and size of home, maintenance, garden
- Location, community, environment, amenities
- Ease of access to services e.g. transport, facilities
- Suitability for people with special needs
- Proximity to work, family, friends
- Potential resale value
- National housing policy

National housing policy

The Department of the Environment and Local Government is responsible for formulating and implementing policy and preparing legislation relating to the provision of a good standard of housing. Main strategies in national housing policy include:

- Supervising and supporting a sustainable national housing programme
- Facilitating the greatest number of households to own their own homes
- Developing and supporting a well-managed social housing sector
- Highlighting the needs of low-income families and neglected areas
- Supporting the Remedial Works Scheme
- Developing and supporting an effective private rented sector

Examples of housing services provided through local authorities include:

- Local authority housing and traveller accommodation
- Accommodation for homeless people
- Support of social housing projects
- Home improvements in private houses
- Low cost housing sites
- Sale of local authority houses to tenants
- Disabled individuals' grants
- Enforcement of rented houses regulations

Schemes designed to help provide homes include: House Purchase Grants, Rental Subsidy Scheme, Mortgage Allowance Scheme, Shared Ownership Scheme, Affordable Housing, Tenant Purchase Scheme

Trends in housing development across Ireland
- Improvements in inner city, urban and large towns
- Development of a variety of home ownership schemes
- Commuting to work from more affordable housing is common
- Development of satellite or dormer towns across the country
- Developers must include green areas and amenities
- Smaller estates have large entrance pillars and sometimes security gates
- Tax-designated status has been given to some homes and developments
- Houses are smaller and more compact with little garden space

Availability – current situation (2003)
- Currently demand for housing far exceeds supply
- Rise in property prices, many individuals unable to buy a home
- More people are able to rent rather than buy property, rents are increasing
- Local authority housing is subject to availability, supply shortage
- Supplies of social and affordable housing are insufficient
- Overcrowding is common among students and young adults in larger urban areas

HOUSEHOLD TECHNOLOGY

Definition
Technology in the home is the application of science through appliances and new resources to make the management and maintenance of the home easier, faster and efficient.

CONTRIBUTION OF TECHNOLOGY TO HOME MANAGEMENT

- Reduction in workload
- Improved quality of home life
- Energy-efficient appliances save money
- Appliances are fitted with safety devices
- Higher standards of food and kitchen hygiene
- Tasks completed quickly, more time for other activities

Technological developments that have contributed to efficient home maintenance and management include:
- Production of plastics and man-made materials
- Creation of easy to care for products, surfaces and fabrics
- Mass production of items, appliances are more affordable
- Use of computer chips in household machines
- Design of appliances e.g. food preparation, laundry, cleaning

- New cooker designs e.g. fan-ovens, double ovens, dual grills
- Automated systems e.g. water-heating systems, lighting systems
- Development of electric tools e.g. drills, paint strippers
- Household security systems e.g. security lights, alarms
- Use of computer packages for budgeting and accounts
- Use of Internet for shopping, banking online, communication

HOUSEHOLD TECHNOLOGY IN ACTION – EXAMPLES OF DEVELOPMENTS

Laundry or washing: washing machines, dryers, irons, washing detergents
Food preparation and cooking: food processors, electric kettles, microwave ovens, refrigerators, deep freeze, cordless appliances
Household cleaning: vacuum cleaners, steam cleaners, new cleaning materials
Materials and textiles: aluminium, cling film, plastics, man-made fibres, special finishes for textiles and other surfaces

General guidelines for choosing household appliances
- Choose a reliable well-known brand, buy from a reputable dealer
- Shop around, compare costs, get value for money
- Consider the budget available, buy the best you can afford
- Check purchase, installation and running costs
- Consider the design, construction and care of appliances
- Check energy-efficiency rating, safety features, additional features
- Consider family needs, size of household, number of people
- Check appliance measurements against space available
- Check if extra services are needed e.g. power points, plumbing, ventilation
- Ask about guarantees and after-sale service

Sources of consumer information
Advertisements, consumer television programmes, manufacturers' leaflets and brochures, sales staff in shops, newspapers and magazines, the telephone directory, word of mouth – friends and family.

HOUSEHOLD APPLIANCES

TYPES OF APPLIANCES

With a motor: food processor, vacuum cleaner, carving knife, washing machine
With a heating element: coffee percolator, electric cooker, deep-fat fryer, electric kettle, frying pan, iron, sandwich maker

THE FOOD PROCESSOR

A food processor is a versatile motor appliance that saves time and energy, speeds up food preparation and is easy to use and maintain.

Construction
Food processors are made up of:
- A motor enclosed in a strong metal or plastic casing
- A plastic or metal bowl with a lockable funnelled lid
- A selection of metal and plastic blades and discs
- A central spindle to hold blades and discs
- A variable speed button/switch with on/off switch
- A flex and 3-pin plug with appropriate fuse

Figure 4.2 A food processor

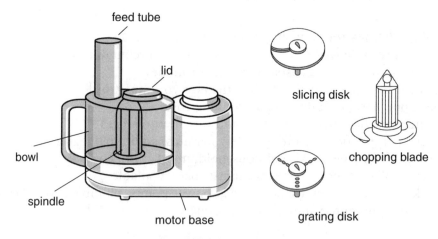

Attachments and uses: steel chopping blade (puréeing fruits, soups, sauces, fine parsley, vegetables, meats). Grating discs – fine, medium, coarse (cheese, cabbage, carrot, potatoes); whisk attachment (meringues, sponge cakes, sauces); juice extractor (fresh orange juice, lemon juice). Liquidiser (soups, sauces, purées); dough hook (bread, pastry, cake mixtures)

Working principle (food processor)
Electricity powers a motor, which drives rotating metal/plastic blades and discs that beat, chop, liquidise, slice and whisk ingredients in an enclosed metal or plastic container. A safety lock system prevents the motor working when the lid is removed. When slicing or grating food the lid is locked into place, the appliance turned on and food is pushed down the funnel of the lid using a plastic 'pusher'. The metal disc slices or grates the food into the bowl.
Size/capacity: standard is 2 litres, smaller and larger capacities are available

Guidelines for use
- Follow manufacturer's instructions
- Never operate with wet or damp hands
- Ensure that bowl and lid are locked securely
- Use attachments for correct processes, slot into place before using
- Never put spoons or fingers down the funnel or near rotating blades
- Use feed tube as recommended
- Never overload appliance, follow instructions
- Prepare food in small quantities when using the funnel
- Stop the appliance, scrape down sides from time to time

Guidelines for care
- Unplug before cleaning, do not use abrasives
- Cool motor before cleaning and storing away
- Do not immerse motor in water, wipe with damp cloth
- Clean blades/discs carefully in hot soapy water
- Dry attachments thoroughly, wipe base with a damp cloth
- Store appliance with lid off and attachments in a dry place

ELECTRIC COOKER

The electric cooker is a large appliance with heating elements.

There are different *types of electric cookers*: free-standing cooker, built-in split level cooker, built-in under worktop cooker, range style cookers and tabletop cookers.

Construction
- Enamelled steel with fibreglass insulation
- Cast iron used in some solid fuel cookers
- Most have a grill, hob and one or two ovens
- Hobs may consist of:
  - Electric radiant rings *or*
  - Sealed/solid hotplates *or*
  - Gas burners *or*
  - Ceramic surface with halogen rings
- Ovens ranging from fan oven, double oven to ovens with auto-timers
- Grills at eye-level, below hob level or built into the main oven

Working principle (convection and fan ovens)
Heat for cooking is transferred by conduction, convection and radiation and is thermostatically controlled. Hobs transfer heat to saucepans by conduction, food cooks by conduction or convection. Grills cook food by radiation. In ovens food cooks by conduction as hot air currents circulate around the oven. In fan ovens

an element is located at the back from where a fan blows hot air around the oven. An even temperature is produced which allows all shelves to be used to produce the same result e.g. sponge cakes. Fan ovens are suitable for batch baking. They heat up quicker, cook faster and are energy-efficient. Conventional ovens have uneven temperatures from the top shelf to the bottom shelf.

Special features
- Energy saving: dual circuit rings, simmerstat rings, dual element rings
- Ovens: catalytic ovens (stay-clean linings), pyrolytic ovens (self-cleaning)
- Removable oven linings: for easy cleaning
- Autotimers: switching on/off the oven automatically

Guidelines for use
- Follow manufacturer's instruction
- Never pull or drag pots across ceramic hobs
- Use energy-saving features e.g. dual grill
- Make full use of the oven, cook complete meal in oven
- Pre-heat the oven before baking
- Time dishes correctly, check during cooking
- Make use of residual heat to finish cooking dishes
- Avoid opening the oven door during cooking

Guidelines for care
- Turn off main switch before cleaning
- Clean regularly, dismantle removable parts, wash and dry
- Wipe up spills immediately, do not allow to build up
- Do not use abrasives on ceramic hobs, use recommended cleaners
- Ventilate kitchen when using oven cleaners, some produce fumes

THE REFRIGERATOR

Refrigerator appliances are designed to keep perishable food fresh for a specific length of time under cold conditions by preventing the action of micro-organisms.
   There are a variety of designs and colours from which to choose:
- Standard fridge
- Larder fridge
- Integrated fridge/freezer

Construction
- An outer layer of insulated enamelled steel
- An inner lining of enclosed moulded polystyrene
- Layer of insulating material between the steel and polystyrene

- Door with magnetic catch and rubber door seals
- Thermostat to control temperatures
- Selection of adjustable plastic coated shelving and storage drawers
- Adjustable door bottle rack and moulded compartments
- An icebox at the top of refrigerator, size depends on model
- Light inside the cabinet which switches on/off automatically

Figure 4.3 A refrigerator

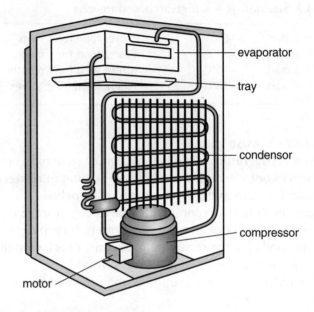

Features
- Variety of sizes, shapes, colours and exterior finishes
- Compartments, adjustable shelves and storage areas
- Chilled drinks dispenser for water and/or fruit juices
- Internal ice-maker and/or external ice dispenser
- Automatic defrost, at intervals in the fridge section
- Zonal refrigeration, different temperatures in different shelves
- Frost-free refrigerators

Working principles (compressor refrigerator)

The *compressor*, at the base of the refrigerator, is activated by an electric motor. It forces the *gaseous refrigerant* (Freon 12 or liquid ammonia) into the condenser. The refrigerant is cooled by the condenser and changes into liquid. From the *condenser* the liquid passes into the evaporator where it is cooled and evaporated into a gas. The liquid refrigerant evaporates by removing heat from inside the refrigerator. The evaporated refrigerant returns to the compressor where the cycle begins again. A thermostat controls the temperature within the cabinet between 0°C and 5°C and disconnects the electricity when it is cold enough. The motor starts again when temperatures rise.

Size/capacity: average is 150 litres, ranges from 50 litres to 280 litres

Methods of defrosting
- Automatic: compressor stops at intervals to allow ice to melt, eliminates build-up
- Manual: controls set to 'off' or 'defrost' until ice melts, controls re-set
- Push-button: button turns off the compressor, ice melts, automatically restarts

Table 4.2 Star ratings – refrigerators and freezers

* 1 star	-6°C	Stores food for 1 week	
** 2 stars	-12°C	Stores food for 1 month	
*** 3 stars	-18°C	Stores food for 3 months	
**** 4 stars	-18°C to -25°C	Freeze fresh food, stores frozen food up to 12 months	

Guidelines for use
- Open refrigerator only when necessary to avoid energy loss
- Always cool warm/hot food before storing in refrigerator
- Cover foods to avoid flavours being absorbed
- Store foods in the recommended area e.g. storage drawer
- Store raw and cooked meats separately (raw meat on a lower shelf)
- Store foods for the recommended time, check contents daily
- Allow for circulation of air around food
- Clean /defrost as directed in the manufacturer's guidelines

Guidelines for care
- Position refrigerator away from any source of heat
- Clean regularly i.e. weekly
- Wash inside with a solution of warm water and bread soda
- Never clean with washing-up liquid or strong-smelling cleaners
- Wipe the outside of the fridge daily
- Defrost according to the instructions, avoid build up of ice
- Wipe up spills immediately, never allow to build up
- Keep the back of the appliance free of dust
- When not in use unplug and leave door open

MICROWAVE OVEN

The types of microwave ovens available are:
- Standard microwave oven – cooks using electromagnetic waves only
- Microwave with grill – cooks with microwave, browns food with grill
- Combination microwave – combines microwave, grill and conventional cooking

Foods suitable for microwave cooking
- Evenly shaped food without sharp corners
- Foods for re-heating e.g. meals, sauces, gravy, soups
- Ready-made meals and individual dishes
- Fish, meat, poultry, fruit, vegetables

Figure 4.4 A microwave oven

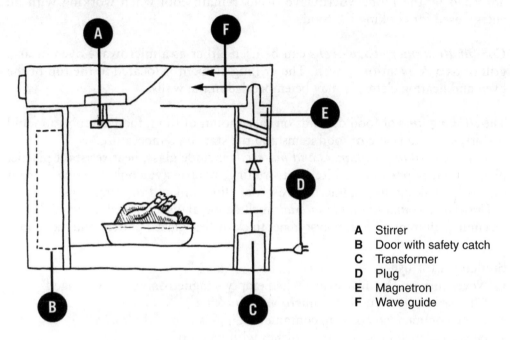

A Stirrer
B Door with safety catch
C Transformer
D Plug
E Magnetron
F Wave guide

Construction
- Control panel (power knob, timer knob, variable power control)
- An enclosed metal-lined steel box – an oven cabinet
- Glass door lined with perforated metal mesh
- Safety lock, seal on door, built-in cooling fan and cavity lamp
- Magnetron to change electrical energy into electromagnetic energy
- Wave guide and wave stirrer to distribute microwaves evenly
- Transformer to increase domestic voltage
- Turntable in some models, rotates dishes with food
- A flexible cord and plug

Special features: temperature probe, automatic programming facilities, browning dish, auto-weight defrost, keep-warm setting, defrost settings, panels with electronic controls

Working principle (microwave, basic model)

A magnetron and rotating blades (wave stirrer) direct high frequency electro-magnetic waves around the microwave oven. The waves are reflected off the walls and penetrate the food to a depth of 2–4 cm. Water molecules in food vibrate very rapidly creating heat which cooks, re-heats or defrosts the food. Water comes to the surface and prevents the food crisping or browning. Heat travels to the centre of the food by conduction. Microwave energy does not produce heat until it is absorbed by the food. Microwave ovens remain cool when working with all energy used for cooking the food.

Combination microwave ovens can be used either as a microwave oven or as a grill or as a conventional oven. The grilling element is located in the top of the oven and heating elements may be embedded in the walls.

The *cooking time* of food depends on the amount of food, food composition and density, size and shape of food items and the starting temperature.

Suitable cooking containers and materials include glass, heat-resistant plastic, plain china, paper plates, kitchen towelling, microwave cookware, ovenproof casseroles, baking dishes, microwave-proof cling-film and roasting bags.

Unsuitable containers and materials include metal dishes, metal trimmed dishes, melamine, aluminium foil, polystyrene, thick dishes, glazed pottery and metal ties.

Guidelines for use

- Never turn on the microwave when empty, magnetron will be damaged
- Choose recipes suitable for microwave cooking
- Use recommended cooking containers e.g. glass, special plastics
- Never use metal containers or dishes with metal trims
- Arrange food in a circle, cover food to speed up cooking
- Turn large pieces of food from time to time during cooking
- Always leave for the recommended 'standing time'
- Use recommended heat-resistant cling film
- Never leave unattended, use oven gloves to remove dishes
- Stir all food to prevent 'hot spots'
- Overcooking food can cause a fire within the cabinet
- Pierce sausages, tomatoes and egg yolks to prevent from bursting

Microwave cooking processes include boiling, steaming, and baking (potatoes), poaching, dry-roasting, defrosting and melting ingredients/foods. *Micro-waving is not suitable* for meringues, many cakes, large quantities of food, pastries, deep-frying, batters and foods dipped in batters.

Guidelines for care

- Follow manufacturer's instructions

- Unplug microwave oven before cleaning
- Do not move oven often as moving damages the magnetron
- Avoid using abrasives, use washing-up liquid or special cleaner
- Wipe around door seal and interior of oven, rinse and dry
- Remove glass turntable, wash in warm soapy water, rinse and dry
- Do not allow spills to build up, wipe up immediately
- Get oven serviced occasionally by a qualified service engineer

Advantages
- A wide variety of foods and meals can be cooked
- Less cooking smells are produced in kitchen
- Economical method of cooking, preheating not required
- Cooks foods quickly, defrosts foods quickly
- Food retains natural colour, flavour and nutrients
- Saves on washing up, saves time and energy
- Foods can be served in dishes in which they were cooked
- Ideal for busy families, safe for children and the elderly to use
- Combination models can brown and crisp foods

Disadvantages
- Foods do not brown satisfactorily in basic models
- Tough cuts of meat cannot be used (will not tenderise)
- Not suitable for fried foods, roast foods, cakes and batters
- Food poisoning could result if food is not cooked properly
- Foods/dishes need standing time before serving
- Extra time needed when cooking larger quantities of food

TEXTILES

USE OF TEXTILES
- Household linens e.g. bed linen, table linen, kitchen cloths, etc.
- Interior textiles e.g. cushions, floor coverings, upholstery
- Clothing

Functions of textiles for clothing purposes
- To enhance ones appearance and give confidence
- To protect against the weather e.g. hats, gloves
- To keep us safe from chemicals, disease, fire, injury
- To keep us dry e.g. waterproof items for outdoor activities
- To identify workers e.g. doctors, gardaí, nurses, soldiers
- To influence others e.g. at interviews, when giving presentations
- To express one's personality

Functions of textiles for household purposes
- To decorate our homes e.g. variety of colours, patterns and textures
- To create a comfortable atmosphere e.g. carpets, cushions, throws
- To provide warmth and insulation e.g. soft surfaces, lined curtains
- To absorb sounds making the home a more relaxing environment
- To provide privacy e.g. curtains, blinds
- To protect us e.g. textiles with flame retardant finishes, oven gloves
- To provide absorbency e.g. bath towels

Selection criteria
When choosing textiles consider the following factors:
- Function of item: end use of textile
- Fitness for purpose: suitability
- Cost: buy the best you can afford
- Fabric properties: check its desirable/undesirable properties
- Care: easy care, washable, dry clean only, stain resistant
- Personal choice: individual preferences for feel and look of fabric
- Aesthetic appeal: appearance, drape and weight
- Safety: flame-resistant, suitability for children's clothing

Scientific principles underlying textile care
Care of textiles depends on the fibre used, yarn, construction and finishes. Follow the instructions given by the manufacturer. The scientific principles underlying the care of textiles at home involves:
- Using detergents that suit the fabrics
- Choosing suitable water temperatures to safeguard fibres, finishes, etc.
- Agitating fabric by hand or by machine to loosen dirt and remove stains
- Adding fabric conditioners to reduce static electricity in synthetic fabrics
- Removing water using a method which will not damage the fabrics or their finishes e.g. drip-drying or spinning or wringing by hand

Textile care labelling codes
Washing
Drying
Ironing
Dry cleaning
Chlorine bleach

Refer to pages 165–6 for further information.

Table 4.3 Properties and care of fibres relative to their general properties

WOOL	
Care required	*Properties*
■ Hand wash or dry clean (read label) ■ Medium machine washing action at 40°C ■ Dry flat to avoid fibres stretching ■ Use a warm iron setting ■ Do not use bleach	Absorbent and soft Resists flames, smoulders slowly Resists static electricity Easily damaged by bleach, hot water Pills easily, scorches easily Shrinks at high temperatures Weak when wet

COTTON	
Care required	*Properties*
■ Hand wash with hot water *or* ■ Machine wash at 95°C (100% cotton) ■ Machine wash cotton blends at 40°C or 50°C ■ Chlorine bleach can be used ■ Press when damp	Absorbent, dyes readily Strong, washes, dries and irons well Burns and scorches easily when ironed Creases easily Cheap cotton becomes limp Shrinks readily if not pre-shrunk

SILK	
Care required	*Properties*
■ Hand wash or dry clean ■ Some knitted silk may be washed in a machine (read label) ■ Do not use chlorine bleach ■ Care needed when ironing, low temperature ■ Use a pressing cloth between iron and silk	Absorbent Resilient, does not shrink Easily damaged by chemicals, careless washing, perspiration, poor handling and moths

LINEN	
Care required	*Properties*

■ Machine wash 40–60°C or dry clean
  (read label)
■ Do not use chlorine bleach
■ Iron at a high temperature when damp,
  press on the wrong side
	Absorbent and dries quickly
	Durable (wears and washes well)
	Resists dirt and grime
	Burns readily
	Shrinks, wears along the creases

ACRYLIC	
Care required	Properties
■ Hand wash or machine wash in warm water 40°C ■ Chlorine bleach can be used ■ Requires little ironing, cool iron if used	Absorbent Attracts dirt Flammable Poor absorbency Loses shape when wet

POLYESTER (SYNTHETIC FIBRE)	
Care required	Properties
■ Machine wash in warm water ■ Wash cotton/polyester blends at 50°C ■ Chlorine bleach may be used	Resistant to creasing, mildew Washes well, dries quickly Non-absorbent, attracts dirt easily Develops static electricity easily

VISCOSE (REGENERATED FIBRE)	
Care required	Properties
■ Machine wash at 50°C ■ Press/iron at low temperatures	Creases easily, must not be wrung out Weak when wet, likely to shrink Absorbent, drapes well

Blends

Different fibres are mixed together to improve the properties of textiles. The care of blended textiles is in accordance with the fibre present in the highest amount or the fibre requiring a gentler treatment.

Finishes that affect fabric care

Finishes applied to textiles, to make caring for them easier, include anti-static, anti-pilling, crease-resistance (easy care), mercerising, shrink resistance and stain resistant finishes.

Safety considerations in the selection of household textile items

All natural, synthetic and regenerated fibres tend to be flammable. Dangers associated with children's clothing and furnishing fabrics are well documented. Non-toxic and durable treatments are applied to fabrics that alter their reactions to flames e.g. coated fabrics and inherent flame-retardant fabrics. Fabrics with flame-retardant finishes will self-extinguish when the flames are removed. They do not multiply the flames. Back-coatings are used on upholstery, carpets and floor coverings.

Proban

This is a durable flame-retardant finish used on fabrics. A chemical compound containing phosphorus and chlorine is applied to the surface of a textile and then treated with ammonia resulting in the formation of an insoluble polymer. Follow the care label instructions when laundering the item.

Effects of fire retardant finishes

Main benefit is the reduced risk of textiles catching fire and burning rapidly. Textiles treated with flame-retardant finishes are more expensive. Some individuals may experience an allergic reaction to the chemicals used in treatments.

Fire Safety (Domestic Furniture) Order (1988)

The Fire Safety Order covers:

- The types of fillings and covers used for upholstered domestic products e.g. armchairs, beds, cushions, pillows, sofas, children's cots and pushchairs
- The labelling arrangements for textile products

Note: It does not cover bedclothes, carpets, curtains, pillowcases and sleeping bags.

The regulations require that manufacturers use Combustion Modified Highly Resilient Foam (CMHRF), covers used must pass a cigarette test or match test and loose covers must pass both tests. All new furniture and re-upholstery done since 1950 come under the 1988 regulations. Regulations are implemented by the Department of Enterprise, Trade and Employment and enforced by the Director of Consumer Affairs.

Products must carry two distinct separate labels (either short or long):

- *Swing or display label*:
  - *Shaped like a red triangle*, printed on both sides, showing that the filling meets the safety requirements, states that a fire resistant interliner has been used but the filling is not match-resistant, and
  - *Shaped like a green square*, printed on both sides, states that filling and covering fabric meet the safety requirements for resistance to cigarettes and match ignition
- *Permanent label*: stitched permanently to the product, provides the name and address of manufacture or importer, manufacturer's item batch number or identification number, date of manufacture or importation, description of filling and cover materials, whether or not a fire-resistant interliner has been included and a warning 'Carelessness causes fire'

Figure 4.5 Furniture labels

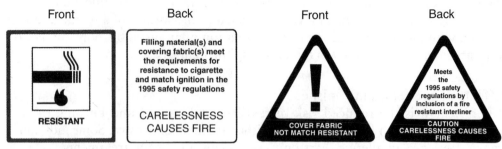

Safety symbols used on household textiles.

Triangular label showing front and back views.

CONSUMER STUDIES

CONSUMER CHOICES

Factors affecting consumer decision-making
Consumers' decision-making is determined by some of the following factors:
- Wants, needs and goals: essentials and non-essentials
- Cost: budget available, value for money
- Household income: single, dual or multiple sources of finance
- Family and friends: how they view a product or service
- Merchandising and advertising: techniques encouraging spending
- Special offers: a specific product or service at a reduced price
- Salespeople: persuading consumers of the value of a product/service
- Packaging: quality, environmentally friendly, interesting
- Labelling: good information on care, energy, nutrition and safety

Merchandising
Merchandising techniques to encourage consumer spending include loyalty schemes, discount offers, sale of special display products, own brand products, special offers and easy-pay systems. Some merchandising strategies encourage unplanned spending on items that are not necessary.

ADVERTISING

Function of advertising
- To sell goods and services
- To inform consumers of new products and make them popular
- To improve the popularity of old products, to increase sales
- To create an environmentally-friendly image
- To promote the company as a consumer-friendly organisation

Advantages of advertising
- Provides consumers with information about a product/service
- Creates interest in new/old products, increases or maintains sales
- Encourages competition among companies, may reduce prices
- Provides a range of employment opportunities

Disadvantages of advertising
- Cost of advertising increases cost of product/service
- Creates a desire in people to buy lifestyle products
- Encourages consumerism, buying of non-essential products
- Puts pressure on low-income groups
- Can re-enforce stereotyping

Note: Refer to 'Packaging and Materials' in 'Food Processing and Packaging'.

THE PURCHASING PROCESS

Classification of main shopping outlets
- Department stores
- Discount stores
- Hyper-markets
- Independent shops
- Multiple chain stores
- Specialist shops
- Supermarkets

Other shopping outlets: auction room, door-to-door selling, markets, house parties and vending machines

Other methods of shopping
- Mail order shopping
- 'Easy-pay' system
- On-line shopping or Internet shopping
- Television buying

RETAIL PSYCHOLOGY

Retail psychology involves the study of how people think when they are making decisions related to the buying of products and services.

Techniques to encourage consumer spending
- In-store stimuli: background music (soft or loud), colours, aromas
- Layout of store: grid layout or free-flow layout

- Product placement: luxury items placed at eye level
- Product blocking: 'blocking' products makes consumers notice them
- Shelf position: highest profit margins products at eye level
- In-store crèche facilities: allow parents to shop in comfort
- Late-night opening: to accommodate other workers and families
- Size of decompression zones: makes consumers adjust to shopping area
- Home delivery service: of use to people without transport
- Car delivery service: help for consumers to take groceries to their car
- *Others*: merchandising strategies

Shopping patterns

Factors that influence shopping patterns include:
- Shopping traditions in the family
- Size of household
- Dietary needs of individuals
- Demand for convenience products
- Time available for shopping
- Dependence on others for transport
- Income e.g. restrictive or non-restrictive
- Environmental awareness
- Marketing and advertising strategies
- Opening times of shopping outlets
- Availability of one-stop shopping

Consumer research

Consumer research involves collecting information from consumers through surveys, interviews, customer panels and questionnaires in order to understand consumer decision-making, satisfaction with products, effectiveness of marketing and advertising strategies, the effectiveness of packaging and displays.

Advantages of consumer research

- Creates a consumer profile e.g. age, gender, income
- Identifies the group most likely to spend money
- Identifies consumers likes and dislikes
- Highlights weaknesses in marketing and advertising strategies
- Identifies current size of markets and the potential market size
- Demonstrates current trends

Figure 4.6 Signs and symbols on consumer products and textile care labelling codes

Hazardous substances or materials

Harmful and irritant

Toxic

Flammable

Corrosive

Quality Symbols

Approved Quality
System/Quality Irish

Guaranteed
Irish

Communauté
Européenne

Design Centre

Caighdean Éireannach/
Irish Standards Mark

BSI kitemark

BSI safety mark

Irish mark of
electrical conformity

Recyclable

Office of Consumer
Affairs

Textile care labelling codes
Washing – The Wash Tub

Symbol	Application
95°	White cotton and linen articles without special finishes.
60°	Cotton, linen or viscose articles without special finishes where colours are fast at 60°C.
50°	Nylon, polyester/cotton mixtures, polyester, cotton and viscose articles with special finishes, cotton/acrylic mixtures.
40°	Cotton, linen or viscose articles where colours are fast at 40°C but not at 60°C.
40°	Acrylics, acetate, triacetate (including mixtures with wool), polyester/wool blends.
40°	Wool (including blankets) and wool mixtures with cotton or viscose and silk.
30°	Delicate fabrics

95° – cotton, linen, hot boil wash

60° – hot wash, cotton, linen or viscose

50° – nylon, polyester/cotton blends

40° – cotton, linen, viscose

40° – (one bar) acrylics, acetate, triacetate

40° – (two bars), wool, wool blends

30° – non-colour fast fabrics, silk

Ironing Codes (cool, warm, hot and do not iron)

 Cool (120°C) acrylic, nylon, acetate, triacetate, polyester.

 Warm (160°C) polyester mixtures, wool.

 Hot (210°C) cotton, linen, viscose or modified viscose.

 Do not iron.

Cleaning Codes
Dry cleaning

 Normal goods dry cleanable in all solvents.

 Normal goods dry-cleanable in perchloroethylene, white spirit, Solvent 113 and Solvent 11.

 Normal goods dry-cleanable in white spirits and Solvent 113.

Some fabrics may be affected by different solvents, e.g. silk.

Handwash

 Articles which must not be machine washed.

Drying Codes (drip dry, dry flat, line dry, tumble dry, do not tumble dry)

Drip dry

 Fibres may stretch or crease if wrung.

Dry flat

 Fibres may stretch if line dried.

 Tumble drying beneficial

 Do not tumble dry

Chlorine bleach

 Do not use chlorine bleach.

 May be treated with chlorine bleach.

CONSUMER RESPONSIBILITY

Consumer responsibilities
Under law consumers have certain rights and responsibilities. Consumers are expected to:
- Be informed when making decisions
- Be familiar with, and understand, consumer protection laws
- Read the labels provided about goods and services
- Examine products and investigate services before buying them
- Understand symbols and warnings on labels
- Use the product as intended and follow the manufacturer's instruction
- Keep receipts and guarantees
- Shop around to get value for money
- Know how to make a complaint

Sources of consumer information
- *Official centres*: The Consumer Association of Ireland, The Office of the Director of Consumer Affairs, The European Consumer Centre, The Ombudsman, National Social Services Board, Food Safety Authority of Ireland, The Irish Goods Council, Citizen Information Centres
- *Points of sale*: shops and showrooms, salespeople, manufacturer's brochures and leaflets, labelling information
- *Others*: libraries, the media, friends (word of mouth), billboards

Consumer rights

Informed consumers are aware that they are entitled to the right to:
- Accurate information (labelling laws, instructions)
- Redress (repair, replacement or refund depending on case)
- High standards of safety (safety symbols, warning symbols)
- Choice (competition is encouraged)
- Value for money (do not confuse cost and value)
- High quality services and goods (merchantable, fit for purpose)

THE CONSUMER AND THE ENVIRONMENT

Consumers have a responsibility to protect the environment by developing a waste management system in the home, which encourages re-using and/or recycling products. Waste management involves prevention, minimisation, re-using, recycling and disposal. There are two forms of energy:
- *Renewable energy*: comes from naturally recurring resources e.g. biomass, geothermal power, hydropower, solar power, wind power
- *Non-renewable energy*: comes from fossil fuels e.g. coal, gas, oil, peat, uranium

Re-use or recycle

Responsible waste management involves:
- Recycling organic and inorganic waste products
- Reusing products in the home e.g. glass jars
- Bringing products to recycling centres/points
- Choose durable re-usable shopping bags
- Choosing products with the EU Eco-label symbol or the green dot
- Selecting 'biodegradable' products, buying 'phosphate-free' products
- Choosing aerosols free of CFCs, using alternatives
- Disposing of freezers and fridges correctly
- Creating a compost heap in the garden

Energy consumption

Energy consumption can be reduced by using the methods listed below.

Appliances

Use energy saving rated appliances, choose appliances to reduce consumption (kettles, toaster), use the 'half load' button on washing machines, unplug televisions and video machines when not in use, avail of 'Nightsaver' electricity etc.

Lighting

Use CFLs, switch off lights when not in use.

Insulation

Lag the hot water cylinder, fix a timer to the immersion, use draft proofing and insulate the house, timers and thermostats on central heating systems, turn down heating thermostats by a couple of degrees, replace old windows with double glazing.

Others

Dry clothes in the fresh air, take a shower instead of a bath, use rechargeable batteries and a charger, add solar systems to new homes, replace fossil fuels with solar, wind or biomass energy.

Air pollution in the home

Air pollution in the home can be reduced by:

- Opting for natural gas instead of oil or coal
- Using water-based paints, avoiding solvent-based products
- Choosing pump-action sprays instead of pressurised aerosols
- Selecting environmentally-friendly products
- Buying energy-saving appliances

Water pollution in the home

Water pollution in the home can be reduced by:

- Opting for phosphate-free detergents and washing powders
- Reducing or eliminating the use of artificial fertilisers on farms
- Avoiding garden chemicals that threaten the water supply

Noise pollution in the home

Noise pollution in the home can be reduced by:

- Turning down loud music, reducing sound of radio
- Locating homes at a distance from transport systems

Global effects of pollution – examples

Pollution has already damaged the rain forests, caused changes in animal and plant life, desertification of vast regions, drought and failure of crops. There has been damage to the ozone layer resulting in increased incidents of skin cancer and global warming with rising temperatures.

Environmental signs and symbols to note

Energy label on white goods	European Union Eco-label
Green dot/repak	Recycling triangle
Organic produce	Fairtrade mark

Environmental organisations: Enfo, Irish Energy Centre, Repak, The Environmental Protection Agency

CONSUMER PROTECTION

Legislation and the courts, statutory government agencies and voluntary agencies protect consumers' rights.

Consumer Information Act, 1978

The act protects consumers against false information or claims about a price, product or service and credit agreements. It applies to advertisements, shop notices e.g. prices, claims made by sales assistants, information provided on labels and APR in credit agreements. Under this act the Office of the Director of Consumer Affairs has the authority to prosecute offenders.

Examples of misleading claims: 100% Pure New Wool, 24-hour service, machine washable or nationwide service when they are untrue

The Sale of Goods and Services Act, 1980

A legally binding contract is formed between the buyer and the seller when a product or service is purchased. The Sale of Goods and Services Act 1980 states that the goods or services should be:
- Fit for the purpose described
- Of merchantable quality
- As described, corresponding to any sample on display

This act also applies to guarantees and notices in shops. When goods are faulty the retailer is responsible for putting things right. A contract exists between the retailer and the consumer. When returning goods each consumer should expect items to be repaired or replaced or a refund, depending on the particular case. Some notices displayed in shops have no legal effect under the act. Consumers are not obliged to accept credit notes when a complaint is valid.

Under this act consumers should expect that services be provided by qualified and skilled people with due care, diligence and safety and materials used should be sound and of merchantable quality.

Under this act *guarantees* should:
- Be legible and refer to specific goods
- Name the person/company offering the guarantee
- Give the company address
- List the duration of the guarantee from date of purchase
- Outline the procedure for claiming a refund
- State what the manufacturer will do, what the customer should expect to receive

- Identify extra charges that might be incurred by the claimant
- Not interfere with the customer's rights

STATUTORY AND VOLUNTARY BODIES CONCERNED WITH CONSUMER PROTECTION

The Office of the Director of Consumer Affairs
The Director of Consumer Affairs:
- Informs consumers about their rights and responsibilities
- Enforces consumer laws and initiates legal proceedings against offenders
- Monitors the Sale of Goods and Supply of Services Act 1980
- Enforces advertising standards, product labelling
- Oversees safety and price displays
- Aims to raise all standards relating to goods and services

The Ombudsman
The Ombudsman, appointed by the government, investigates and deals with unresolved complaints against government departments and offices e.g. Health Boards, local authorities, An Post, etc. Valid complains are reported by the Ombudsman to the department in question and recommendations are made to resolve the matter. The Insurance Ombudsman of Ireland deals with complaints relating to insurance companies. The Ombudsman for Credit Institutions investigates complaints against institutions providing credit.

Small Claims Court
The Small Claims Court is a system within the local District Court for dealing with small claims. The claim must not exceed €1,270 and the cost to the consumer is €7.62. Complaints are dealt with quickly by the Small Claims Registrar who tries to settle the dispute before referring the matter to the court. A solicitor is not required.

National Standards Authority of Ireland (NSAI)
The NSAI is a state organisation setting standards relating to safety and quality in industry in Ireland, providing reports, carrying out research and endeavouring to ensure that Irish products meet EU and international standards.

Citizen Information Centres
Citizen Information Centres provide an independent, free, confidential service supplying information on a variety of topics that are of concern to citizens e.g. consumer affairs, family law, health services, housing, income tax, local organisations and services, redundancy and social welfare.

Consumer Association of Ireland
The Consumer Association of Ireland is a non-profit-making, independent, non-governmental organisation representing Irish consumers. It provides consumer information, works towards improving consumer legislation, represents consumers within industry, government bodies and state bodies and runs a Consumer Personal Service. A monthly magazine, *Consumer Choice*, provides information on a variety of products and services available in Ireland.

European Consumer Centre
The European Consumer Centre is a walk-in centre run by the Director of Consumer Affairs to provide information and advice to consumers on rights under Irish and European law. The Director of Consumer Affairs and the European Commission jointly fund it.

Other bodies concerned with *consumer protection* include: Advertising Standards Authority of Ireland (ASAI), trade associations and organisations, Free Legal Advice Centre, the Law Society of Ireland, the media (newspapers, magazines, radio, television).

Procedure to follow when making complaints
- Do not use the product if you notice a fault
- Stop using the product if it develops a fault when in use
- Return the product and the receipt to the retailer
- Request to speak to the person in charge if the assistant is unable to help
- Explain the nature of the problem, produce the product and receipt
- Keep to the facts and calmly ask what the retailer with do to solve the problem
Solution: might involve replacement, refund or repair

Procedure to follow for complaining in writing
If the problem is not solved put the complaint in writing to the manager or director, outlining clearly:
- Item purchased (manufacturer's name, make, model)
- Date of purchase
- Copy of receipt of purchase (keep the original receipt)
- Nature of the problem
- Outline of return visit to the shop, name of the person spoken to
- Action you expect the company to take
- Keep a copy of the letter.
- If everything fails, consider taking legal advice or legal action or consider using the small claims procedure

Outline of the small claims procedure

Claimant completes an application form with three sections:

- Claimant's name, address and telephone number, respondent's information
- Facts of the claim
- Form is signed and sent to the District Court Office
- Small Claims Registrar registers the application
- A copy of the claim and notice of the claim is sent to respondent
- Undisputed claims are settled without going to court
- Registrar tries to settle disputed claims
- If a settlement is not reached the matter is set for a court hearing
- Respondents are informed if the matter is resolved in the claimant's favour
- Respondents are given about four weeks to pay claimants
- Consumers may have to take their complaint to a higher court should the respondent fail to pay the money awarded

CHAPTER 5 — Social Studies

SOCIOLOGICAL CONCEPTS

Sociology is a systematic scientific study of the organisation and functioning of human society.

Society is a group of people who share a common culture or way of life.

Social groups can be defined as the units or groups of people who are linked by a shared way of life or a common purpose. Social groups may be primary or secondary.

Primary social groups are small groups of people who see each other frequently and whose relationships are seen as permanent e.g. family and close friends.

Secondary social groups are larger groups of people involved in more impersonal and less permanent relationships e.g. school community, members of trade unions, voluntary organisations and work groups.

Culture describes the beliefs, customs, language, norms, mores, values, roles, knowledge and skills passed on from one generation to another.

Norms are the accepted established patterns of behaviour i.e. the social rules that people are expected to follow e.g. going to school.

Mores are the accepted customs, norms and values that are considered important by a society.

Values are the beliefs held by a society about what is 'right' and 'wrong'.

Role is the expected appropriate pattern of behaviour of an individual according to status or position.

Role model is a person whose patterns of behaviour are followed by others.

Status refers to the position held by people relative to others within the society and the respect or prestige given to the position by others.

Social stratification is the way society is organised into different groups according to gender, income, occupation, race, etc.

Socio-economic groupings is the classification of people according to income and wealth e.g. lower-income, middle-income and higher-income groups

Social mobility refers to the movement of people between socio-economic groupings because of changes in education, income, occupation and social circumstances.

Kinship refers to the blood relations that exist between people.

Socialisation is the process whereby people learn how to fit into society in the family, school, local community or workplace. It is a life-long process of development.

Social change refers to changes that take place in a society due to events (national or global) or scientific and technological developments.

Social controls are the methods (sanctions, rewards or punishments) used to make people follow the acceptable norms, mores and values of society.

Social institutions are the organised arrangements accepted as part of society e.g. family, educational system, religious institutions.

DEFINING THE FAMILY

FAMILY DEFINED

The family is 'the basic unit of society which acts as a support for its members and transmits values from one generation to the next'. The *Irish Constitution* defines the family as the 'natural, primary and fundamental unit group of society'. The family is a social institution that exists in all societies in different forms. The *Family of Origin* is the family in which we grow up. The *Family of Procreation* refers to the families we form as adults in order to have our own children.

Examples of family forms
- Married couples without children
- Married couples with children
- Cohabiting couples with children
- Single parents with children
- Grandparents with grandchildren
- Communal families

FAMILY STRUCTURES

MODERN FAMILY STRUCTURES

The main *types of family structures* are nuclear, extended, blended, lone-parent and foster families.

Some characteristics of the nuclear family
- Located in areas of rapid social change
- Accepting of change more easily than extended family

- Based on a modern family structure, small in size
- Mobile, moves for a variety of reasons e.g. career
- Economically dependent on a small number of people
- Subject to change in family structure
- Independent, democratic and egalitarian, flexibility in roles
- Less reliable in a crisis, more isolated than extended family
- Short-lived, children move away from home

Some characteristics of the extended family
- Located in areas where social change is slow
- Based on the traditional family structures, large in size
- Located in one area, one house or houses close together
- A large family (provides an economic advantage)
- Long-lasting and reliable in a crisis
- Based on clearly defined social divisions
- Authoritarian in control and patriarchal

Some characteristics of the blended family
- Based on combinations of biological, step-parents and children
- Emerged as a result of increased rates of divorce and separation
- Mobile e.g. two family groups merge to form a new family group
- Flexible roles for family members
- Discipline may become a source of conflict
- Links with multiple sets of grandparents and family groups
- Relationship with non-resident parent may be difficult
- Can be more isolated than nuclear or extended family
- Conflict may result between remarried mothers and daughters
- Balancing financial commitments across two families is difficult

Some characteristics of the lone-parent family
- Generally headed by women, some men head one-parent families
- Results from death, divorce, separation, unplanned pregnancy, spouse in prison
- Problems e.g. stress, financial difficulties, cost of childcare
- Increased workload, may feel isolated and rejected
- Reduced ability to work outside home for some parents
- Greater risk of poverty, may be living in inadequate housing
- Increased dependence on state benefits

BRIEF OVERVIEW OF FAMILY LIFE IN IRELAND

Overview of pre-industrial Irish families
Family form: extended family the more usual family form.
Family size: tended to be large, children viewed as an economic benefit.

Economic status: households functioned as residential and work units. The father controlled the finance.

Roles: household tasks organised along segregated roles. Authority was gender related, vested in the father (patriarchal). Sons had higher status than daughters.

Position of women: women considered inferior legally and socially to men. Marriages were often arranged for females and dowries offered.

Employment: work opportunities were limited and determined by level of education. Access to education was limited without finance. Emigration was common.

Religion: strict religious upbringing.

The home: introduction of rural electrification in 1946 and water schemes in the 1960s improved home life for women and children.

Overview of post-industrial Irish families

Family form: nuclear families emerged, families became more urban based. Families more isolated.

Family size: smaller in size, child mortality decreased. Children no longer looked on as economic assets. Regulations were put in place to reduce child labour.

Economic status: better standard of living overall in the last thirty years. Life expectancy has increased, with improved nutrition and healthcare. Children's future secured through education. Increase in educational initiatives and opportunities for all.

Roles: husband viewed as breadwinner, wife as the homemaker and carer. Romantic love became the basis for marriage. There was a decrease in arranged marriages. Focus on children, their development and family life. Decline in status and role of older members of families. More egalitarian roles emerging in the last fifteen years.

Position of women: many women at home caring for the family. Improved life expectancy and family planning.

Employment: increase in number of married women in the workforce from the 1970s. Increases in wages, reduction in working hours, increase in leisure time.

Contemporary Irish families

Family form: increase in lone-parent and blended families. Decline in nuclear and extended family structures. Introduction of divorce, increased rates of separation. Fall in marriage rates and an increase in co-habitation. Families are geographically mobile.

Family size: smaller family size, more reliable methods of family planning.

Position of women: increased numbers of married women in the workforce. Emergence of problems associated with 'dual-career' and 'dual income' families.

Roles: demand for greater gender equality in the home and workplace.

Religion: influence has declined over the past fifteen years.

Other: state now supporting family functions e.g. financial, education and socialisation. Use of Internet to keep in contact with family and friends. Increase in social problems.

SOCIAL, ECONOMIC AND TECHNOLOGICAL CHANGES AFFECTING THE FAMILY

Social changes
- Decline in extended families, increase in new family structures
- Egalitarian roles replacing strict traditional segregated roles
- Acceptance of divorce and separation
- Decrease in religious influence, emergence of a more secular society
- Focus on individualisation, personal choice emphasised
- Improved educational opportunities, improved work opportunities
- Equal pay legislation encourages women to develop careers
- New demands for child-care options
- Increase in leisure time, more time to spend with family
- Cultural diversity increasing in Ireland
- Safety of children has become a problem

Economic changes
- Cost of raising a family has increased, smaller family sizes
- Increased cost of buying home, both partners must work
- The family is now a unit of consumption rather than production
- Child-care arrangements tend to be expensive
- Improved state support for the elderly and lone-parents
- People move jobs several times, the 'job for life' is disappearing
- More money spent on comfort within the home
- More disposable income to spend on holidays, etc.

Technological changes
- New employment opportunities in the IT sector
- Modernisation of home, work and communications
- Reduces time spent doing monotonous tasks
- Advances in communication technology e.g. on-line shopping
- Danger associated with children using Internet is causing concern
- Television provides a 'window' to rapid changes in society
- Mass production has reduced cost of products

THE FUNCTIONS OF THE FAMILY

Physical and reproductive functions
The family provides the basic physical needs for survival, food, clothing and shelter. Within the family adult sexual behaviour is regulated and by having children families ensure the survival of the human race.

Nurturing, rearing and emotional function

The family cares for the emotional and psychological development of the child, providing reassurance, encouragement, love and security. A child will develop a well-balanced personality in a safe, secure and loving environment.

Supplementary assistance: state support is available through child benefit and access to social workers, Community Mothers Programme and foster care for families experiencing difficulties.

Economic function

Adults within the family work to earn money to provide for the members of the family who are not self-sufficient.

Supplementary assistance: state support is provided for the elderly, disabled, unemployed and for those suffering from long-term illness through state supported institutions, financial allowances and benefits.

Educational/intellectual function

The family is the first location for early learning. It later supports the state education of children by supervising homework, praising and encouraging the child to work to the best of her/his ability and by providing a stimulating home environment.

Supplementary assistance: the state provides free education to the child from the age of five, supported by the parents, in primary and secondary education and provides the services of psychologists to assess children experiencing difficulties in school. Nurseries and playgroups are available to those who can afford them.

Socialisation function

The family is the primary centre of socialisation. It introduces the child to the beliefs, culture, language(s), norms, traditions and values of the society in which they live. The family acts as an agent of social control by showing children what is acceptable and unacceptable behaviour.

Supplementary assistance: nurseries, playgroups and the education system support the socialisation function of the family as the child gets older and attends school on a full-time basis. The Family Resource Project run by the state through the Health Boards provides parenting courses and a variety of services within local areas.

Protective function

Families protect and care for the young, elderly and individuals with special needs.

Provision of assistance: the state provides support for families, the elderly and individuals with special needs e.g. home help, public health nurse, sheltered accommodation, sheltered working environments and the Family Support Workers Scheme. The Child Care Act, 1991 reflects a system that is child-centred.

MARRIAGE

Marriage may be defined as a voluntary, legally binding union between a man and a woman to the exclusion of all others.

Examples of cultural variation in marriage arrangements
Choosing a partner: mutual consent of couple, marrying someone of the same background, arranged marriages e.g. Hindus, Sikhs, Muslims, endogamy (particular race, religion, social class)
Number of partners: monogamy, serial monogamy, polygamy (polyandry or polygyny), group marriages, serial polygamy
Locality: where couples live after marriage, patrilocal, matrilocal, neolocal
Transfer of inheritance: eldest son, between spouse and all offspring, inheritance to children born outside marriage

Rights and responsibilities within marriage
Within marriage each partner is entitled to:
- The company of the other
- Conjugal rights
- Cohabit or live together
- Loyalty and faithfulness to each other
- Financial maintenance under Maintenance of Spouses and Children's Act, 1976
- Joint guardianship and custody of children born within the marriage
- Inheritance on the death of a spouse under Successions Act, 1965
- Protection under the Family Home Protection Act, 1976
- Protection under the Domestic Violence Act, 1996

Cohabitation refers to couples living together without being married.

Validity of a marriage in Ireland
Under Irish legislation:
- Those over 18 years of age who are unmarried *or* widowed *or* have an Irish divorce *or* whose foreign divorce is recognised in Ireland *or* who have a state annulment can marry
- The marriage must be voluntary, partners must be of the opposite sex, not too closely related
- Advance written notice of three months must be given to the Registrar of the district in which the marriage will take place
- The marriage must take place in a registered building e.g. registry office, church, synagogue and in the presence of an appointed person, the couple and witnesses must sign the register immediately after the ceremony

PREPARATION FOR MARRIAGE

The home
Young people form their ideas on marriage early in life based on positive or negative experiences within the home. Parents are the first role models for married life. An unhappy home life with poor role models produces individuals who may have difficulty in relating to others and maintaining lasting relationships. Desirable qualities for forming happy relationships will be obvious to those who experience a caring and loving home environment.

The school
Social and personal development programmes have been introduced in schools. These are designed to facilitate discussion on relationships. Examples include the Relationship and Sexuality programme (RSE), Health Education and subject areas such as Religion and Home Economics.

Pre-marriage courses
A number of groups offer pre-marriage courses e.g. Accord Catholic Marriage Counselling Service, Marriage and Relationship Counselling Services, etc. Areas for discussion include relationships, roles and responsibilities, children, family planning, finance, home management, marriage and family law. The expertise of doctors, financial experts, lawyers, marriage counsellors and home economists are employed in order to provide couples with practical examples and advice.

BREAKDOWN OF MARRIAGE

Reasons for marriage breakdown
- Vulnerability of the modern family structures
- Marrying for the wrong reason e.g. pregnancy
- Unrealistic expectations associated with romantic love
- Social problems e.g. alcoholism, gambling
- Abusive relationships, marital violence
- Couples grow apart, expectations change over time
- Changing role of women, increased financial independence

CHOICES AVAILABLE AFTER BREAKDOWN OF MARRIAGE

Marriage counselling
Couples experiencing problems avail of marriage counselling to get help in solving difficulties and to prevent marital breakdown. Accord, Marriage and Relationship Counselling Service and Family Mediation Service provide marriage and relationship counselling. Trained professionals help couples to communicate difficulties in a non-threatening environment and to reach resolutions through discussion.

Family mediation

The Family Mediation Service is designed to help couples who have decided to separate or divorce, to communicate, negotiate and reach agreements about parenting arrangements, custody and access, financial matters, maintenance, the family home and property in a co-operative and non-threatening atmosphere. The Department of Social, Community and Family Affairs funds this service and legislation states that solicitors must inform clients seeking separation or divorce about this service.

Legal separation or deed of separation

Legal separation involves couples drawing up a legal written contract or agreement outlining future arrangements for parenting, custody and access, residence of family and financial matters. Both partners must agree to all terms. The written contract is signed in front of witnesses.

Civil legal aid

The Legal Aid Board provides couples who are involved in separation and divorce proceedings with the assistance of solicitors and barristers. Income must be below specific levels to qualify for Civil Legal Aid and a small contribution is expected from the individuals.

Judicial separation

When a couple fail to agree on the terms of the separation, or when one person wants a separation, the Judicial Separation Act, 1989, (amended by the Family Law Act, 1995) allows for an application to be made to the courts for a decree of judicial separation. Grounds for a judicial separation include adultery or desertion, unreasonable behaviour, spouses living apart for one year prior to application and an absence of normal marital relationship for one year prior to application. The court may make orders regarding access to and custody of children, the family home and family finance.

Legal nullity

A state law of nullity declares that the marriage never existed. *A marriage is void* if either of the parties were already married, parties are of the same gender, one of the parties is under age, formal requirements were not followed or there was an absence of consent. *Grounds for annulment* include impotence, non-consumption, homosexuality, alcoholism, drug abuse, lack of consent, psychiatric problems and lack of attention to legal formalities. A person is free to remarry after being granted a state annulment.

Church annulments

Church annulments are not recognised by the state, remarriage by either partner may be bigamous.

Divorce

The courts may grant a decree of divorce under the Family Law (Divorce) Act, 1996, if the parties have lived apart for four of the five previous years, no prospect of reconciliation exists and proper financial provision will be made for the spouse and dependent members of the family. Solicitors acting on behalf of the parties are obliged to discuss the possibility of reconciliation, mediation and the options of a judicial separation with their clients.

Effects of marital breakdown on spouses
- Feelings of guilt, failure and rejection, emotional trauma
- Low self-esteem, isolation and loneliness
- Financial pressures, loss of family home
- Pressure of child care and work

Effects of marital breakdown on children
- Feelings of insecurity, division of loyalties
- Emotional problems, loss of contact with one parent
- Loss of home and friends

Effects of marital breakdown on society
- Breakdown in society, traditional family unit undermined
- Increase in one-parent families
- Dependency on state support e.g. housing
- Increase in juvenile delinquency

FAMILY AS A CARING UNIT

Characteristics of traditional family roles
- Segregated roles for men and women, boys and girls
- Division of labour based on segregated roles
- Women took care of the home and children
- Father made all financial decisions
- Men rarely involved in rearing of children
- Father fulfilled an authoritarian role

Characteristics of modern family roles
- Increased equality between men and women
- Household tasks not based on segregated roles
- Males and females equally involved in household tasks
- Fathers involved in rearing of children
- Husband and wife make decisions together
- 'Dual career' women experience role conflict
- Conflict may arise if husband/wife expect traditional roles to be the norm

LIFE-CYCLE OF FAMILY ROLES

Roles and responsibilities of children
- To learn how to behave in an acceptable manner
- Older children can be role-models for younger siblings
- To follow the rules set down by parents
- To help out with basic tasks e.g. making their beds
- To learn about responsibility e.g. tidying toys away
- To become socially competent

Role and responsibilities of adolescent
- To become more responsible for themselves
- To help out in the home in preparation for life
- To learn from role conflicts that may arise
- To use independence and freedom wisely

Roles and responsibilities of parents
- To provide for a child's physical, psychological and social needs
- To teach children what is right and wrong, to set clear limits
- To balance discipline with encouragement and love
- To be a positive role model for other family members
- To provide a stimulating and secure environment for the family
- To spend time together as a family e.g. talking, playing games
- To modify the role as children get older; be provider and friend

Gender Roles
Gender refers to being male or female. *Gender role* refers to the pattern of behaviour expected from a man or woman. *Gender equity* means treating men and women equally at home, at school and in the workplace.

Gender roles and the family
Traditional stereotyping gender roles are reinforced by:
- Assigning different household tasks to girls and boys
- Reinforcing the view that cooking is a female only activity
- Encouraging separate types of play/games for boys and girls
- Suggesting that boys are independent, ambitious and strong
- Suggesting that girls should be content, sensitive and dependent
- Encouraging girls to take up 'caring' professions
- Encouraging boys to consider scientific professions

FACTORS AFFECTING FAMILY ROLES

Social factors
- Increases in 'dual career' mothers, 'dual-career' families
- Changing role of women in the home, more independent
- Increased importance of education, greater social mobility
- Shared roles within the family, men and women
- Smaller families, more resources spent on children
- Shorter working week, more time to spend with children
- Recognition of adolescence as a period of transition
- Child care provided by grandparents

Economic factors
- Increase in standard of living, dual-income families
- High house prices and high cost of child care
- Children do not have to work as in the past
- Adolescents may choose to work part-time
- State benefits provided through social welfare

Role conflict
Role conflict occurs when roles are not easily defined and when one role interferes with another. 'Dual career' women experience role conflict when a family role interferes with the demands of their work role. For men a role conflict might arise when they are no longer the 'breadwinner' in the family because the wife has a better paid job or because he has become unemployed.

RELATIONSHIPS

Child/parent relationship
- Provides for the child's physical, psychological and social needs
- Is the most important first relationship
- Depends on parent's ability to care for and love children
- Emphasises honesty, justice, loyalty and maturity
- Develops warm relationships and a sense of responsibility
- Provides praise, security, approval and acceptance
- Develops self-esteem and confidence in the child

The rights of children within the family
Under the UN Convention on the Rights of the Child, children are entitled to:
- Protection from abuse and neglect
- Education within the family
- Free primary and secondary education
- Freedom from any form of discrimination
- Provision for special physical or emotional needs

- Be allowed to develop physically, spiritually and emotionally in an atmosphere of freedom and dignity

Conflict between adolescents and adults
- Conflict arises in the transition between childhood and adulthood
- Learning about responsibility, independence and decision-making
- Adolescents object to the imposition of rules
- Parents worry about the influence of the peer group, changes in attitudes and mood swings, alcohol, drugs, boy/girl relationships
- Parents may have a 'child' with a new personal value system
- Adolescents may become more independent, outspoken and challenging
- Adolescents and parents seem to have little in common
- Parents may not be sufficiently informed about recent changes in the world of adolescents e.g. music, fashion etc.

Dealing with generational conflict (child/parent) – guidelines
- Maintain an open system of communication within the family
- Develop a fair system of discipline which is consistent
- Set limits, boundaries should be clear
- Avoid confrontation, wait until people are calm
- Never use physical punishment
- Provide a calm atmosphere where the young person feels secure
- Consider the issue from both points of view
- Check what each person wants
- Examine the possible solutions
- Negotiate and compromise if possible

Good communication
- Determines the quality of the relationships between family members
- Ensures that all family members can express their ideas, feelings and thoughts in a safe environment where their views are valued
- Requires the development of good listening skills
- Supports a positive approach to solving disagreements
- Enables young people and older people to reach an agreed solution together

THE ROLES OF OLDER PEOPLE

Older people within families play an important role by:
- Passing on norms, mores and values from one generation to the next
- Enriching society through sharing knowledge and life experiences
- Spending free time with grandchildren
- Providing a child-care option for their adult children
- Offering financial assistance to young family members

Grandparent/grandchild relationships

The relationship between grandparents and grandchildren tends to be relaxed and fun. It is a very special relationship. Grandparents teach grandchildren how to respect older people. There are less rules and regulations and the relationship tends to be less formal. Grandchildren learn how to communicate and negotiate with adults.

Quality of life

To maintain a quality of life older people need:
- An acceptable level of privacy
- Independent lifestyle to maintain self-esteem
- Freedom to make their own choices
- Recognition of their role within the family and society
- Clarification in relation to role expectation
- Protection and care if unable to look after themselves
- Involvement in family life, not excluded or ignored

Problems

Problems associated with getting older include deterioration of eyesight, hearing, memory, mobility, loneliness, change in status, change in roles and reduced income.

Accommodation

Accommodation options for older people include:
- Living at home alone
- Living with family
- Home care in their own home
- Sheltered housing scheme in the local community
- Residential care (private or public nursing home)

Services/allowances for older people

Current services are old-age pension (contributory, non-contributory), medical card (means tested), living alone allowance, butter allowance, free electricity allowance, free travel pass, fuel allowance, over-80 allowance, telephone rental allowance, visits by the Public Health Nurse and access to health centres.

Causes of generational conflict
- Each generation values what they consider to be acceptable
- Conflict arises over views of norms, mores and values
- Young people may accept changes parents reject
- Each generation living in the family may feel threatened by the other
- Young people may feel misunderstood
- Older people (grandparents) may feel undervalued
- Grandparents may question the parenting skills of their children

FAMILY MEMBERS WITH SPECIAL NEEDS

A key function of the family is to look after its most vulnerable members, those with physical, emotional or mental disabilities.

Examples: deafness, blindness, cerebral palsy, Down's Syndrome, emotionally disturbed, epilepsy, polio, multiple sclerosis, spina bifida and limb defects

Causes: lack of oxygen at birth, genetic disorders, infections at birth, side effects of drugs, degenerative disease and the natural ageing process

The main *problems faced by people with special needs* are cost of disability, social isolation, poor access to buildings and transport, low self-esteem, limited employment because of access, inadequate facilities and discrimination.

Responses of families to those with special needs
- Modifying the family home and car to provide ease of access
- Encouraging self-esteem and confidence from a young age
- Helping and assisting the person with disabilities each day
- Encouraging independent living, working in sheltered workshops

Statutory services
- Comhairle
- The Equality Authority
- The National Disability Authority
- The Rehab Group

Voluntary services for special needs – some examples
- AHEAD – Association for Higher Education Access and Disability
- Associations for Special Disabilities e.g. blindness, cystic fibrosis
- Central Remedial Clinic (combination of state and voluntary funding)
- Disability Federation of Ireland
- National Association for the Deaf
- National Council for the Blind of Ireland
- The Irish Wheelchair Association
- Schizophrenia Ireland Group

Othe supports available: community health board services, disability allowances, reserved jobs in public sector employment, sheltered workshops, special needs schools, wheelchair access and special facilities in buildings

FAMILY LAW

The Family Law (Maintenance of Spouse and Children) Act, 1976
This entitles dependent spouses and children (under 18 years *or* 23 years if in full time education) to financial support from his/her partner. Applications are made

to the District Court which decides on the amount of maintenance to be paid based on income and needs.

The Family Home Protection Act, 1976
The Family Home Protection Act states that neither spouse can mortgage, sell, lease or transfer the family home without the consent of the other, regardless of whose name is on the title deeds to the house. This act does not cover cohabiting couples.

Domestic Violence Act, 1996
The Domestic Violence Act states that a spouse/partner or anyone in the family home may apply to the courts for a safety, barring or protection order against another family member who is putting an individual's safety at risk. Violence in the home is a crime. Offenders can be charged under the Domestic Violence Act, 1996. Those who may apply include spouses, children, cohabiting partners, a parent of an adult child and a Health Board. Alleged offenders may return to the family home when the barring period has ended.

The Judicial Separation Act, 1989
Spouses who fail to agree on the terms of a Separation Agreement may apply to the court for a judicial separation. The judge makes the decisions regarding custody and access, maintenance, division of property, etc. Grounds for a judicial separation are:
• Adultery or desertion
• Unreasonable behaviour
• Spouses living apart for three years before application
• Absence of normal marital relationship for one year
• No chance of reconciliation (counselling/mediation services suggested)

The Child Care Act, 1991
The Child Care Act outlines a range of regulations, which provides for the protection of children who are seriously at risk (neglected, assaulted, ill-treated and sexually abused). A child is defined as being less than 18 years of age. Children who are abandoned or orphaned may be taken into care. Health Boards supervise the provision of foster care. A Supervision Order may be granted to a Health Board for the monitoring of children 'at risk'.

Children's Act, 1997
The Children's Act enables unmarried fathers to become joint guardians of a child without going to court. A joint statutory declaration outlining the arrangements is completed in the presence of a Commission for Oaths or a Peace Commissioner.

Services for families in difficulty: Accord, Family Aid, Family Mediation Service, Gingerbread Ireland, Legal Aid Board

Making a will
The Succession Act, 1965, outlines what should happen in the case of an individual dying and leaving a will, or without leaving a will in the following cases:
- An individual with a spouse and no children
- An individual without a spouse but with children
- An individual without a spouse or children

Cohabiting couples have no entitlements unless a will has been made.

Reasons for making a will
The main reasons for making a will are that your wishes are carried out, money and property go to those you wish to have them. Making a will eliminates family stress and disagreements when a person dies.

Procedures for making a will
- Employ a solicitor
- Make a list of assets, their current value and their location
- Choose an executor. It is recommended that two executors be appointed.
- Compile a list of beneficiaries (who should have your assets) to include names, dates of birth and contact addresses
- Divide the estate (cash and specific property) between the beneficiaries
- Keep in mind restrictions imposed by the Succession Act, 1965
- Outline your wishes regarding funeral arrangements and burial place
- Draw up the will in a written form
- Sign it in the presence of two witnesses (witness does not need to know contents)
- Keep it in a safe place, the bank or solicitor's office

Inheritance Tax/Capital Acquisition Tax
Property inherited on the death of any person may be subjected to Capital Acquisition Tax. Currently inheritance from a spouse is not liable for inheritance tax. For other beneficiaries there is a tax-free threshold based on the relationship to the dead person and above that threshold tax must be paid at stated rates.

CHAPTER 6 — Elective: Housing

HOUSING STYLES

Early nineteenth century, 1800–50

Table 6.1 Early nineteenth-century housing styles, 1800–50

Urban housing styles	Rural housing styles
■ Large four-storey town houses, large Georgian two-storey houses, accommodation over shops, two-storey terrace houses to small cramped single-storey cottages. ■ A variety of shapes and sizes reflecting the social standing of the owners. ■ Simplicity of design and construction. ■ Local materials used, walls made from stone and covered with a layer of lime plaster. ■ Brick common in urban areas, timber used for flooring, slate for roofs, the entrance door formed the focal point of the building.	■ Numerous single-storey thatched cottages, a small number of big estate houses and a number of bigger single-storey and two-storey stone farmhouses. ■ Cottage roofs thatched with reeds, straw or hay, two or three rooms, small windows and open turf fires. ■ Wealthy farmers had a parlour, two storeys with slated roofs and at least five rooms. ■ Front door was split in two to allow light in and to keep animals and poultry out. ■ Estate houses had many rooms, servant quarters and were decorated to a high standard.

Late nineteenth century and early twentieth century (1850–1920)
- Different architectural styles influenced new home designs
- Two-storey slated houses were built in rural and urban areas
- Greater variety in building materials due to new transport systems
- Brick mouldings, bay windows, stone and door mouldings
- Terraces of small cramped houses were home to the working classes
- In towns, terraced houses and cottages were built around main streets
- Terraced houses had small back gardens, tiny front gardens
- Poor people lived in city tenements in overcrowded conditions
- Wealthy families moved to fashionable suburbs or the countryside
- Subsidised housing was provided under the Local Government Act, 1898

Early to mid-twentieth century (1920–50)
- Terraced style replaced with detached or semi-detached house
- Emergence of housing estates and the bungalow
- Less emphasis on ornate architectural styles
- Changes in the building materials used e.g. tiles replacing slate
- Rural electrification scheme changed life and homes in rural areas

Mid-twentieth century onwards
- Housing estates became more common (public and private)
- Increase in local authority housing schemes
- Private houses in a variety of designs
- Insufficient amenities and facilities provided for new developments
- Emphasis was on provision of houses not on design or facilities
- High-rise blocks of flats were provided by local authorities as a solution
- The 1963 Planning Act focussed on setting better standards
- Concept of residential, commercial and industrial zones developed
- Local authorities built housing estates in the suburbs
- Average house size smaller and sites more expensive
- No distinct common style, a mix of classical, modern and post-modern
- New materials/finishes e.g. plastic, double glazing, fibreglass

Popular housing styles in Ireland
Housing options include apartments/flats, townhouses, housing developments, dormer bungalows, single-storey or two-storey homes. These can be terraced, semi-detached or detached in a variety of architectural styles. Homes can be custom-made, refurbished second-hand houses, timber framed, prefabricated or a developer's design.

FACTORS INFLUENCING THE CHOICE AND LOCATION OF HOME

Social and cultural factors
- Personal likes and dislikes e.g. aesthetic requirements
- Family tradition and influences (norms and values)
- Preferred location, proximity to family, work and facilities
- Desire for a sense of community – neighbours and friends
- Size of home depends on life-cycle of family members
- Special needs' requirements e.g. disabilities

Economic factors
- To rent, to share, to buy or to build
- Availability of skilled workers if building or refurbishing
- Sufficient funds to cover all the costs involved in building/buying

- Cost of furnishing, decorating and maintaining a home
- Potential for resale, long-term or short-term investment
- Availability and range of local materials

Environmental factors
- Location, the surroundings and amenities
- Building laws and regulations if building a home
- Energy efficiency of house (insulation, double glazing)
- Choice of sustainable materials when building
- Potential for alternative energy sources
- Proximity to large trees, river or flood plains
- Radon gas levels in the area
- Quality of light within and around the house

HOUSING PROVISION

HOUSING REQUIREMENTS – VARIATIONS IN NEED

Priorities for families with children
Financial circumstances, number in the family, ages of family members and stage of life cycle determine the specific needs of each family.
- Sufficient living and sleeping space
- Adequate bedroom and bathroom facilities
- Secure outside play area, garage and/or garden shed
- Easy access to schools, parks, library and leisure facilities
- Good system of public transport (bus, train, dart)

Priorities for single people
- Renting an apartment or a room rather than buying
- Sharing a house with others (common option for students)
- Buying a flat or house and inviting others to share it
- Easy access to work, recreational and entertainment facilities

Priorities for the elderly
- Accommodation on one level or a converted room downstairs
- Chair lift fitted on stairs, if necessary in a two-storey house
- Downstairs bathroom with handrails fitted
- Non-slip easy to care for surfaces
- Safe lighting and heating systems
- Close proximity to shops, post office, entertainment, etc.
- Good public transport system, easy access to family and friends
- Alarm-communication system in case of emergency

Priorities for people with disabilities
- Housing to suit the specific disability
- Ramp access on all external doors, no steps
- Wider doorways to allow for wheelchair access
- Toilets showers and baths with support rails
- Low-level kitchen units, light switches and electric sockets
- Easy to manipulate window and door handles
- Handrails fitted along stairs and corridors

Housing for homeless people
A person who has no accommodation available to him or her, and those who are living in night shelters without access to accommodation, are considered to be homeless. Most homeless people are single men. Homelessness is associated with mental illness, poverty, unemployment and breakdown in family relationships, violence in the home, alcoholism, drug abuse, marriage breakdown and lack of access to the local authority housing list.

Accommodation for homeless people is provided by:
- *Voluntary organisations*: The Simon Community, Focus Ireland, Threshold
- *Local authorities*: housing, flats, hostel-type accommodation, bed and breakfast

EVALUATION OF HOUSING PROVISION IN IRELAND

Distribution of housing
- Ireland has a high home ownership (80% approx.) when compared to other EU countries. This is changing into older homeowners and younger tenants due to the rapid increases in house prices.
- Prices have risen because of economic growth, shortage of serviced lands, relatively low mortgage interest rates, increased numbers of investors and changes in family structures.
- Demographic changes have resulted in 30% of the population living in Dublin, 65% in cities and towns, and 35% in rural areas. Numbers on the local authority housing lists continue to rise.

Distribution may be categorised into owner-occupied housing, private housing, rented accommodation, social housing and rural or urban housing.

Quality of accommodation
The quality of house building is governed by The Building Regulations Act, 1991, and the national building guarantee scheme, 'Homebond'. The quality of accommodation varies according to the type of house.
- *Local authority housing*: accommodation varies from flats to four-bedroom family homes. Increased funding has resulted in the development of high quality accommodation but some older flats and houses are not up to standard.

- *Private rented housing*: minimum standards are set down under the Housing Act, 1992, a range of accommodation is available, standards vary according to the rent charged, rented properties must be registered under the Housing Regulation, 1996. Student and lone-parent accommodation is frequently below standard.
- *Owner-occupier housing*: quality is determined by the family, some elderly people are living in poor quality accommodation.

Comparative costs of buying and renting

Table 6.2 Comparative costs of buying and renting

Renting	Buying
Initial costs ■ Agency fee (if used to find property) ■ Deposit (usually one month in advance, returned at end of tenancy)	**Initial costs** ■ Deposit ■ Lending agency fees (application fee, survey, searches, mortgage fees, indemnity bond) ■ Legal fees (fee plus 1–2% of property price plus VAT, land registry fees, legal searches) ■ Stamp duty (government tax, check current rates, may change in Budget) Buyers survey (private survey)
Continuous/on-going costs ■ Weekly/monthly rent ■ Household expenses (gas, heating, phone electricity, television, etc.) ■ Contents insurance (personal items, paid annually) ■ Maintenance charges for a common area	**Continuous/on-going costs** ■ Mortgage repayments monthly ■ Mortgage protection policy ■ Household insurance (building and contents) ■ Maintenance/repairs (variable) ■ Local charges (water, refuse charges) ■ Ground rent (for leasehold properties) ■ Management charges

Adequacy of housing provision to meet housing demands
- High demand for home ownership, demand outstrips supply
- Inadequate supply of affordable housing for owner-occupiers
- Increase in house prices has resulted in more people renting
- Shortage of rental accommodation, cost has increased
- Numbers on local authority housing lists have increased
- Lack of accommodation for the elderly, homeless and students
- Dramatic increase in refugee population

Government response to housing crisis

The government introduced the Planning and Development Bill, 1999. It states that up to 20% of land zoned for residential use must be used for the development of social and affordable housing. Land zoned for residential housing must include plans for community, shopping, transport and utility services. Local authority housing schemes must also cater for the housing needs of lone-parent families and the elderly.

SOCIAL HOUSING PROVISION

Local authorities

Local authorities are the main providers of a range of social housing which cater for a variety of needs at affordable prices. Factors taken into account by the local authorities are household size, income, current accommodation (if any), its condition, and special circumstances e.g. age, disability, etc. Those accepted are put on a housing list. Houses are allocated when they become available.

There are other local authority options for example: affordable housing scheme, local authority loans for house purchase and improvements, low-cost housing sites, mortgage allowance scheme, private rented housing, shared-ownership scheme and the tenant-purchase scheme.

Voluntary housing

Non-profit-making schemes approved by the Department of the Environment and Local Government are operated by voluntary housing bodies. Based on local needs a variety of housing projects/services is provided under two schemes:
* *Capital Assistance Scheme*: small units for people with special housing needs
* *Rental Subsidy Scheme*: rented accommodation for families on low-income
    Tenants are not allowed to buy their rented homes but under certain conditions may return the house to the voluntary housing body and quality for benefits under the local authority schemes e.g. shared ownership and affordable housing.

Co-operative housing

A group of people forms a co-operative to build their own homes at an affordable price. The individuals within the co-operative work together to meet the needs of a small group of people. The costs of the site, materials, builder and solicitor are shared.

Examples of co-operative housing options are:
* Co-ownership housing co-operatives
* Home-ownership building co-operatives
* Rental housing co-operatives

Provision of local amenities and services for housing developments

The Department of the Environment and Local Government and the local authorities, based on the number of developments, decide on the amenities needed in an area. Key amenities expected by people include community centres, play areas and parkland, refuse collection, schools, shops, street lighting and transport systems.

BUILDING AND DESIGN

Factors influencing the choice of location (site)
- Slightly sloping, bright and sunny site with pleasant views
- Orientation and aspect, well drained with no areas of dampness
- Free of flooding from rivers, drains and artesian pools
- Secure, not too isolated, near a road, urban or rural
- Cost of site – budget available
- Building regulations and local development plan

Factors influencing the choice of house style
- Size and orientation of site
- Suitability of design for the landscape
- Finance available, traditional or modern design
- Exterior finishes and landscaping
- Energy-efficient design
- Suitability for family size and lifestyle
- Building regulations and planning permission

The costs involved in building a house can be categorised as:
Initial or start-up costs: site, architect, surveyor and planning application
Construction or building costs: builder, site work, drainage, septic tank, blockwork, timber-work, roof, windows and doors
Service connection costs: electricity, water, telephone and/or gas
Fittings and fixtures: bathroom, kitchen, appliances, electrical, heating and plumbing, flooring, tiling, fireplace/s, security system, painting and decorating
External: driveway, paths, landscaping, external lights and garden shed

PLANNING PERMISSION

Planning permission is necessary for new homes, alterations to existing homes, change of use of a home e.g. B&B, conversion of garages. Porches to the front or back of a home, extensions to the back of a house under 23 sq. m, TV aerial and satellite dishes up to one metre are generally exempt.

Types of planning permission
- *Outline planning permission* – finding out if the authorities agree in principle
- *Full planning permission* – full details of plans submitted for consideration

Summary of planning permission process
- Apply to planning authority with building plans, site map and fee
- Publish notice of application in national or local paper
- Erect notice on site/development following specific guidelines
- Application is put on the planning register for public to view
- Inspection of site by planning authority officials
- Planning authority examines application
- A notice of intention is issued to applicant
- Written objections by public may be lodged within one month
- A grant of permission is issued if there are no objections

Bye-law approval: bye-law approval is required for some internal alterations, extensions and outbuildings. It ensures the safety of the structures.

PROFESSIONAL SERVICES WHEN DESIGNING AND BUILDING A HOME

Architects design, co-ordinate and supervise the building of homes.

Structural engineers advise on how to overcome serious building problems and difficulties when carrying out alterations, they may work in conjunction with the architect.

Surveyors carry out site surveys, structural surveys of buildings ('snag' list) and complete surveys for lending institutions before mortgages are granted.

Solicitors, specialists in the legal procedures involved in buying a site or a house, checking deeds, title, planning permission, processing documentation and dealing with registering of properties.

Builders are responsible for site preparation, construction work and finishing of building by employing trades people and/or subcontracting the work.

Books of house plans are a cheaper option to employing an architect. Order by post, house designs, site maps and all details for building.

FACTORS THAT INFLUENCE HOUSE DESIGN

Aesthetic factors
- Visually pleasing design that fits into the landscape
- Orientation of building to suit the aspect of the site
- The elements and principles of design
- Quality of natural light within the building
- Layout and arrangement of rooms
- Architectural details (external and internal)
- Materials used e.g. local stone

Environmental factors
- Shelter from the elements e.g. wind
- Maximise natural sunlight on site
- Potential to harness solar energy
- Use of natural materials in the building
- Position of trees, landscaping of garden

Family requirements (current and future)
- Adequate for current family needs:
  - bedrooms, bathroom/s, shower, toilet/s,
  - living room, play area, study area
  - kitchen and dining area
- Suitability of rooms for multiple uses
- Suits the needs of a person with a disability
- Potential to meet the changing needs of the family

Energy efficiency
- Design of energy-efficient heating system
- Zoned heating systems, solar heating or underfloor system
- Installation of thermostats on radiators and timer controls
- Adequate insulation (windows, doors, roof, walls, floor)
- Double-glazed windows to reduce heat loss
- Fitting a lagging jacket on the hot water cylinder
- Energy-efficient appliances and use of night-saver electricity
- Tiled conservatory floors absorb daytime heat and release it at night

Ergonomics
Ergonomics is the study of the relationship between people and the environment in which they work e.g. the amount of space they need to work efficiently and effectively. Ergonomics is important in room planning in order to ensure that all activities are catered for in the design. For example a kitchen work sequence involves food storage, preparation and washing, cooking and serving areas are organised to keep walking to a minimum. The area between fridge, cooker and sink is called the work triangle.

Table 6.3 Initial and maintenance costs of a home

Initial costs – examples	Maintenance costs – examples
■ All costs involved when buying/building ■ Painting & decoration – low-maintenance ■ Furnishing – quality, long-lasting ■ Equipment – best you can afford ■ Landscaping the garden – years . . . ■ Building a garage – optional	■ Monthly mortgage ■ Insurance – annually or with mortgage ■ Service bills (regularly) ■ Painting and decorating (inside/outside) ■ Replacing furnishings and equipment ■ Garden – ongoing and can be expensive

Technological developments

Technology has contributed to a variety of changes in house design. Examples include use and development of:

- Computer Aided Design (CAD) to draw/modify plans
- New streamlined kitchen, bathroom and bedroom fittings
- Light sensor systems, time controls, thermostatic controls, under-floor heating, computerised programmes for appliances, electric showers, centralised vacuum-cleaner systems
- New building materials with special finishes e.g. heat-resistant
- Easy to maintain surfaces, e.g. new types of paints, floorings
- Remote control networks for heating and lighting systems
- Security systems e.g. phone-watch alarms, electronic gates, security lights

REGULATION OF HOUSE BUILDING STANDARDS

Building Regulations Act, 1991

Under the Building Regulations Act, 1991, strict rules have been set for the following: design and construction standards, materials used, foundations, stability, insulation, windows, drainage and sewage-treatment system, chimney flues and hearths, ventilation, fire and weather resistance, light, heating and ventilation. Compliance with the regulations must begin at the design stage. The local authority is responsible for enforcing the regulations.

Homebond Certificate – The National House Building Guarantee Scheme

- Issued to homes built in accordance with the National House Building Guarantee Scheme and the Department of the Environment and Local Government
- Guarantees against major structural faults to house within ten years, repairs are done free of charge by the builder
- Builders pay a fee to register houses initially
- Officials from the Department of the Environment inspect houses
- Builders issued with a Homebond Certificate if all is in order

- Lending institutions require new houses to have a Homebond Certificate. This scheme has contributed to improvements in building standards in Ireland

Floor Area Certificate
The Floor Area Certificate is given by the builder to the purchaser to indicate that the floor area of the house does not exceed 125 sq. m. It was a requirement for first-time buyers.

Grant provision
Government grants are available in building situations. Building standards are specified under these grants:
- State housing grants
- Thatching grant
- Improvement grants

DESIGNING THE HOUSE INTERIOR

ELEMENTS AND PRINCIPLES OF INTERIOR DESIGN

Table 6.4 Elements and principles of interior design

Elements	Principles
Colour, pattern, texture, form	Balance, emphasis, proportion, rhythm

Colour
Colour can:
- Create a visual unity and visual interest
- Be cool or warm to the eye
- Visually alter the shape/size of a room
- Conceal unattractive features, emphasise the best features

Types of colour schemes
Contrasting: colours directly opposite each other
Harmonious: colours next to each other on the colour wheel
Monochromatic: shades or tints of the same colour
Neutral: 'non-colours' such as white, cream, beige, brown, grey

Pattern
Decorative designs that add interest to plain surfaces e.g. pattern on carpets, arrangement of objects, are called patterns. Small patterns suit small rooms, large patterns suit large rooms. When using several patterns in one area link them using

colour, texture or themes. Too many patterns create visual clutter but related patterns of different scales work well together.

Function of pattern
Patterns can add interest, create atmosphere, emphasise particular features and disguise unattractive features.
Types of patterns: abstracts, checks, floral, geometric, motifs, printed textural patterns, self-pattern weaves, stripes and trellis

Texture
Textures can be described as the feel or touch of a surface. Textures can be:
• Soft or hard
• Rough or smooth
• Matt or shiny
• Absorbing or reflecting

Functions of textures
Textures can create balances in a room when combined with pattern to provide an accent and yet be functional. They influence how we see colour e.g. shiny glossy surfaces reflect light making the surface look brighter, flat painted surfaces absorb light making the surface look darker.

Form
The term 'form' refers to the shape and line of an object.

Table 6.5 Forms

Shapes	Examples of use
Circle	Stools, tables, tableware
Rectangle	Equipment, furniture, rooms
Square	Equipment, furniture, rooms, shower trays
Triangle	Hipline of roof
Line	Examples of effects
Curved	Softens hard edges, creates a sense of comfort
Diagonal	Creates movement, tends to be harsh
Horizontal	Makes rooms or objects appear wider, easy on the eye
Vertical	Increases or narrow the height of a room or object

PRINCIPLES OF DESIGN

Balance
Balance refers to the organisation and relationship between colours, patterns, textures, room lines and shape, proportion and emphasis to produce an attractive setting. No one object dominates the design (colour, pattern and texture). There are three types of balance (a) symmetrical, (b) asymmetrical and (c) radial.

Emphasis
Using an object or special area of interest within a room to draw attention to it and to create a focal point e.g. fireplace.

Proportion and scale
This is the relationship between the size of the room and all the objects in it. The objects in a room should be the right height and size relative to the scale of the room.

Rhythm
Rhythm creates a sense of unity and harmony by repeating or alternating colours, patterns or texture, or using a number of objects similar in style or shape in the room.

FACTORS INFLUENCING INTERIOR DESIGN

Aesthetic and comfort factors
To have rooms that are pleasing to the eye, it is essential to use the elements and principles of design effectively. Colours, patterns, textures, proportions, internal features, soft furnishings, fabrics and furniture, may be used to create a comfortable welcoming look. For comfort it is important that heating, lighting and ventilation arrangements suit the needs of the family.

Ergonomics
By examining the functions and use of rooms it is possible to plan layouts which suit the space and size of the room. Many activities take place in a home e.g. hobbies, work, eating, sleeping and study. It is important to lay out the room in a way that maximises the space and allows people to carry out activities efficiently and in comfort.

Family size and circumstances
The following need to be considered: number and age of family members, areas for play and study, choices and preferences of each family member e.g. colours, family income, number of people working, practical, durable and easy clean surfaces, current and future needs, conversion of attic, garage or bedroom. Bigger families need to make maximum use of space. When building a house ensure some flexibility in the design for future needs.

Special needs

The elderly and the disabled may have specific needs to be considered when planning room layouts. Key factors to consider are accessibility, safety, levels for door and window handles, light switches, space to manoeuvre a wheelchair, floor coverings and width of doorways. Depending on the need, more specific interior design modifications may be necessary.

Cost

The family budget will play a key role in the final design. People may choose to decorate a home room-by-room. Others working on a limited budget may first choose the essentials for the whole house and add the finishing touches later as money becomes available. Well chosen inexpensive fabrics and furniture can be made to look attractive. Costs can be reduced if family members do some of the work e.g. painting.

Environmental awareness

Materials used should be environmentally friendly. The use of natural materials for curtains, flooring, soft furnishings and furniture are widely available. Organic paints tend to be more expensive. Stone and timber have many uses and are less expensive than brick. Plastics and synthetic finishes are not environmentally friendly. Choose energy-efficient lighting, heating, CFC-free refrigerators and solar panels.

ROOM PLANNING

The key factors to consider when planning a room are:
- Aspect of room
- Layout and functions of room
- Size and stage of family
- Storage requirements
- Traffic flow
- Existing furniture and new furniture
- Heating, lighting and ventilation
- Ease of maintenance
- Safety and hygiene

FLOORING AND FLOOR COVERINGS

Floor coverings may be hard or soft:
- Hard: ceramic tiles, quarry tiles, slate, stone, wood
- Soft: carpets, rugs

Choosing floor covering – general rules

When choosing floor coverings consider the following:

- Function of room, rooms have different requirements
- Traffic in room, 'wear and tear', durability
- Budget available, cost involved (buying and fitting)
- Ease of maintenance, easy to keep clean, hygienic
- Non-slip, safe underfoot for children and the elderly
- Hard-wearing, durability, value for money
- Insulating properties (noise and heat)
- Suitability for existing interior décor

CARPETS

Types: woven (e.g. Axminster and Wilton), tufted, bonded and carpet tiles
Fibres: a variety of natural, man-made and blend fibres are used. 80% wool and 20% nylon blend provides an excellent balance of characteristics (high performance or durability, colour retention and comfort). Carpets with a higher percentage of man-made fibres are not as durable as wool

Table 6.6 Types of flooring

Selections/grade	Uses and properties
Light domestic	Bedrooms (warm and comfortable)
Medium domestic	Bedrooms, dining rooms, study (warm and comfortable)
General domestic	Dining rooms, living rooms (hard wearing, non-slip)
Heavy domestic	Halls, landings, stairs, living rooms (hard-wearing, durable)
Luxury/contract	All areas in the house except kitchens and bathrooms

WOODEN FLOORING

Types of woods used in flooring
Soft woods: birch, pine, spruce
Hardwoods: ash, beech, cherry, oak, maple
Types of timber flooring: block (different patterns e.g. basket weave), cork/timber (cork on a plastic sub-layer with a layer of wood veneer), mosaic (tongue-and-grooved tiles formed from narrow strips of wood), strip (tongue-and grooved flooring in hardwood or softwood), laminated wood floors, solid and semi-solid flooring

Properties
- Resilient and comfortable underfoot
- Durable, hardwearing and easy to maintain
- Noisy especially upstairs
- Resistant to acids, alkalis and heat
- *Suitable for asthma sufferers*
Uses: bedrooms, children's rooms, halls, study, living rooms and dining rooms

VINYL

Types: clear PVC-faced vinyl (solid in sheet or tile form), foam-backed vinyl (cushioned in sheet form only), slip-resistant vinyl (solid in sheet or tile form).

Properties
- Resilient, warm underfoot
- Easy to clean and maintain, replaceable
- Hardwearing, durable, quiet, good insulator
- Non-slip when dry, some forms can be slippery when wet
- Acid, alkali, grease and water resistant
- Damaged by heat and weight of furniture, dents easily

Uses: bathrooms, children's rooms, kitchens, halls, porches, playrooms and utility rooms

CORK

Cork is a natural material harvested from the bark of cork oak trees and is available in different colours and shades.

Properties
- Comfortable and warm
- Quiet and resilient underfoot
- Easily marked
- Acid, alkali and water resistant

Uses: sealed for use in bathrooms, children's rooms, kitchens and playrooms

NATURAL FLOORING

This type of flooring, made from 100% plant fibre, provides comfort, insulation, resilience and warmth underfoot. The types of natural flooring are coir, jute, seagrass and sisal.

Properties
- Coir: tough and hardwearing
- Jute: soft underfoot
- Seagrass: hardwearing, soft and resilient underfoot
- Sisal: hardwearing, anti-static

Uses: bedrooms, living rooms, study, playrooms, not recommended for kitchens

HARD FLOORING

Types and properties
- Ceramic: hardwearing, easy to clean, long-lasting, cold underfoot, resistant to chemicals, heat and water
- Quarry/flagstones: frost-proof, cold underfoot, lacks resilience
- Slate: non-slip, stain resistant, long-lasting, cold underfoot
- Terracotta: hard underfoot, easy to clean, long-lasting
- Terrazzo: noisy underfoot, hardwearing, easy to clean
- Marble: absorbs liquid, discolours easily, slippery when wet
- Stone: hardwearing, cold underfoot, some varieties stain easily

Uses: kitchens, halls, bathrooms and conservatories

WALL FINISHES

Walls may be covered with paint, paper, tiles, wood panelling, metal, glass or fabrics (silk).

Choosing wall finishes and coverings

When choosing wall finishes and coverings consider the following:
- Function of the room, suitability for the room
- Durability and resistance to dirt and stains
- Overall room decoration
- Within the budget available
- Care and maintenance
- Trends, varieties available

Paint

Table 6.7 Types of paint

Types Water-based paints	Properties and uses
Kitchen and bathroom paints	Anti-mould/fungus, anti-condensation, resistant to grease *Uses*: walls and ceilings
Vinyl emulsions	Matt (dull finish, non-washable), silk (shiny finish, washable), egg-shell (flat matt finish, very durable) *Uses*: kitchen, bathrooms, ceilings and walls
Textured paint	Rough stone texture, contain plastic fibres *Uses*: uneven walls and ceilings
Thixotropic emulsions	Non-drip, thick paint, only one coat required, colours cannot be mixed *Uses*: ceilings ⟶

Solvent-based paints	
Gloss	Shiny finish, durable, not suitable for uneven walls
	Uses: walls, windowsills, woodwork, cupboards/presses
Polyurethane	Durable, difficult to apply, dries quickly
	Uses: woodwork e.g. skirting boards, doors, furniture
Satin finish	Durable, washable, needs no undercoat
	Uses: ceilings, walls, metal, wood

Other paints/products: anti-mould/fungus paint, bituminous paint, exterior paint, flame-retardant paint, floor and step paint, radiator paint, primer, undercoat paint, anti-woodworm treatments

Paint effects: colour washing, dragging, freehand painting, ragging, rag-rolling, spattering, sponging, stencilling, stippling

WALL COVERINGS

Paper – types and properties

Lining: improves uneven surfaces for papering or painting, hung horizontally

Printed: by machine or hand, price depends on thickness of paper, range of designs

Embossed: design pressed into surface, paint over after hanging, suits uneven walls

Washable: water-resistant surface which can be wiped with a damp cloth, do not soak

Woodchip: cheap, paint over after hanging, suits uneven walls

Vinyl

Ready-soaked vinyl: soak to moisten dried paste on back, use in small rooms

Vinyl: tough, hardwearing, waterproof, washable, use in all areas

Textured vinyl: two types, blown vinyl (natural textures, washable, durable) and sculptured vinyl (looks like ceramic tiles, spongy to touch)

Wall tiles

General purpose wall tiles: use on own or with co-ordinating tiles

Mosaic panels: suitable for covering small or large areas

Patterned tiles: patterns stand out e.g. fruit, flowers

Special shapes: cross, diamond, honeycomb, triangle, rectangle

Tile panel: set of tiles forming a decorative panel surrounded by plain tiles

Others: border tiles, dado tiles, slip tiles

FURNITURE

Choosing furniture
When choosing furniture consider the following:
- Function and décor of the room
- Style, colour and personal preferences
- Design – attractive yet functional
- Construction – well-made joints, smooth finishes
- Space available for built-in or free-standing furniture
- Budget available, buy the best you can afford
- Consider cost versus quality
- Quality and durability of the materials used
- Quality symbols and safety symbols
- Guarantees, delivery arrangements

Styles and uses
Antique: bedroom, dining room, occasional furniture, hall-stands, writing desks
Fitted: bathroom, kitchens, bedrooms, home office, study
Modern: chairs, bedroom furniture, tables and chairs (dining and kitchen)
Traditional: bedroom suites, tables and chairs (dining and kitchen), hall tables, doors
Upholstered: armchairs, dining chairs, headboards, sitting room suites, sofas, stools

Choosing upholstered furniture
Upholstered furniture should:
- Be easy to clean, stain-resistant, durable
- Carry flame-resistant labels
- Be made with strong, sturdy and durable frames/structures
- Have high-density padding or filling to hold its shape
- Have taut and strong webbing or springs
- Have removable covers for ease of cleaning

Fabrics used: cotton, linen, synthetics, velvet, wool and leather

Choosing chairs and tables
Chairs and tables should:
- Be comfortable, well-designed and constructed
- Support neck, back and shoulders (chairs)
- Have arms at a comfortable height for user
- Have strong legs with grain going downwards
- Be attractive and easy to clean
- Be well constructed with secure joints
- Be adequately sealed, heat and stain resistant

Choosing beds
- Firm but not too hard, comfortable
- Supports the back
- Longer than the user

SOFT FURNISHINGS

Examples
Bed linen, cushions, curtains, duvets, kitchen accessories e.g. tea cosy, oven gloves, loose covers, table linen, throws, are examples of soft furnishings.
Fabrics used: cotton, linen, silk, wool, acrylics, draylon, rayon, polyester

Properties of fabrics
- Closely woven and pre-shrunk
- Colour fast, fade resistant, dirt and stain resistant
- Drapes well, durable and long-lasting
- Easy to care for and maintain
- Flame resistant, flame-retardant

Curtains
Purpose/function
- To enhance the décor of a room
- To provide privacy
- To keep out light
- To prevent heat loss

Curtain styles
- Net curtains (sill length, full length, café-style)
- Main curtains (sill length, full length)

Suitable fabrics: cotton, linen, synthetics, velvet and wool
Fitments: poles, tracks, wooden pelmets or valances, tie-backs
Headings: pencil pleats, pinch pleats, smocked, standard pleats, tabs

Blinds
A selection of fabrics may be used depending on the style and budget e.g. calico, chintz, cotton, linen. Fabrics can be plain, textured, patterned or self-patterned.
Types: Austrian or festoon, roller, Roman, Venetian and vertical blinds

Duvets

The warmth value of a duvet is measured in togs, higher togs for winter, lower for summer. Combination duvets with different tog ratings are available, one half has a higher tog rating, the other half has a lower tog rating, zipped together. Fillings are loosely packed to trap air to keep in body heat. Filling is kept in place in channels.

Fillings: down, down and feather, pure cotton, pure silk, synthetic

Pillows

A variety of shapes and sizes are available (rectangle, square, v-shaped). Made from natural or synthetic fillings. Price is generally an indicator of quality. Pillows provide support for the head, neck and back.

Fillings: down and feather, feather, foam, latex, synthetic

Bed linen

Duvet covers, sheets and pillowcases come in a variety of colours, patterns and fabrics. Fabrics used include plain or brushed cotton, linen, silk, polyester and blends. Fabrics should be absorbent, colour fast, pre-shrunk, smooth and closely woven with an easy care finish (washable, drip-dry, easy iron). The basic types of sheets are flat, fitted and semi-fitted. Buy the best quality you can afford, they will wear better and last longer.

MATERIALS USED IN THE HOME (TYPES, PROPERTIES AND USES)

Cotton

Types: broderie anglaise, chintz, denim, gingham, muslin, organdie, seersucker
Properties: absorbent, dyes readily, hard-wearing, strong, washes, dries and irons well, crease and stain-resistant finishes available, easy to sew, shrinks
Uses: bed linen, curtains, cushions, tea towels, table linen, bath towels

Linen

Types: fine linen, damask, linen union, linen blends
Properties: expensive, absorbent, durable, launders well, cool, creases easily, resists dirt and grime, wears along creases
Uses: bed linen, curtains, table linen, pelmets

Silk

Types: brocade, dupion, faille, organza, raw silk, shantung, taffeta
Properties: expensive, luxurious, lustrous surface, absorbent, varied textures, drapes well, resilient
Uses: bed linen, curtains, cushion covers, bed-spread or throw

Wool
Types: gabardine, mohair, tweed, worsted
Properties: absorbent, resist flames (smoulders slowly), resilient, holds its shape, warm, wears well, mixes well with other fibres
Uses: blankets, curtains, cushion covers, upholstery

Man-made textiles
Types: acrylic, polyester, nylon, viscose (acetate, rayon), PVC-coated fabric
Properties: cheaper than natural fabrics, properties vary with different fibres, for example:
- Acrylic launders well, is durable, light, resistant to creases mildew and moths
- Nylon is durable, strong, launders well, is crease resistant and resilient, pills, is uncomfortable in warm atmospheres, damaged by sunlight, bleach and hot water
- Polyester is resistant to creasing, mildew and moths, warm to touch, launders well, develops static electricity

Uses: bed linen, curtains, cushion covers, fillings, shower curtains, table linen

Glass
Types: blown, cut, plate, heat-resistant glass, soda lime glass, stained glass
Properties: breaks and chips easily, durable, hard-wearing, heat-resistant (pyrex)
Uses: cabinet doors, coffee makers, cookware, conservatories, mirrors, shower doors, tableware, teapots, windows and doors, packaging for food and drink

Metal
Types: aluminium, brass, copper, iron, silver, stainless steel
Properties: excellent conductor of heat
Uses: cutlery, utensils, furniture, light fitting, saucepans, windows

Thermosetting plastics
Types: Bakelite, melamine, polyester
Properties: hard and rigid, resistant to chemicals, oils and grease, good insulators
Uses: electric plugs, sockets and switches, worktops, handles on kettles and saucepans, kitchenware, laminated kitchen worktops

Thermoplastic plastics
Types: polythene, polystyrene, non-stick finishes
Properties: easily moulded, easily cleaned, does not corrode, rot or rust, resistant to acids, alkalis, waterproof
Uses: bins, buckets, non-stick surfaces, food packaging, tableware, utensils

Hardwoods
Types: ash, beech, elm, oak, mahogany, rosewood
Properties: slow-growing strong trees with fine grains and hard surfaces, expensive, durable, resistant to decay, can be attacked by woodworm
Uses: kitchen, dining room and bedroom furniture, doors, flooring, staircases

Softwoods
Types: fir, larch, pine, spruce
Properties: fast-growing trees with softer, coarser grain, cheaper than hardwoods, warps easily, damaged by heat
Uses: fitted kitchens and bedroom units, kitchen tables and chairs, skirting boards, doors, staircases

Man-made boards – examples, properties and uses
Chipboard: easily damaged by moisture, rough surface, inexpensive furniture
Hardboard: strong, hardwearing, inexpensive, used for backing in furniture
Medium density fibreboard (MDF): easily machined into shapes, no grain, used for furniture and mouldings
Plywood: stronger than chipboard, laminated or veneered, used in furniture, roofing, wall-panelling

THE ENERGY-EFFICIENT HOME

Energy supports cooking, central heating, water heating, lighting and all appliances.
Sources of energy: electricity, gas, oil, solid fuels
Fossil fuels: coal, natural gas, turf (peat), fuels from crude oil

ENERGY SUPPLIES TO THE HOME, SOURCES AND SUSTAINABILITY
Electricity
- Electricity is a clean efficient energy
- The Electricity Supply Board (ESB) is the main supplier
- Sources of generation are hydropower, imported coal, natural gas, oil, peat (turf)
- Supplies heat, light and power to households countrywide
- Appliances are powered by electricity, power cuts are inconvenient

Advantages: easily available, clean, efficient, labour-saving, energy-efficient when controlled by thermostats, reliable, option of off-peak electricity
Disadvantages: dries the air, expensive, inconvenient if there is a power cut
Sustainability: electricity in itself will not run out but the fuel used to generate it may cost more as supplies of coal, natural gas, oil and peat are used up. Alternative renewable sources of fuel are being investigated e.g. solar, wave and wind.

Gas

A gas field is produced from accumulations of hydrocarbons. There are two types, natural gas and Liquefied Petroleum Gas (LPG). Used as a fuel to generate electricity, central heating and hot water.

Natural gas

- Natural gas is brought ashore to a national grid pipeline by Bord Gáis
- Available in main urban centres of Ireland
- Arrives in the home via a mains pipe to a service pipe
- Meter measures home use in cubic metres, bill based on therms used

Liquefied petroleum gas (LPG)

- Supplied in pressurised tanks and small cylinders
- Useful for areas not served with natural gas
- Purchased from UK, Saudi Arabia and Whitegate (refinery in Cork)

Advantages: clean, environmentally-friendly fuel, accessible to households, efficient, storage not required
Disadvantages: dries the air, unpleasant odour, danger of gas leaks, not available to some centres of population, coal-effect fires expensive to run, requires good ventilation
Sustainability: natural gas is a non-sustainable fuel, sources are being used up rapidly, research is being carried out to find a suitable substitute

Oil

Oil is used to generate electricity, for home heating, cooking and hot water.
Advantages: easy to store, instantaneous heat, clean and efficient system of heating
Disadvantages: non-renewable source of energy, boiler needs regular servicing, requires ventilation
Sustainability: non-sustainable resource, reserves take millions of years to form

Solid Fuels

- **Coal** – the use of bituminous coal is prohibited in some parts of Ireland as a method of reducing levels of pollution and smog. Consumers must use low-smoke fuels instead. Most coal used in Ireland is imported.
- **Peat** has a similar formation to coal. Peat forms in bogs. It is cut into sods, dried and referred to as 'turf'. Bórd na Móna supplies turf and briquettes to urban areas.

Uses: solid fuel ranges, open fires, stoves
Advantages: affordable, creates a focal point in a room, no connection fees

Disadvantages: dirty, storage area required, inefficient, difficult to control, labour-intensive, chimneys need cleaning, mining coal and harvesting turf damages the landscape, contributes to air pollution

Sustainability of coal and peat: non-sustainable and non-renewable forms of fuel, reserves worldwide are dwindling rapidly, research is currently being carried out to find an effective method for converting coal into an 'oil-like' fuel

Wood
Wood is a renewable source of energy from trees e.g. fir, pine and spruce. Woodlands are planted under government schemes.

FORMS OF RENEWABLE ENERGY

Biomass: main sources are forestry, wood industry residue and energy crops

Geothermal energy: harnessed from heat released from the earth's crust

Hydropower: fast-flowing water passing over turbines generates electricity; low running costs, high initial costs, clean, efficient and renewable resource

Solar power: energy captured from the sun, useful for space and water heating, a renewable sustainable form of energy

Wind: energy generated by high masts with propellers rotating at high speeds, problems associated with the wind farms in Ireland concern noise pollution and their visual impact on the environment, a renewable form of energy

Uses of renewable energy
- Design of buildings to maximise solar energy
- Ground source heat pumps heat drawn from the earth
- Solar panels provide space and water heating
- Wood stoves, ranges and fireplaces for space and water heating

EMISSIONS

Effects of emissions on the environment
The effects of emissions has resulted in acid rain, global warming/greenhouse effect, climate change, pollution, smog and health problems e.g. asthma, bronchitis, sinusitis.

Acid rain
The burning of fossil fuels produces carbon monoxide, carbon dioxide, nitrogen oxides and sulphur dioxide. These combine with water vapour to produce carbonic, nitric and sulphuric acid. These acids dissolve in the rainfall to earth damaging buildings and soil, destroying forests, trees, plants, fish and insects.

Greenhouse effect

The greenhouse effect is caused by the action of certain gases in the atmosphere as a result of human activity (burning of fossil fuels, use of fertilisers). The effects of the greenhouse effect/global warming on the environment are changes in the climate, crop production and yields, pest control, rising sea levels, extinction of some plants and animals.

Smog

Smog is a combination of fog and smoke from cars, chimneys (burning of fossil fuels) and factories. It contains harmful gases, reduces the amount of sunlight reaching earth and affects plants.

Ways of reducing emission levels

- Learn about inter-governmental agreements and obligations
- Choose cleaner environmentally-friendly fuels e.g. natural gas
- Promote alternative renewable sources of energy e.g. wind, solar power
- Choose 'ozone-friendly' products, avoid aerosols with CFCs
- Use energy-efficient lighting systems and appliances
- Install energy-efficient space and water heating systems
- Eliminate the burning of rubbish or lighting of bonfires

THE ENERGY-EFFICIENT HOME

An energy-efficient home is designed and built to use energy effectively, reduce energy bills, reduce fuel emissions, pollution and waste, provide a clean comfortable environment and provide the consumer with good value for money.

Potential energy inefficiencies in the home – examples and solutions

- High watt bulbs waste energy when a lower energy bulb would be sufficient
Solution: replace with CFLs or lower wattage bulbs

- Lights on in rooms when not in use wastes money and energy
Solution: turn off lights when not required, replace with CFLs, use timers for indoor lights and sensors on outdoor lighting

- Dripping hot water taps waste money and energy
Solution: fix taps, replace washers or buy new taps if necessary

- Baths use twice as much water as shower, heating water is expensive
Solution: shower rather than a bath or take baths occasionally

- Old appliances have higher water and energy consumption than newer models
Solution: buy energy-efficient models when replacing them, use *Nightsaver* electricity to reduce cost of running appliances, use lower temperature washes

- Hot water cylinder without a lagging jacket wastes energy and money
Solution: buy and fit a lagging jacket

- A badly insulated house loses heat through the roof, windows, doors and floors
Solution: insulate house, draught-proof windows, doors and floors, etc.

- Old heating systems are inefficient if not serviced regularly and updated
Solution: service regularly, fit timers and thermostats, lower thermostat settings on boilers and radiators by a degree or two to save fuel, install a zonal system of central heating, fit a timer to immersion heaters

- Cooking only one item in an oven, using a grill to toast bread, running a dishwasher or a washing machine for a few items, heating a full kettle to make one cup of coffee and allowing ice to build up in fridges and freezers waste energy
Solutions: fill up the oven, use a toaster, wait until the dishwasher is full, use the economy button on the washing machine when washing a few items, boil the minimum amount of water in the kettle, defrost the fridge and freezer regularly

Other strategies to improve energy inefficiencies
- Do not leave television on standby mode
- Close windows and doors in the evening
- Pull blinds and curtains to keep heat inside
- Wear extra clothes when it is cold
- Cool food before placing in the refrigerator
- Use economy buttons on all appliances
- Reheat food using a microwave oven
- Buy a slow cooker, use a pressure cooker
- Use pots that suit the size of the cooking ring

Figure 6.1 Eco symbols

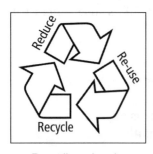

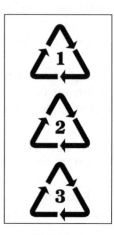

| Recycling triangle | Blue flower symbol | Green dot | PET label |

SYSTEMS AND SERVICES

ELECTRICITY

Household electricity supply
- ESB service cable provides the home with electricity
- Service cable connects to a sealed ESB fuse box in the home
- ESB fuse box can only be opened by employees
- From the sealed fuse box electricity flows through the meter
- A second meter may be present if off-peak electricity is used
- Meter records the amount of electricity used
- Meters are located in sealed external boxes for meter readings
- From the meter, electricity flows to the consumer unit, located indoors
- Consumer unit contains mains switch, fuse box, miniature circuit breakers, residual current devices
- Current is supplied to the various power points and lights around the house

Types of electrical circuits
Radial circuits are used for large appliances e.g. cookers, immersion heaters, each appliance has its own fuse.

Ring circuits – a number of sockets are attached to a continuous wire passing around the house forming a ring circuit. It goes from the consumer unit all around the house and back again. Branches off a ring circuit are called spurs. The total number of sockets attached to ring circuits should not exceed the fuse strength.

Figure 6.2 A ring circuit (a)

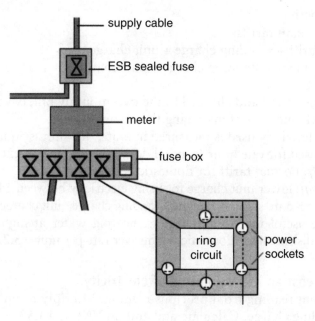

Figure 6.2 A ring circuit (b)

Terminology
Amperes: rate of flow of the electric current
Current: flow of electrons or electricity
Kilowatt-hour: measurement of a unit of electrical consumption
Voltage: pressure or force driving the electric current through the wire
Wattage: measurement of rate at which different appliances use electricity

Tariffs and costing
There are two main tariffs:
- Standard tariff + standing charge + unit charge
- Nightsaver tariff + standing charge + unit charge

Standing charge: fixed and charged to the two-monthly bill, covers upkeep of the supply network and cost of managing the accounts
Unit charge: electricity used is measured in units, one unit is equal to 1,000 watts of electricity used for one hour (general domestic charge = 12.20c inc. VAT)
Standard tariff: normal tariff for domestic customers
Nightsaver tariff: lower unit charge for using electricity between 11 p.m. and 8 a.m. (12 midnight to 9 a.m. summer), higher standing charge, unit charge less than half the standard rate, useful for storage heaters, heating water at night, using washing machines and dishwashers (domestic Nightsaver rate per unit = 5.22c inc. VAT)

Working out cost and consumption of electricity
Subtract present reading from previous reading. Multiply result by the unit cost. Add the standing charge. Calculate and add on VAT at 13.5%.

Safe use of electricity

Appliances, flexes, plugs

- Buy electrical appliances with recognised safety symbols
- Ensure equipment is always in perfect conditions
- Replace damaged equipment, flexes, plugs, sockets and switches
- Unplug all appliance at night before going to bed
- Never overload the circuit
- Service equipment regularly

Electricity and water

- Do not mix electricity and water
- Never handle appliances etc. with wet hands
- Never immerse appliances in water
- Unplug kettles before filling

Bathrooms

- Do not use portable electrical heaters or radios in bathrooms
- Electric showers must be wired separately, protect with RCD
- Use the recommended lights and shaver sockets in bathrooms
- Use pull cords for wall-mounted heaters and shavers

Bedroom

- Do not repair an electric blanket, check regularly for wear and tear
- Place electric fires in a safe place
- Never 'warm' clothes near or on electric fires
- Keep electric fires away from bed linen and curtains
- Never run flexes under carpets or rugs

Kitchens

- Avoid trailing flexes across cooker hobs and sinks, and across the floor
- Unplug a toaster before releasing jammed toast
- Never leave electric frying pans and deep-fat fryers unattended
- Avoid overuse of adaptors and extension cables

SAFETY FEATURES AND SYMBOLS

Safety features include double insulation on appliances, earthing and fuses, miniature circuit breakers, residual current devices and shuttered sockets. Appliances carrying the double insulation mark have a two-core flex without an earth wire, and are doubly insulated.

Figure 6.3 Double insulation safety symbol

Fuses

A fuse is a deliberate weak link that melts (blows) when a fault occurs due to too much current passing through it. This breaks the circuit and stops the electrical current. Fuses are found in appliances and in the fuse box and are made of glass or porcelain. Each fuse protects a specific size of circuit.

Examples of fuse ratings: 6 amp – lights, 16 amp – socket outlets (radial), 20 amp – water heater, 35 amp – cooker (ring)

Miniature circuit breakers (MCBs) and residual current devices (RCDs)

MCBs are a safety feature that contain the trip switches that interrupt the circuit and disconnect the current when a fault occurs or the circuit is overloaded. Trip switches can be reset when the fault has been found and sorted out. MCBs also contain RCDs (residual current devices) which provide additional protection by detecting current leaking to earth due to a fault in the circuit e.g. faulty appliances or cables.

Earth wires

When a fault occurs, electricity passes from the appliance through an earth wire and runs to the metal plate buried in the ground, rather than passing through the user and causing electrocution or death.

WATER

Water for human consumption must be clear, colourless, odourless, free of pathogenic bacteria and have a pleasant taste. In cities and towns the local authority provides the water supply to each home. In rural areas water for home use is supplied from deep wells and rural water schemes.

Figure 6.4 Water treatment process

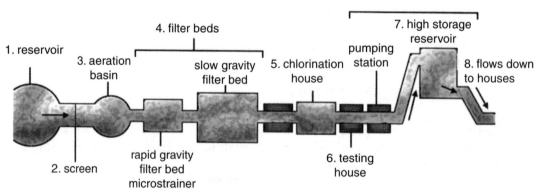

Table 6.8 Water treatment system

Stages	What happens during each stage
Screening	Impurities in water such as floating debris are removed
Sedimentation	Chemicals are added to remove remaining impurities
Filtration	Water is filtered to remove suspended matter
Chlorination	Chlorine is added to kill bacteria
Fluoridation	Fluoride is added to strengthen teeth and reduce tooth decay
Softening	Chloride of lime is added to soften hard water
Testing	Treated water is tested for quality and pureness

Household water supply

Water from reservoirs is brought to the main pipes. The mains pipes bring water to the service pipe at the house. A stopcock outside the house controls the supply (on/off). A service pipe enters the house near the kitchen sink and a connecting pipe brings fresh water to the cold tap. A pipe brings the water to storage cisterns or attic tanks. These tanks are made of galvanised iron or plastic. A ball valve controls water levels or rate of fill and an overflow pipe takes away excess water in emergencies. Water in the attic storage tank is not drinking water. Storage tanks should be covered and insulated. Do not insulate under the storage tank. Water pipes should be lagged.

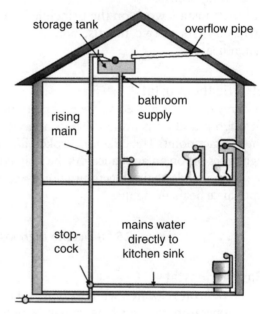

Figure 6.5 Cold water supply

HEATING

Thermal comfort control

Thermal comfort may be controlled by using:
- A data term controller – combines the controls for the whole house
- Thermostats – gas or electric
- Time clocks or programmes – times selected by user
- Zone controls – each area has its own thermostat and timer

Table 6.9 Levels of thermal comfort

Bathroom	15–20°C
Bedroom	15°C
Corridors	13–15°C
Kitchen	15–20°C
Living Room	21°C (lower if there is an open fire)

THERMOSTATS

Thermostats are devices that control temperature levels. There are two types of thermostats, electrical thermostats and gas thermostats.

Underlying principle
All thermostats work on the principle of a bimetallic strip (brass and invar). This strip consists of two metals, bonded together, which expand at different rates when heated.

Electric thermostat

A bimetal strip is heated as the electricity flows through it and on heating it bends away from the contact point. The circuit is broken and the light goes off on an appliance. As the strip cools contact is made again. Electricity flows and the appliance heats up again.

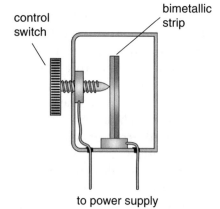

Figure 6.6 (a) Electric thermostat

Gas thermostat

A rod of invar is located within a brass tube. As the temperature rises the brass expands, pulling the invar rod with it. A valve at the end of the invar rod controls the flow of gas. As temperatures fall the brass contracts and the valve opens releasing the flow of gas again.

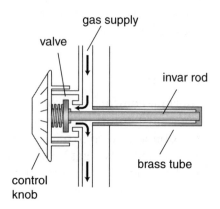

Figure 6.6 (b) Gas thermostat

Uses: cooker, deep-fat fryer, electric blanket, heating systems, hot-water cylinder, immersion heaters, iron, kettle, radiator thermostats, toaster, tumbler drier, washing machines

HEATING OPTIONS AVAILABLE FOR THE HOME

Factors to consider when choosing a heating system
- Space heating requirements based on size and use of rooms
- Costs, the budget available for installation, running and servicing
- Convenience, labour saving and fully automated e.g. oil fired
- Level of control (partial, full, zones)
- Safety of system, installed by a professional
- Reliability, annual servicing by a professional is recommended
- Environmentally-friendly, efficient system and fuel e.g. gas
- Availability, delivery and storage of fuel

Table 6.10 Heating options available for the home

Systems/heaters/appliances	Options
Portable heaters	Bottled gas heater, convector heater, fan heater, radiant heater, electric or oil-filled radiator
Fixed heating appliances	Electric/gas coal-effect fire, solid fuel stoves and ranges, storage heater (electric), wall-mounted heater
Central heating systems – some combine water and space heating	Wet system: boiler fuelled by gas, oil or solid fuel Dry system: electric under-floor heating, warm air system
Solar energy	Solar collector unit absorbs heat from sun and it is used to heat space and water

SCIENTIFIC PRINCIPLES UNDERLYING ONE SYSTEM OF CENTRAL HEATING

Small bore wet system
A small bore wet system combines central heating and indirect heating of domestic hot water. Heating the radiators is referred to as primary circulation, heating of the water is the secondary circulation. The underlying scientific principles involved in central heating are convection, radiation and the expansion of liquids when heat is applied to water.
- Cold water is heated in the boiler by convection
- Hot water rises from the boiler, passes through a coil of pipes in the hot water cylinder, indirectly heats the water in the cylinder (secondary circulation) and then moves to the radiators
- Cooled water returns to the boiler and the cycle begins again
- An electric pump keeps the water circulating
- The same water circulates in the primary system at all times. Steam from the boiler escapes into the feed and expansion tank located in the attic

Figure 6.7 Central heating system

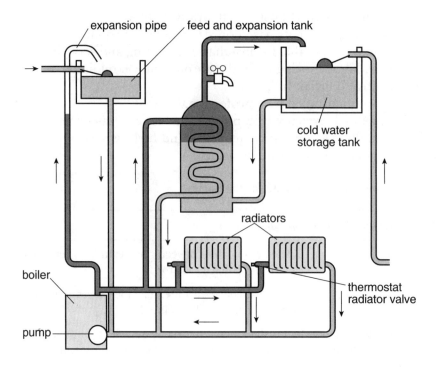

INSULATION

Underlying principle
Insulation is used to prevent or slow down heat loss from the home. It traps the heat within the home. Insulating materials are bad conductors of heat e.g. air, fibreglass, polystyrene (sheets and pellets) and wool.

Heat loss in a house

Table 6.11 Heat loss in a house

Area of house	House without insulation
Roof	25–35%
Walls	25–35%
Windows	10–15%
Doors	10%
Floors	10–20% – depends on type
Ventilation	25%

The building Regulation 1997 (Conservation of Fuel and Energy) states that all buildings must meet minimum standards of energy efficiency.

Methods of insulation

Attic insulation

To insulate the attic choose from the following methods: blown insulation, fibreglass or blanket insulation, foam insulation, loose fill insulation. Storage tank and pipes in the attic must be lagged or insulated.

Draught-proofing

There are many forms of draught-proofing.
- Doors: brush excluder, flap excluder, fabric snake excluder
- Door and window frames: fill cracks with filler or flexible sealant
- Door and window openings: adhesive strips, metal or plastic strips, sealant
- Fireplaces: use a fire screen
- Floors: fill gaps with wood fillers or papier maché, cover with felt and carpet
- Letter boxes: letter box seal

Wall insulation

Cavity walls

The cavity (5–10 cm) between the two layers of blocks or bricks are fitted with polystyrene sheets or pumped with liquid polystyrene foam.

Solid walls

Solid walls can be insulated internally using fibreglass blankets between wooden battening frames and covering with plasterboard. External insulation involves positioning fibreglass between wooden battens attached to the wall, covering it with metal mesh and putting a waterproof layer over it.

Windows – double-glazing

Double-glazing refers to the space between two panes of glass, in a window, filled with air that prevents heat travelling from inside the room to the outside pane. There are two types *gas-filled double-glazing*, the gap is filled with inert gas e.g. argon. *Low-emissivity glazing* where the outside of the internal pane is coated with special material that keeps heat inside but allows light through.

Hot-water cylinder

Cover the hot-water cylinder with a lagging jacket to keep the water hot for longer, to save energy and reduce energy bills.

VENTILATION

Purpose of ventilation
- To provides a supply of oxygen-rich fresh air
- To prevent condensation and reduce humidity levels
- To control air temperature
- To remove stale air with impurities e.g. CO_2, smoke
- To remove contaminants such as micro-organisms
- To remove cooking smells and other odours

Underlying principle
All systems of ventilation are based on the scientific principle that warm air rises and cool air rushes in to takes its place. Convection currents are formed as fresh air enters at the lower openings in a room and hot stale air escapes through higher air outlets in windows or walls.

Characteristics of good ventilation
- Air is replaced at least once every hour
- Temperatures should not drop too much
- Draughts should not result

Signs of inadequate ventilation
- Risks of infections e.g. respiratory, colds
- Lower levels of concentration
- Feeling tired and drowsy, getting headaches
- Increased humidity and condensation levels
- Damage to walls, paintwork and wallpaper e.g. mould

Condensation
Water vapour turns into water droplets and drips down all shiny cold, non-absorbent surfaces, e.g. mirrors. Condensation is caused by large amounts of steam in bathrooms and kitchens with poor ventilation and shiny smooth cold surfaces.

The *effect of condensation* include respiratory problems, damaged paintwork, wallpaper and wooden surfaces and metal equipment (rusting), dangerous slippery floors, mould on ceilings, clothes, walls and wood, and damp insulation materials.

Preventing condensation
Avoid overuse of shiny smooth surfaces e.g. tiles. Choose absorbent soft furnishing fabrics and carpets. Control moisture content of the air, open windows and vents. Improve system of ventilation, use cooker hoods and extractor fans. Choose a condenser dryer or vent the clothes drier to the outside. Improve the system of insulation. Increase room temperature and use efficient heating systems.

Humidity is the amount of water vapour contained in air: low levels in cold air, high levels in warmer air. Low humidity ranges from 20–50% moisture, high humidity is greater than 90%.

Methods of ventilation

Artificial: air conditioning, cooker hoods, extractor fans
Natural: air bricks, cooper's disc, doors, fires and fireplaces, vents, windows

ARTIFICIAL VENTILATION

Extractor fans

Underlying principle
A pull cord activates the fan with its rotating blades, opens the shutter and starts a motor. Blades rotating at high speeds create a suction action and draw stale air from the kitchen or bathroom. Fresh air takes the place of the stale air. Reverse actions allow some extractor fans to be used in summer to draw in cool air. Extractor fans should be placed away from the main door into the room, and as high on the wall as possible. Bathrooms or lavatories without windows must have extractor fans fitted to a wall or ceiling and ducted to the external wall.

Cooker hoods

Cooker hoods are positioned over cookers. They have a control switch, which can be set to different speeds, and a light switch.

Types of cooker hoods

Ductless hood
Ductless hoods consist of a metal canopy, a metal filter, a charcoal filter and a fan. The filters remove grease and cooking smells. Air is then re-circulated. They are generally fitted on internal walls. The metal filters need regular cleaning, the charcoal filter replacing occasionally.

Ducted hood
Ducted hoods remove stale air. They consist of a metal canopy, charcoal filter, grease filter, centrifugal fan and duct. Stale air is conducted along a duct fitted in an external wall. The charcoal or fabric filters need to be replaced at least twice a year. This type can remove more humidity and heat than the ductless type.

LIGHTING

Good lighting is needed:
- To see what we are doing
- For visual comfort

- To prevent accidents and see in the home at night
- To emphasise objects and add to interior décor
- To create atmosphere within the home

Properties of light and their application
Absorbed: dark colours and matt surfaces absorb light rays, dark colours, rough textures and matt surfaces create a warm atmosphere in living rooms and dining rooms

Diffused: all non-reflective surfaces scatter light in different directions e.g. enclosed, opaque glass light shade in a bathroom or kitchen

Dispersed: light passed through a prism is broken into its different colours e.g. glass blocks, crystal lampshades

Reflected: light falling on shiny surfaces bounces back e.g. ceramic tiles, mirrors, uplighters

Refracted: the ray of light bends as it passes through ridged or thick glass or plastic surfaces e.g. frosted glass on front doors or windows

Natural lighting
Natural lighting enters the home through doors, windows and glass bricks with areas of the room furthest away from windows getting a minimum amount of light. The actual amount of light getting into a room depends on the size of the windows, aspect of the room and colour scheme. South facing rooms get more light than rooms with other aspects.

ARTIFICIAL LIGHTING

Tungsten filament bulbs
Filament bulbs consist of thin curled tungsten filaments supported by wires within a clear or opal glass bulb. Argon gas fills the bulb and prevents the tungsten filament from vaporising, as it becomes white hot when the bulb is switched on.

Bulb wattage: 25w to 200w, last for about 1,000 hours, glass is clear, pearl or coloured

Figure 6.8 Tungsten filament bulb

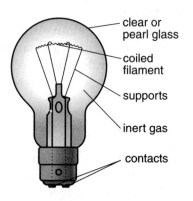

clear or pearl glass

coiled filament

supports

inert gas

contacts

Advantages
Tungsten filaments bulbs are inexpensive and widely available, easy to fit, replace and dispose of, light instantly, and are easily dimmed.

Disadvantages
Tungsten filaments bulbs are expensive to run, have a short lifespan, and are suitable for indoor use only.

Tungsten halogen bulbs

Tungsten halogen bulbs are similar to tungsten filament bulbs except this bulb consists of glass filled with halogens. The filament heats to a high temperature, it lasts about 3,000 hours. Low-voltage tungsten halogen bulbs are small lights with a sparkling effect due to the quartz glass reflecting the light in a narrow beam. Frequently used to emphasise or highlight objects within a room.

Advantages
Tungsten halogen bulbs are similar to natural daylight, compact, have a long lifespan, give instant light and can be dimmed. There is a good variety of wattage and types.

Disadvantages
Tungsten halogen bulbs are expensive to buy, there is poor availability, they are suitable for indoor use only.

Standard fluorescent tubes/bulbs

A glass tube, consisting of an inner coating of phosphor, lights up when the electrodes at each end cause vaporisation of the mercury present, when the light is turned on. The phosphor absorbs the ultraviolet light produced by the mercury. Wattage and price increase with the length of the fluorescent tube. Lengths vary from 30 cm to 2.5 m. Fluorescent tubes are available in straight, circular or curved shapes.

Figure 6.9 Fluorescent tube

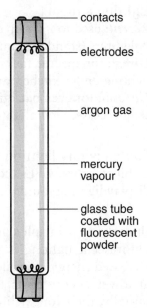

Advantages
The fluorescent tube lasts for about 8,000 hours, and is cool in operation. It is suitable for use next to wood. Energy-efficient, it give bright shadowless light, lasts 3–4 times longer than filament bulbs and gives out more light.

Disadvantages
The fluorescent tube uses highly toxic chemicals. They hum and flicker as they weaken. There is a time delay between switching on and lighting, the light looks harsh and clinical, not environmentally friendly.

Compact fluorescent lights (CFLs)

CFLs are energy-efficient bulbs, which last eight times longer and use 80% less energy than filament bulbs. CFLs operate on a low wattage, are energy efficient and useful in kitchens and in the hall, stairs and landing areas. Range of sizes from 7–23w, light output similar to 40–100w filament bulbs.

Advantages
CFLs are long lasting compared to other types, energy-efficient, economical in the long-term, fit traditional light fittings. They come in a variety of shapes and sizes.

Disadvantages
CFL light is not instant, it takes a few minutes to reach brightness, not suited to areas where lights are turned on/off frequently. Less light produced in cold conditions, light output decreases with age, ugly shaped long bulbs, may not suit all shades, unsuited to use with dimmer switches.

Principles for planning lighting systems
Consider the following principles:
- Maximising natural light
- Devising a lighting plan based on the function of each room
- Creating visual comfort, avoiding light that is too harsh and bright
- Installing fittings correctly, employing a qualified electrician (safety)
- Aesthetically pleasing practical and accent lighting

Lighting a room
Accent: used to light up displays or an area in a room e.g. table lamps, spot lights, uplighters (standard lamp, wall mounted)
Direct: for specific tasks e.g. reading, board games e.g. desk lamp, recessed strip lighting under kitchen units, standard lamp
General: for even background lighting in a room e.g. ceiling pendant, recessed or semi-recessed downlighters in the ceiling

Contemporary lighting developments
Cabinet lights, CFLs, cornice and cove lighting, desk lamps, dimmer switches, display lighting, outdoor/garden lighting, recessed ceiling lights, track lighting.

Underlying principles and uses of energy-efficient lighting
Fluorescent lighting is more energy-efficient than filament bulbs. CFLs have increased energy-efficiency. The low wattage of CFL bulbs can produce more light at lower energy costs than other bulbs. Though CFLs are expensive to buy initially, their longer life saves money and energy when compared to filament types. CFLs are useful in locations which require that lights be left on for long periods of time e.g. all-night security system, hall area.

CHAPTER 7 — Elective: Social Studies

SOCIAL CHANGE AND THE FAMILY

THE IMPACT OF SOCIAL AND ECONOMIC CHANGE ON THE FAMILY

Significant social, economic and technological changes have impacted on family life in Ireland in the following ways.

Settlement patterns from rural to urban
People move from rural areas to urban areas because:
- Mechanisation of farming has resulted in a decrease in agricultural jobs
- New employment opportunities in urban-based companies
- Industrial estates and third-level colleges are generally located in urban areas
- Urban areas tend to have a wide variety of amenities and facilities
- Infrastructure in rural areas is inadequate for many businesses
- Decline in rural populations is resulting in school and service closures
- Essential services e.g. hospitals are located in cities and large towns

New patterns in the last 5–8 years
- Young people are moving to affordable housing in country towns
- These young people travel to work by train or car
- Decentralisation of government departments to rural areas
- Not all companies choose to be located in large urban areas
- Increase in problems e.g. lost time, traffic congestion, pollution, fatigue and stress

Reduction in working hours
- Changes in legislation has resulted in a reduction in working hours
- Additional hours worked may attract overtime pay (in some cases)
- Flexibility in how hours are worked e.g. flexitime, term-time, job-sharing
- Job-sharing permits parents to share childminding and caring for the elderly
- Increased leisure time due to decreased working hours
- Improvement in quality of home life

Increases in leisure time
Decreased working time and increases in disposable income has resulted in people spending more time doing things that they like. Leisure activities include education, entertainment, sport and more relaxing activities. A new service industry has developed around leisure activities employing thousands of people.

Improvements in the provision of education
- Education is accessible to all individuals for a longer period of time
- Pre-school education has been improved
- Education at primary and secondary levels is free
- New programmes and a wider range of subjects are available
- Majority of young people sit the Leaving Certificate Examination
- Wide selection of courses at third level to meet demands of the job market
- Grants for third level students available subject to a means test
- Increased numbers of Institutes of Technology countrywide
- Adult education and concept of lifelong learning is becoming acceptable

Improvements in the provision of social welfare
As a result of improvements in the economy the government was able to increase benefits. Changes in family life has resulted in the state providing support to groups who are unable to look after themselves either in the short-term or long-term. Some examples of improvements in social welfare include Child Benefit, Family Income Supplement, One Parent Family Payment, Supplementary Welfare Allowance, Unemployment Assistance and Supplementary Welfare Allowances.

Changing attitude to marriage
- No social pressure on couples to marry
- Increase in number of couples cohabiting
- Religious and social influence not as strong
- Divorce legally recognised

Changing attitude to parenting
- Women establishing careers before having children
- Both parents involved in child rearing
- Equality of responsibility for children
- Maternity and paternity leave is available
- Unpaid parental leave available to look after children
- Children dependent on parents for a longer period of time
- Corporal punishment illegal as a method of discipline
- Parenting is shared by mothers, fathers, crèche providers and childminders
- Grandparents playing a 'parenting role' for grandchildren

Changing attitude to traditional roles
- Traditional role of breadwinner changing
- Women work outside the home, dual-careers
- Increase in number of dual-earner families
- Roles tend to be more egalitarian than in the past

- Many women are financially independent
- Women are better educated and want to have careers

Improved pay and conditions of work – some developments
- Introduction of minimum wage, minimum standards and PRSI
- Rights of workers to be protected by trade unions
- Introduction of Employment Equality Act, 1998
- Legislation for working hours, pay rates and conditions
- Introduction of Health and Safety at Work Act, 1989
- Flexible working hours, shorter working hours
- The Protection of Young Persons (Employment) Act, 1996

Increased participation of women in the workforce
- Acceptance by society of women working outside the home
- Improved education opportunities (at all levels)
- Better employment opportunities for women
- Women do not have to retire on marriage
- Equal pay and improved salaries
- Increase in number of women lone-parents

Women working outside the home may experience:
- Improved standard of living, increased financial security
- Greater independence of their children
- Role conflict between home and work
- Difficulties when arranging child care (cost and choice)
- Stress because of work overload (home duties/paid work)

Women working outside the home contribute to the economy by bringing a range valuable skills, knowledge and experiences to the workplace.

Legislation on equal pay and employment opportunities
The Employment Equality Act, 1998, prohibits discrimination under gender, marital status, family status, sexual orientation, religious belief, age, race, disability and membership of the travelling community.

Unemployment figures depend on current economic conditions. Economic conditions vary from year to year. Employment opportunities vary from region to region. Companies close, go into liquidation or move to new locations. Investment in Ireland by large international companies varies depending on government grants and tax incentives.

EDUCATION

Purpose of education
- Contributes to one's emotional, intellectual, physical and moral development
- Transmission of culture and knowledge by providing a broad education
- As a method of socialisation, children learn how to interact with others
- Reinforces what parents have already taught them at home
- Agent of social control, children learn expected patterns of behaviour
- Provides preparation for work by developing responsibility, skills etc.

Factors that influence educational achievement
- Child's abilities, combination of inherited and attained abilities
- Family size, large families may not be able to afford third-level education
- Attitudes, norms and values transmitted within the home
- Value placed on education, local employment and unemployment rates
- Good parenting, parental support, parental attitude
- Parents' level of education and parental relationships with school
- Peer group attitude to education determines participation and quality of work
- School environment e.g. relationships, amenities, class size, discipline

EDUCATIONAL PROVISION – THE IRISH EDUCATION SYSTEM

Pre-school
Through play and interaction with others children develop intellectually, physically and socially. They develop independence, self-control, self-esteem and responsibility. Parents can choose from Montessori schools, nurseries, crèches or day care centres, play groups to pre-school programmes in primary schools. Children are not obliged to attend a pre-school playgroup. Pre-schools must register with the local Health Board. Pre-schools must be healthy, hygienic and safe environments.

Early Start Pre-school Programme
The Early Start Pre-school Programme is an educational programme set up in areas of particular disadvantage. These programmes lay a solid foundation for the future of children who may not succeed in education. Primary school teachers, child-care assistants, pupils and parents work together. Class size is around fifteen. The programme is funded by the state, grants are provided for necessary resources. Pre-school classes are provided for children in inner-cities and for travellers.

Primary schools
Types
The following primary schools may be mixed or single sex with a particular ethos:
- State-assisted National Schools, mainly denominational

- Some private primary schools exist where parents pay fees
- Gaelscoil
- Special schools for children with special needs

Overview
- Curriculum is child-centred and set (broad-based)
- Teaching and learning methods are activity-based
- Lays a foundation for the child's development
- Considers individual differences, interests and needs
- Wide range of subjects in the curriculum
- French, German or Italian may also be available for senior classes
- Skills developed include reading, writing, speaking, listening, mathematical, spatial, artistic, musical, etc.
- Learning support and resource teachers may be attached to the school
- No formal exams at the end of primary school

Secondary schools
The options available to parents are Community and Comprehensive schools, Secondary schools or Vocational schools. Ownership and management structures differ across the schools. A five or six year programme is on offer (transition year adds a year). A wide range of academic, technical and vocational subjects are offered.

SUMMARY OF PROGRAMMES ON OFFER

Junior Certificate Programme
Three-year programme, range of subjects, variety of levels (foundation, ordinary level and higher level).

Transition Year Programme
May or may not be compulsory, a wide selection of non-state examination subjects including mini-company, work experience, range of sport activities.

Established Leaving Certificate
Two-year programme, five to seven subjects, structured set programmes; points gained may be used to access third-level education.

Leaving Certificate Applied
Preparation for work examination, modular approach over two years, general education subjects, practice skills and vocational preparation and work experience, can lead to PLC courses.

Leaving Certificate Vocational Programme

Two-year programme, five subjects at least (two vocational subjects, one European language), three compulsory link modules (enterprise education, preparation for work, work experience), can lead to PLC courses, courses in Institutes of Technology or Universities.

Post-Leaving Certificate Courses (PLCs)

Courses are one or two years full-time and students must have completed the Leaving Certificate. Courses are offered by VEC and by other local schools. Integrated general, technological and vocational based programmes are available. Certification provided by the National Council for Vocational Awards (NCVA). PLC courses can lead to employment or further education on selected courses.

THIRD-LEVEL EDUCATION

Types of institutions

Universities: National University of Ireland (UCD, UCG, UCC), University of Dublin, Trinity College (TCD), Dublin City University (DCU), University of Limerick (UL)

Institutes of Technology: fourteen in total e.g. Athlone, Carlow, etc.

Dublin Institute of Technology: there are many colleges within the DIT system

Colleges of Education: St. Patrick's College, Drumcondra, Mary Immaculate College, Limerick, St, Catherine's College of Home Economics, etc.

Private colleges: charge fees, variety of certificate, diploma and degree courses

ADULT AND SECOND CHANCE EDUCATION AND TRAINING

Participants may be:
- Adults who may have been early school leavers
- Adults who may have literacy problems
- Adults rejoining the workforce having reared their children
- For professional reasons, to increase job prospects (promotion)
- Keeping up to date, new skills required in the workplace

Sources of adult and second-chance education and training
- Courses in community and comprehensive schools – PLCs
- Adult Literacy Community Education Schemes (ALCES)
- Back to Education Programmes (plus Back to Education Allowance)
- FÁS (education, training and personal development courses)
- Oscail (distance education programmes, diploma/degree courses, DCU)
- Senior Traveller Training (early school leavers)
- Teagasc

- Vocational Training Opportunities Scheme (skills-based courses)
- Youthreach (early school leavers)

The *National Association for Adult Education* (AONTAS) is active in promoting, developing and supporting educational initiatives in adult education.

SPECIAL NEEDS EDUCATION

Special needs education covers a range of disabilities including autism, dyslexia, the emotionally disturbed, mild and moderate to severe learning disabilities, hearing or visual difficulties and physical disabilities. Depending where children live, they may be educated in:
- A state special school
- Special classes in primary school
- An integrated class

Research favours integration into mainstream schools with support structures.
- Special provisions may include learning-support teachers, resource teachers and special-needs assistants
- Interpreters, learning aids, special equipment and other assistance is available
- Visiting teachers for pupils with hearing or visual difficulties or children with Down's Syndrome may be allocated to schools

A dilemma exists for parents when choosing special needs or mainstream education

Deficiencies in special education

Communication between mainstream and special schools is poor. Support services are inadequate for many children and their parents. Educational provision is lacking for some children with special needs.

EQUALITY OF OPPORTUNITY

The Irish Constitution states that all individuals are entitled to an education. Free education was introduced in 1967 in order to reduce the inequality in access to education. Exclusion may be caused by the following factors:
- Gender inequality, socio-economic status, place of residence, school, leaving school early, cost of education

Contemporary initiatives in improving the accessibility of education
- Early Start Project
- Pre-school for travellers
- Disadvantaged Area Schools' Scheme

- Home-School-Community Liaison Scheme
- Breaking the Cycle Programme
- Early School Leaver Initiative (primary)
- Learning Support/Remedial Teaching
- Youth Encounter Projects
- Travellers' Education Needs
- Stay in School Retention Initiative (post-primary)
- Junior Certificate School Programme
- Leaving Certificate Vocation Programmes
- Leaving Certificate Applied Programmes
- Youthreach
- Adult Literacy Programmes
- Community Training Workshops
- Community Training Programme
- Back to Education Allowance
- Traveller Training Centres
- Vocational Training Opportunities Scheme (VTOS)

WORK

Work may be defined as:
- Paid work – financial reward for work done, salary or a wage, carried out in a designated place, full-time, temporary or part-time, employer/employee
- Unpaid work – no financial reward, voluntary activity e.g. household duties
- Voluntary work – higher status unpaid work e.g. working in the local community

Table 7.1 Attitudes to work and work attainment

Extrinsic	Intrinsic satisfaction
■ Provides clothing, food and shelter (basic needs)	■ Makes individuals and families independent
■ Is a measure of success in life	■ Confers respect and status
■ Prevents boredom	■ Satisfies psychological and social needs
■ Social unacceptability of being lazy	■ Develops self-esteem and confidence
■ Value placed on contributing to society through work	■ Provides interest and satisfies basic drives within us

Work ethic
Background, educational achievement, life goals and parental attitudes determine a person's work ethic. A work ethic will be reflected in a person's views on

absenteeism, punctuality, commitment to work, meeting deadlines, respect for authority, etc.

Variations in working conditions according to occupation
Variations in working conditions depend on the occupation and employment sector. Some sectors involve non-manual work while others involve heavy manual jobs. Examples of sectors include:
- Blue-collar workers
- Professional workers (white-collar workers)
- Service workers
- Farmers and farm workers

Changes in pattern of work and work availability
- Employment in area of information technology
- Flexibility in working hours
- Improved gender equality, less gender specific
- High levels of education and training required
- New opportunities for lifelong learning and training
- Migration and immigration patterns

Improved working conditions
Improvements have been achieved in the work place because of the following:
- Trade unions looking after workers' rights
- Introduction of the Health and Safety at Work Act
- Availability of early retirement
- Family friendly schemes e.g. flexible working hours
- Reduction in maximum weekly working hours

Maternity and adoptive leave
- Ten weeks leave for adoptive parents
- Fourteen weeks for maternity leave
- Fathers entitled to unpaid paternity leave

Increased automation
The use of machinery and computers to carry out tasks, originally done by hand, is referred to as 'automation'. New technology is applied in a variety of areas, e.g. manufacturing, accountancy, food production, banking, administration and architecture.

Advantages of automation
- Increase in quality and productivity
- Increase in leisure time
- Creation of new jobs
- On-going demand for upskilling
- Elimination of monotonous tasks
- Working from home e.g. teleworking
- Safer and healthier working environments

Disadvantages of automation
- Demand for more educational qualifications
- Increase in unemployment in some sectors
- Loss of some traditional jobs, de-skilling
- Fewer opportunities to socialise with others
- Increase in supervisory roles, reduced job satisfaction

THE DECLINE IN PRIMARY AND SECONDARY INDUSTRIES

Examples of industries
- Primary industries: agriculture, fishing, forestry, mining
- Secondary industries: construction and manufacturing sectors e.g. building companies and suppliers to the industry, businesses established by Irish people, food production (agri-business), multinational companies e.g. oil, technology, hotel groups

Factors influencing the decline in these industries
- Shortage of qualified staff
- Relocation of companies to other countries
- Competition between Ireland and other countries
- Replacement of production and manufacturing skills by IT
- Decline in manufacturing has resulted in increases in service industries

Reasons for increase in work in service industries
- Decreases in primary industries, increase in service industries
- New developments in construction and manufacturing
- Transnational companies setting up branches in Ireland
- Availability of government grants for multinational companies
- Increase in disposable money has resulted in increased spending
- New jobs created e.g. household services, media, music, technology
- Better standard of living and increased expectations
- More employment in the leisure and entertainment industry

Increased educational requirements
- Leaving Certificate is the minimum qualification
- Many jobs require third-level qualifications
- Exclusion of early school leavers
- People without qualifications are likely to be unemployed
- Unskilled people may be unemployed or in low-paid jobs
- Existing qualifications may be updated at work
- A lack of suitably trained graduates exists in some areas

Increased participation by women in employment
Increased participation may be as a result of the following:
- Removal of the 'marriage ban' in 1973
- Acceptable that women work outside the home
- Improvement in flexible work patterns
- Women availing of third-level educational opportunities
- Introduction of the Employment Equality Act, 1998

Points to note
- Female participation in paid employment is below EU average
- Less opportunities to advance to top of many professions
- Restricted access to executive positions
- More women participating in lower-paid employment
- More women in service industries, clerical, education and health
- More women represented in some areas than men

Improved working conditions – some examples
Improvements in working conditions have taken place due to the following factors:
- Safety, Health and Welfare at Work Act, 1989
- National Minimum Wage Act, 2000
- Parental Leave Act, 1998
- The work of the Health and Safety Authority
- Shorter working days, set hours for the working week
- Entitlement to overtime for some jobs

Flexibility in working hours
Examples of flexibility in working hours include banked overtime, career-breaks, job-sharing, flexible hours and parental leave.

Role of voluntary work/organisations in the community
- Acts as a pressure groups e.g. protecting a specific group
- Highlights inadequacies in state support for necessary services
- Draws on the personal experiences of people in the community

- Focuses local attention on community needs
- Works with agencies responding to community needs

Benefits of voluntary work to the volunteer
- Develops expertise and skill as a volunteer
- Sense of personal reward in helping others
- Develops self-esteem and self-worth
- Encourages sharing of knowledge and experiences
- Provides opportunities to meet others
- Reduces boredom for those unemployed and retired

Benefits of voluntary work to the community
- Creates a caring atmosphere in the community
- Empowers a community to care for its vulnerable members
- Assistance is always at hand in an emergency
- Builds a sense of belonging and friendship within a community
- Services are provided which might not be funded by the state

Examples of voluntary organisations
Aid for Parents under Stress, AIM, Alone, Barnardos, Cherish, CMAC, Council for the Status of Women, Combat Poverty Agency, Cura, Focus Point, National Youth Council, The Samaritans, The Simon Community and the Society of St Vincent de Paul.

The Protection of Young Persons' (Employment) Act, 1996
The Protection of Young Person's Act aims to protect the rights of employees under the age of 18 years and to ensure that work does not affect schoolwork. The act provides the following strict guidelines:

Minimum age
Young people under 16 cannot be employed full-time, 14–15 year olds may work part-time during the school term, during school holidays (with a three-week break) and as part of an educational work experience programme.

Table 7.2 Maximum working hours per week

	14 years	*15 years*
Term-time	Nil	8
Holidays	35	35
Work experience	40	40

The act also provides guidelines for rest breaks, starting and finishing times. A breach of the act may result in a fine. It should be noted that the act is not applied to specific groups e.g. defence forces, relatives involved in farming, fishing, etc.

WORK AND FAMILY RESPONSIBILITIES

Reconciling employment with family responsibilities has been affected by changes in society.

Changing gender roles within the family
There has been a movement away from fixed segregated gender roles to more egalitarian roles. Roles are less clear with parents and children actively involved in a variety of family activities and household duties. Parents are more conscious of the importance of not reinforcing or encouraging the stereotyping of gender roles when rearing children.

DUAL-EARNER FAMILIES AND FAMILY LIFE
Factors influencing the increase in the number of dual-earner families include:
- Increased financial commitments e.g. property is expensive
- Better education, individuals want to use their qualifications
- Improved employment opportunities, particularly for women
- Fulfilment of personal needs e.g. independence, social
- Ambition e.g. career advancement a priority

Dual-career families enjoy higher living standards, more egalitarian roles within the family, greater equality for the mother and the father in rearing of the children. Some children may be more independent and confident. Others develop problems with self-esteem, poor behaviour and low achievements at school.

Impact of dual-earner families on family life
Problems faced by dual-earner families might be: role overload, role conflict, high child-care costs, inadequate child-care services, marital breakdown, reduction in leisure time, children unsupervised until parents return home (latchkey children).

Role overload
Role overload occurs when a person finds the demands of fulfilling multiple roles in a limited amount of time stressful e.g. being parent, spouse and employee. Role-overload may occur if one partner/spouse is responsible for household duties, child care and paid full-time employment outside the home.

Role conflict
Balancing the demands of household duties, child care and work may result in role conflict when an individual prioritises one role above the other. The individual may feel guilty about letting people down as a result of work or family commitments.

Avoiding role overload and role conflict
Role overload and role conflict may be avoided by sharing household and child-care duties between the parents and dividing the household tasks/chores among the parents and children. A list of 'who does what' ensures that everyone does their fair share. Good communication and the development of a sense of responsibility among family members will help eliminate conflict related to unfinished household duties.

CHILD-CARE FACILITIES

The options
Demand for suitable child-care facilities has resulted from increasing numbers of women working outside the home. Parents choose from a number of child-care options such as:
- Childminders (grandparents, neighbours, friends, au pairs)
- Nurseries and crèches (babies, toddlers, young children)
- Playgroups and play schools (toddlers, young children)
- Montessori or Froebel Nursery schools (children from 3–5 years)
- Naoinrai
- After-school care groups (for school-going children)
- Au pairs and nannies

Family requirements for child–care facilities
The factors which determine requirements include:
- Family circumstances and parental preferences
- Age of the child
- Preferred environment, home, minder's home or a registered facility
- Knowing the minder and if registered with the local Health Board
- High standards of hygiene and safety
- Cost of child-care arrangements
- Qualifications and experience of staff
- Number of children being cared for at the same time
- Needs of special child

Note:
(a) National Children's Strategy, November 2000, published by the Irish government.
(b) Childminding Ireland (1983) is the National Body for childminding and is funded by the Department of Health and Children.
(c) National Children's Nurseries Association (NCNA), (1988), supports providers of day-care facilities.

EVALUATING TWO CHILD-CARE OPTIONS

Quality child care provide children with a comfortable, home-like atmosphere that meets developmental, educational, emotional, physical and socialisation needs.

Option 1 – childminder

Childminders provide full or part day care in the child's home or in their own home during the parents' working day. Childminders may not have a formal qualification in child care but have experience of children, perhaps are mothers themselves. They have a duty of care for the children in the absence of parents. Childminders should have insurance cover to protect the child and themselves. Childminders must have access to a phone and backup arrangements with parents if the child becomes ill or should they themselves become ill. Childminders should:
• Like, understand and have experience of child care
• Be of good character, trustworthy and caring
• Accept direction/guidance from parents
• Be familiar with the needs and rights of the child
• Not smoke or take illegal substances

Guidelines

Good practice guidelines with recommendations for childminders and their homes/premises are available from Health Boards. It is recommended that the childminder gain relevant qualifications (including a First Aid Certificate), be informed about current child-care practices, understand the importance of all aspects of child development and join Childminding Ireland. The childminder's home should be safe, clean, well ventilated, safely heated, have adequate play and sleep areas. The childminder should follow recommended guidelines with regard to discipline, toys and recreation.

Advantages of childminders
• Familiarity with own home if child is cared for in it
• Childminder's home becomes an extension of the child's home
• Special bond develops between the childminder and child

- Individual attention, on a one-to-one basis
- Childminder might be more flexible about collection times
- Childminder may do some light housework and shopping

Disadvantages of childminders
- Lack of training, qualifications, insurance cover, First Aid Certificate
- Children may need to be dropped off early each morning
- Parents left without child-care option if childminder gets ill
- Child may form a closer bond with the childminder than parents
- Conflict with regard to discipline

Option 2 – crèche
Crèches provide day care for babies and young children from a few hours to a full day. The aim is to provide children with 'a home-from-home' environment catering for their emotional, intellectual, physical and social development. Crèches must comply with standards and regulations set down by the Department of Health Child-Care (Pre-School Service) Regulations 1996.

Guidelines
The 1996 Regulations and the Local Environmental Health Officer set out the requirements regarding the correct staff/child ratio, space requirements, design, layout and equipping of the crèche (areas e.g. kitchen, play, sleep/rest) and safety. All rooms must be clean and hygienic. Kitchens should be separate to play areas and the water supply should be sufficient to meet the demands of the crèche.

Advantages of a crèche
- May be attached to workplace
- Definite opening and closing hours
- Qualified personnel (child-care, early childhood education)
- Qualified nurse on duty or personnel qualified in first aid
- Supervision of each individual child
- Educational play activities (formal and informal)
- Opportunities to socialise with other children of different ages

Disadvantages of a crèche
- Rigid drop off and collection times
- More than one child attends, some have large numbers
- Children exposed to a variety of infectious diseases
- Alternative arrangements must be made when a child is sick
- Not all crèches cater for babies and toddlers
- Tends to be more expensive than the childminder option

LEISURE

DEFINING LEISURE

A balanced lifestyle includes some leisure activities. Education for leisure begins with parents at home. 'Education for leisure' is provided through school, clubs, scouts and other groups. *Leisure time* refers to the time left over after essential work and household activities have been completed. It is unpaid time offering individuals a chance to spend time on activities they view as enjoyable.

Function and value of leisure in today's society
- To promote emotional, intellectual, physical and social development
- To encourage relaxation and creativity
- To create a sense of satisfaction and wellbeing
- To reduce or prevent boredom
- To promote the development of new skills
- To set good example for children
- To maintain a healthy body and mind

Influences on leisure patterns
Social influences: influences of socio-economic groups, trends, income, education
Cultural influences: choice of activities based on how one is raised
Occupation: working hours influences time available for leisure, relationship between leisure and work (extension, neutral, opposition)
Disposable income: many leisure activities cost money, young people tend to spend more on leisure than young couples buying a home or couples with children; older couples with grown up children, no mortgages, may have more disposable income to spend on leisure activities
Trends: based on advertising and popularity
Age: influences types and amounts of leisure activities, may be linked to personal interests, physical wellbeing, family life-cycle, disposable income, time available
Gender: less stereotyping than in the past but some activities are still linked to men or women, dual-career women tend to have less leisure time

Role of leisure activities in development
People may develop in the following ways:
Emotional: sense of belonging, confidence, self-esteem, satisfaction
Intellectual: skills of analysis, decision-making, interpretation and observation
Physical: levels of energy, fitness and muscle strength, new skill, weight control
Social: skills of communication, listening and negotiation, social interaction, new friendships

Types of leisure activities in local communities
Physical: outdoor or indoor activities e.g. aerobics, cycling, football, golf, health clubs, hill walking, golf, rugby, squash club, sailing, swimming
Less physical: art classes, bridge, chess, cinema, fishing, theatre, evening classes, debates, drama, quizzes, restaurants, photography, visiting museums and galleries
Others: holidays and travelling, Irish Countrywomen's Association (ICA), politics, voluntary (St Vincent de Paul)

Evaluation of leisure facilities
When evaluating *two* leisure facilities in your own local community examine the following:
- Type of leisure facility e.g. leisure centre, golf club, gym
- Membership fees for individuals, two adults and/or family
- Cost of participation, immediate and on-going
- Value for money, regularity of use, number of activities, personal needs
- Time required, each day, a few times a week, weekends, occasional
- Emotional benefits e.g. relaxation, reduces stress
- Physical benefits e.g. new skill, improves health and wellbeing
- Social benefits e.g. meeting new people, reduces social isolation

UNEMPLOYMENT

Definition
Unemployment refers to people who are without a paid job.

Extent of Irish unemployment – summary
- Mid-1980s: unemployment figures rising worldwide
- Late-1980s: highest unemployment figures in Europe
- 1990s: decline in unemployment due to 'Celtic Tiger' and foreign investment
- 2000: increase in unemployment, may be due to downturn in the global economy, long-term unemployment decreasing due to government intervention, lack of education, poor skills and a lack of employment makes finding a job difficult

Government strategies to reduce unemployment
- Raising of the school leaving age
- Training and skills development programmes
- Introduction of minimum wage
- Partnership for Prosperity and Fairness 2000

Types of unemployment
- Short-term (lasts up to six months)
- Long-term (ongoing for a long period of time)

Causes of unemployment
- Increased automation and new technologies
- Changes from manufacturing to service industries
- Increase in the working population e.g. women, young people
- Lack of skills, demand for higher education qualifications
- Recession, companies moving abroad, downsizing
- Geographical, less employment in rural areas
- Seasonal jobs in agriculture, construction and tourism
- Low wages are a disincentive to work
- Reduced demand for products and services
- Age profile, employers focus on younger graduates
- Residual, some people may not be able to work

Effects of Unemployment on the Individual, Family Unit and on Society

On the individual
- Sense of rejection following each unsuccessful interview
- Financial problems, worry about bills, poverty
- Relationship problems, rows, strained relationships
- Lowering of social status and identity, social isolation
- Decline in self-esteem and confidence
- Health problems such as depression, anxiety and stress
- Antisocial behaviour e.g. crime

On the family
- Children may suffer emotionally and psychologically
- Can shape children's views of employment/unemployment
- Financial problems leading to poverty and insecurity
- May interfere with children's education, educational disadvantage
- Loss of the family home and lowered standards of living
- Tension, possibly violence in the home
- Strained relationships and in some cases marital breakdown

On community/society
- Increase in poverty and inequality
- Continuation or increased growth of the 'black economy'
- Emigration and migration

- Alcoholism, crime, drug abuse, homelessness and mental illness
- Lowering of living standards in the community
- Unstable communities with high unemployment levels
- Increased demands made on the state and the tax payers
- Children of unemployed parents are more likely to be unemployed themselves

POVERTY

Definitions of poverty

Absolute poverty refers to people who do not have the minimum food, clothing and shelter resources in order to survive e.g. people who are starving. Absolute poverty is the same in every society and is based on a universally agreed minimum.

Relative poverty is the term used to describe situations where people are surviving below the accepted standard of living in a particular society/country taking into account the cultural, social and physical needs of individuals.

Consensual poverty refers to a level of deprivation or poverty perceived by the majority of a large group to be unacceptable. It is an indication as to how a group defines poverty within the context of their society.

Poverty line describes the minimum income required to afford the basic necessities of life in a society. It is calculated from national survey information on disposable income. People can experience poverty at different stages in life depending on life-cycle of family, illness, unemployment etc.

Groups most at risk of poverty
- Large families with one income
- Lone-parent or single-parent families
- Long-term unemployed
- Low-paid workers
- Marginal groups e.g. homeless, traveller families
- Older people, elderly, pensioners
- People with disabilities or illnesses
- Refugees, ethnic minorities
- Small farm households on non-viable lands (invisible poverty)
- Families in large public housing estates with few amenities
- Women and children

EXTENT AND DISTRIBUTION OF POVERTY

- Poverty in Ireland is measured using the 'poverty line'. The poverty line is set at half of the average income
- Relative income poverty lines are set at 40%, 50% and 60% of the average household income in Ireland

- Poverty decreased in the late 1960s and early 1970s. High unemployment and economic recession in the late 1970s and early 1980s resulted in an increase in poverty. Poverty levels continued to decrease during the 1990s
- Between 1987 and 1997 the percentage of people living under the poverty line had reduced

Families or individuals may experience poverty if they live in isolated rural households, underdeveloped rural communities, large local authority estates or a 'poverty black spot'.

Indicators of deprivation
- Eight indicators compiled by the Economic and Social Research Institute
- There are different types of indicators, monetary and non-monetary
- Indicators are used to identify basic lifestyle deprivation, secondary lifestyle deprivation and housing deprivation.

THE CAUSES OF POVERTY
- The 'vicious poverty cycle' or 'cycle of deprivation'
- A culture of poverty (anti-authority, fatalistic and present-oriented), unbroken from generation to generation
- Unequal distribution of education, power and wealth
- The social welfare system, benefits may be too low, dependency culture
- Lack of life chances e.g. education, quality housing, employment
- Industrial, technological and social changes
- Economic recession and unemployment
- Inability to manage household finances
- Large family sizes, one-parent families
- Cost of housing and housing shortage

The cycle of deprivation or the cycle of poverty
- Born to poor parents
- Living in poor housing or/and a poor area
- Inadequate diet resulting in dietary problems
- Little encouragement from parents
- Few books in the home
- Poor educational achievement or inadequate education
- Leaving school early (without Leaving Certificate)
- Unemployed or low-paid job
- Marrying early
- Having a large family themselves

Figure 7.1 The cycle of poverty

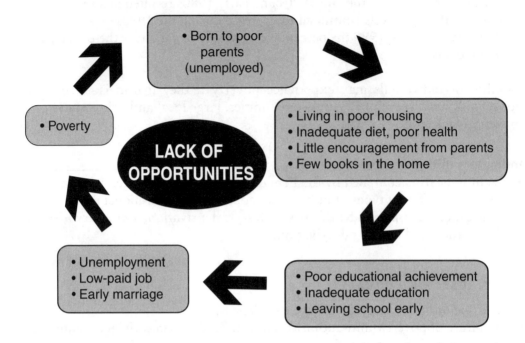

The poverty trap
The poverty trap refers to unemployed people or people in low-paid employment who suffer from financial deprivation. They may receive a number of state benefits but on return to work or an increase in income may lose benefits.

The effects of poverty
- Poor housing
- Inadequate nutrition, poor diet
- Low educational achievement and educational disadvantage
- Physical and psychological illnesses
- Stress and family relationship problem
- Poor self-esteem and confidence
- Fewer employment opportunities

STATUTORY AND COMMUNITY RESPONSES TO CREATING EMPLOYMENT AND ELIMINATING POVERTY

The main responses are in the areas of job creation, consultation, education (resources and training), financial support, modifications to the tax system, decentralisation and rural development.

Statutory responses
- Social Welfare Assistance and Benefit
- Schemes for low-income families
- Social welfare for households with children
- Social welfare for lone-parents, those with disabilities
- Schemes for the unemployed

Anti-poverty statutory activities
- The National Anti-Poverty Strategy (NAPS)
- The Combat Poverty Agency
- The Community Development Programme
- The Local Development Programme

Key areas within social policy
- Tackling educational disadvantage
- Investing in education
- Job creation and employment
- Eliminating poverty in urban and rural areas

Community and voluntary responses
- Community-based educational training and employment initiatives
- Community employment
- Co-operatives and cottage industries
- Voluntary organisations (Focus Ireland, Society of St Vincent de Paul, The Simon Community)

Creating employment – statutory responses
- County Enterprise Boards
- Enterprise Ireland
- Employment Supports
- FÁS
- Forfás
- IDA and Foreign Investment
- Student Summer Jobs Scheme

Foreign investment supports: finance, grants, facilities, IDA, taxation

Creating employment – community-based opportunities
- Area-based partnership scheme
- County Enterprise Board
- FÁS Services
- First Step
- Social Employment Scheme (SES)

HOME ECONOMICS – SCIENTIFIC AND SOCIAL

HIGHER LEVEL

2.00 to 4.30

280/320 MARKS

Instructions to Candidates

Section A There are **twelve** questions in this section.
Candidates are required to answer any **ten** questions.
Each question carries 6 marks.
Write your answers in the spaces provided on the examination paper.

Section B There are **five** questions in this section.
Candidates are required to answer **Question 1 and any other two questions.**
Question 1 is worth 80 marks.
Questions 2, 3, 4 and 5 are worth 50 marks each.
Write your answers in the separate answer book provided.

Section C There are **three** questions in this section.
Candidates are required to answer **one** elective question to include
Part A and either Part B or Part C.
**Candidates who submitted Textiles, Fashion and Design coursework
for examination may <u>only</u> attempt Question 2 from this section.**
Electives 1 and 3 are worth 80 marks each.
Elective 2 is worth 40 marks.
Write your answers in the separate answer book provided.

Section A

Answer any <u>ten</u> questions from this section.
Each question is worth 6 marks.
Write your answers in the spaces provided.

1. (a) Complete the diagram showing the basic chemical structure of an amino acid.

$$H$$

$$R \text{———} C \text{———} COOH$$

$$NH_2$$

(b) What is an essential amino acid?

essential amino acid cannot be manufactured
by the body and must be taken in by food
e.g. leucine

2. (a) State <u>two</u> functions of ascorbic acid (Vitamin C) in the diet.

(i) prevents Scurvy

(ii) Helps with absorption of iron

(b) State how Vitamin C assists the absorption of iron.

_____

_____

3. State <u>one</u> possible effect on the body of each of the following dietary deficiencies.

Dietary deficiency	Possible effect
Lack of Thiamine (B_1)	Fatigue Beri-Beri
Lack of Folic Acid	Problem with unborn babis
Lack of Cabalamin (B_{12})	Aneamie

4. (a) Name the **three** main nutrients found in the endosperm of the wheat grain.
    (i) Protein
    (ii) B groups
    (iii) Starch.

(b) Explain the term *gelatinisation*.

It is when Starch is mixed with liquid and heated, the Starch cells burst and absorb water, this causes the mixture to thicken.

5. (a) What is irradiated food?

It is a preservation method. Radioactive rays are passed through the food.

(b) State **two** effects of irradiation on food.
    (i) Destroys Bacteria
    (ii) It prolongs shelf life of food.

6. Explain the following and give an example of the use of each.

Biodegradable packaging Breaks down into the raw materials of nature

Use Paper bag - bread
Modified atmospheric packaging Air is removed and replaced with a controlled mixture of Gas and pack is heat-sealed
Use Fresh meat.

7. Identify **two** contaminants that may enter the food chain and in each case state a likely source and the possible effect on the body.

Contaminant	Source	Effect on the body
(i) lead	Saucepans	The brain.
(ii) Bacteria		

8. In relation to each nutrient listed, recommend **two** good sources for a vegan diet.

Nutrient	Sources for vegan diet	
Protein	Nuts	TUP
Calcium	Soye milk	Suya Cheese
Iron	Green leafy vegebables	wholemeal products

9. Explain **each** of the following:

Annuity mortgage _____

_____

Endowment mortgage _____

_____

_____

10. (a) State **three** advantages of credit buying.
   (i) Do not have to carry loge amount of money around
   (ii) Take advantages of discounts
   (iii) Con buy products pay later

   (b) Identify **three** areas controlled by the Consumer Credit Act (1995).
   (i) _____
   (ii) _____
   (iii) _____

11. (a) List **two** desirable properties of a fabric for upholstered furniture.
   (i) Comfortable
   (ii) long - lasting

(b) What information does the following label convey to the consumer?

RESISTANT

_____
_____
_____
_____
_____
_____
_____
_____
_____

12. In relation to the environment explain and give an example of each of the following:

Renewable resource This is a resource that will not run out

Example wind

_____

Non-renewable resource This is a resource that will run out

Example Oil.

Section B

Answer Question 1 and any other two questions from this section.
Question 1 is worth 80 marks.
Questions 2, 3, 4 and 5 are worth 50 marks each.

1. *'Fish and other seafood is becoming a more popular choice as an alternative to meat.'*
   Consumer Choice, June 2001

   The following chart provides information on the types of fish consumed.

   Estimated Consumption of Seafood in Ireland, 1997–2001 (*live weight tonnes*)

Fish type	1997	1999	2001
Salmon and trout	7,500	11,500	12,500
White fish	36,850	34,500	33,125
Tuna	4,100	6,200	7,100
Shellfish	3,490	4,050	4,565

   (Bord Iascaigh Mhara)

   (a) Using the information provided in the table comment on the consumer trends in fish consumption. Suggest reasons for such trends.

   (b) Give a detailed account of the nutritive value of fish.

   (c) State why oily fish is recommended for the diet of a person with coronary heart disease.

   (d) Oily fish is a good source of Vitamin D.
   Give an account of Vitamin D and refer to (i) properties, (ii) biological functions and (iii) recommended dietary allowance (RDA).

   (e) Give an account of **six** key factors that consumers should consider when buying fresh fish **and** fish products.

2. 'In Ireland during 1998 and 1999 almost 2,000 people became ill from infectious gastroenteritis, a form of food poisoning. The commonest sources of infections were restaurants, hotels and takeaways. Some outbreaks also occurred in private homes.'

Food Safety Authority of Ireland

(a) List **five** guidelines that should be followed to ensure the safe preparation and storage of food in the home.

(b) Explain how a Hazard Analysis Critical Control Point (HACCP) system can benefit a catering business in the prevention of food poisoning outbreaks.

(c) Differentiate between (i) infectious food poisoning and (ii) toxic food poisoning.

(d) Name and give a detailed account of any **one** type of food poisoning bacteria. Refer to (i) sources of infection, (ii) high-risk foods and (iii) symptoms.

3. *Brian and Helen Jones live with their two children, Colm, (4) and Niamh (2). Both parents work full time and have a combined net monthly income of €3,250. They also receive child benefit of €250 per month. Their mortgage repayment is €600 per month. They commute to work using the family car. Colm and Niamh attend the local crèche each day.*

(a) Outline the considerations that the Jones family should take into account when planning their household budget.

(b) Using the information given above, set out a monthly budget for the Jones family to ensure efficient management of financial resources.

(c) Give details of **one** health insurance scheme that you would recommend for this family. Give reasons for your choice.

(d) State how the family functions as a financial unit within the economy.

4. *A responsible consumer will make informed choices when selecting goods and services, will know how to get best value for money and know how to seek redress if things go wrong.*

   (a) Discuss **three** factors that affect consumers' decision-making when selecting goods and services.

   (b) Name **two** types of retail outlets where household appliances can be purchased. State **one** advantage and **one** disadvantage of each outlet.

   (c) Set out details of a study that you have undertaken on a household appliance with a heating element. Refer to:
   (i) working principle
   (ii) guidelines for using the appliance
   (iii) energy efficiency.

   (d) Outline the role of the Sale of Goods and Supply of Services Act (1980) in protecting the consumer should the product prove faulty.

5. *The 2002 Census of Population reveals the following results:*
   - *the number of divorced persons has trebled since 1996*
   - *the population is getting older*
   - *average family size has reduced to 1.6*

   (a) Describe **four** main functions of the family in modern society.

   (b) Explain how the role of older people within the family has changed as a result of social and economic factors.

   (c) Outline the historical development of the family in Ireland from the beginning of the twentieth century to the present day.

   (d) State how the family is protected by the Family Home Protection Act (1976).

Section C

Answer one elective question from this section.
Candidates who submitted Textiles, Fashion and Design coursework for
examination may <u>only</u> attempt Question 2.

Elective 1 – Home Design and Management
Candidates selecting this elective must answer 1(a) and either 1(b) <u>or</u> 1(c).

1. (a) *Ireland has one of the highest rates of home ownership in Europe.*
   The illustration below shows the new house types built in Ireland in 2002.

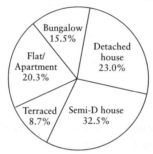

New House Types (whole country) 2002

(Department of the Environment,
Heritage and Local Government.
Annual Housing Bulletin, 2002).

   (i) Analyse <u>three</u> factors that have contributed to the distribution of new
       house types as shown in the pie chart above.
   (ii) Outline (a) the social, (b) the cultural and (c) the environmental factors
        that influence the choice of housing styles.
   (iii) Describe the procedure involved in obtaining planning permission to
         build a house.
   (iv) State the benefits of the National House Building Guarantee Scheme.

and

1. (b) *Excessive ventilation is as undesirable as insufficient ventilation as it can
   lead to low room temperatures, excessive draughts and high heating bills.*

   (i) State the importance of adequate ventilation in a house.
   (ii) Explain how natural ventilation is provided in a modern house.
   (iii) Suggest a suitable method of artificial ventilation for a kitchen. Explain
         the underlying principle of the suggested method.

or

1. (c) *The efficient use of energy is the responsibility of every consumer.*
In relation to energy use in the home give details of:
   (i) potential energy inefficiencies and strategies for improvement
   (ii) the effects of fuel emissions on the environment.

Elective 2 – Textiles, Fashion and Design

Candidates selecting this elective must answer 2(a) and either 2(b) or 2(c).

2. (a) *Clothing is often used to create an impression.*
   (i) Sketch and describe a formal outfit suitable for a teenager to wear to an interview.

   (ii) Indicate:
   (a) how the principles of design have been applied
   (b) how the design of the outfit reflects current fashion trends.

and

2. (b) *Different fibres are often blended together to produce a fabric that exhibits the most desirable characteristics of the fibres used.*

   Write up a profile of a blended fabric under the following headings:
   • Fibre composition
   • Yarn production
   • Fabric properties
   • Suitable uses of the fabric.

or

2. (c) (i) Discuss the contribution of Irish designers to the success of the clothing industry in Ireland.

   (ii) Outline the role played by the craft industry in Irish fashion.

Elective 3 – Social Studies

Candidates selecting this elective must answer 3(a) and either 3(b) **or** 3(c).

3. (a) *'In a post-industrial society increasing emphasis is placed on the ability to continuously acquire knowledge, skills and competencies in an environment of constant change.'*

Report of the Taskforce on Lifelong Learning, 2002

(i) Discuss the factors that affect educational achievement.

(ii) Name and give details of **two** initiatives that have improved access to second-chance education.

(iii) Analyse the possible reasons why many people return to education having concluded their initial education and/or training.

and

3. (b) *'40% of parents with young children use childcare regularly.'* CSO, 2003

(i) (a) Name **two** types of childcare available in your locality.
   (b) Outline the key considerations a parent should take into account when evaluating a childcare option.

(ii) Discuss the factors that have contributed to the increased participation of women in the workforce.

or

3. (c) *Changing work patterns have led to increased leisure time.*

(i) State the factors that influence family leisure patterns.

(ii) (a) Name **two** leisure activities available in your community for teenagers.
   (b) Analyse how **each** activity named contributes to the physical, social and emotional well-being of teenagers.

HOME ECONOMICS – SCIENTIFIC AND SOCIAL

HIGHER LEVEL

MARKING SCHEME AND SUMMARISED EXEMPLAR ANSWERS

Section A
Answer any ten questions from this section.
Each question is worth 6 marks.

1. (a)   (4)

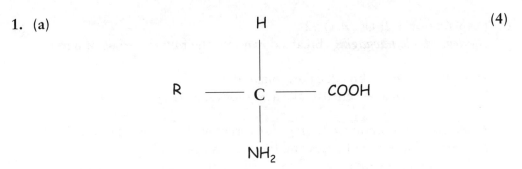

(b) Cannot be manufactured by the body, therefore must be obtained from the food we eat.   (2)

2. (a) Manufactures collagen; Helps absorb iron; Antioxidant; Fights infection; Maintains gums, bones and teeth; Prevents scurvy, Healing of wounds. (4)
   (b) Acts as a reducing agent, changes iron from its ferric form which is found in food into Ferrous form which can be absorbed by the bloodstream i.e. non-Haem iron into Haem iron.   (2)

3.   (6)

Dietary deficiency	Possible effect
Lack of Thiamine (B_1)	Beri Beri; Fatigue; Depression and Irritability; Memory loss
Lack of Folic Acid	Associated with birth defects and Spina bifida; Affects the growth and repair of body cells; Anaemia
Lack of Cobalamin (B_{12})	Pernicious anaemia; Nerve damage; increased susceptibility to disease

4. **(a)** (i) Starch (ii) Protein (Gluten) (iii) B group Vitamins and Vitamin E. (3)
   (b) When starch is mixed with liquid and heated, the starch cells burst
   and absorb water, this causes the mixture to thicken. (3)

5. **(a)** Irradiation is a preservation method. Radioactive rays are passed
   through food. (2)
   (b) (**Two from:**) (4)
   - Destroys bacteria and parasites
   - Vitamins can be destroyed.
   - It prolongs the shelf life of food.
   - It is also used on vegetables to prevent sprouting and on fruit to slow
     down ripening.
   - Free radicals and reactive molecules can develop in foods.

6. **(Explanation = 2; Use = 1) x2** (6)
   Biodegradable packaging Breaks down into the raw materials of nature

   Use Paper bag — bread, cakes, sugar, flour
          Cardboard — cereals, take away foods, eggs

   Modified atmospheric packaging Air is removed and replaced with
   a controlled mixture of gases and the pack is heat-sealed.

   Use Fresh meat, fish, fruit and vegetables, baked goods and cheese.

7. **(Identify =1; Source =1; Effect = 1) x2** (6)

	Contaminant	Source	Effect on the body
(i)	Mercury	Shell fish – industrial pollution of coastal waters	Damage to the central nervous system. Muscle wasting.
(ii)	Lead	Plumbing	Damage to the central nervous system. Muscle wasting.
(iii)	Tin and aluminium	Toothpaste, baking powder	Thought to affect Alzheimer's disease.
(iv)	Lubricants	Industrial waste	Nausea, Damage to the central nervous system.
(v)	Pesticides, herbicides, insecticide, chemicals and processing gas	From use of chemicals in agriculture, industry and households	Nausea, Damage to the central nervous system. Muscle wasting. →

(continued)

Contaminant	Source	Effect on the body
(vi) Hormones, Antibiotics	Animals injected to treat infection/disease	Increases basal metabolism. Can cause heart disease. Causes resistance to antibiotics.
(vii) Bacteria	Lack of hygiene	Nausea, vomiting

8. (6)

Nutrient	Sources for vegan diet
Protein	Textured vegetable protein, Soya beans, Pulse vegetables, Nuts
Calcium	Sesame seeds, Broccoli, Spinach, Fortified flour, Soya milk, Nuts, Vegan cheese, Calcium supplements, Fortified juices
Iron	Leafy green vegetables, Wholemeal products, Prune juice, Fortified juice, Nuts, Iron supplements

9. (2 points @ 3 marks each) (6)

Annuity mortgage Most common type of mortgage. Principal and Interest are paid monthly over a fixed period. Available at a fixed interest or variable rate that fluctuates.

Endowment mortgage This involves taking out a Life Assurance policy to cover the term of the loan. The proceeds of the policy are used to pay off the loan. During the term the borrower pays interest on the loan and a premium on the policy.

10. (a) (Three from:) (3)
   (i) The consumer has use of the goods before they are paid for
   (ii) Allows people to have goods they could not otherwise afford
   (iii) Enables consumers to meet unexpected costs and emergencies
   (iv) People can take advantage of special sales or promotions
   (v) No need to carry around large sums of money.

(b) (Three from:) (3)
   (i) Credit agreements should give the APR and outline how it was calculated
   (ii) Leases must be in writing and signed by all parties

(iii) Advertisements for credit must include a list of information which leaves the consumer in no doubt about extra charges, total cost of credit and number of instalments

(iv) Consumers entering a credit agreement must have a 10 day cooling off period during which they can withdraw from the agreement

(v) Bank charges

(vi) Mortgages

(vii) Money lenders

(viii) Conditions re: contacting borrowers

11. (a) (Two from:) (2)

(i) Durable (ii) Comfortable (iii) Resilient
(iv) Stain resistant (v) Hard wearing

(b) Materials meet the requirements for resistance to cigarette and match ignition (4)

12. (Explanation = 2 marks; Example = 1 mark) x2 (6)

Renewable resource A resource that will always be in supply
Example – Wind power, Water, Solar power, Biomass etc.

Non-renewable resource A resource than will be depleted
Example – Oil, coal, gas etc.

Section B
Answer Question 1 and any other two questions from this section.
Marks
Question 1 is worth 80 marks. Questions 2, 3, 4 and 5
are worth 50 marks each.

1. (a) (Expect 4 points @ 5 marks each) (20)

Salmon and Trout: More people are aware of the health benefits of oily fish and also due to increased fish farming etc.

White fish: Depletion of white fish stocks, due to over fishing of waters, Fishing laws, useful as part of healthy diet etc.

Tuna: Canned tuna mainly available in 1997. Influence of travel and eating abroad. Cost.

Shellfish: Fish farms. Trendy recipes. Influence of foreign travel. More afford-able etc.

(b) (Expect 4 points @ 3 marks each) (12)

Protein: High biological value.

Fats: Oily fish high in polyunsaturated fatty acids and Omega 3 fatty acids. No fat present in white fish

<u>Vitamins:</u> All fish high in B group vitamins. Oily fish rich in Vits A and D.
<u>Minerals:</u> Phosphorous, iodine and potassium found in most fish. Calcium found in fish of which the bones are eaten
<u>Carbohydrates:</u> No carbohydrates found in fish

(c) Polyunsaturated fatty acids (PUFA's) found in oily fish including Omega 3, are associated with reducing cholesterol and risk of heart disease. **(6)**

(d) **Expect 3 properties @ 3 marks each = 9** **(24)**
Expect 3 functions @ 3 marks each = 9
RDA = 6 marks
<u>Properties:</u> fat soluble/insoluble in water; heat stable; not affected by O_2; not affected by acids and alkalis
<u>Functions:</u> aids absorption of Calcium; healthy bones and teeth; prevents rickets/osteoporosis; normal cell growth; regulation of Calcium levels in the blood; regulation of immune system etc. Functioning of healthy nerves and muscle contractions.
<u>RDA:</u> Children = 7 – 10µg Adolescents = 15µg Adults = 10µg

(e) **(Expect 6 points @ 3 marks each)** **(18)**
2 points should relate to fresh fish; 2 points to fish products and any other 2 points
- Buy fresh fish in season
- The flesh of fresh fish should be plump and the eyes bulging. Scales should be moist and unbroken
- Medium size fish have the best flavour
- Buy from a reliable source
- Fish should have a fresh smell
- Mussels should not be open
- Smoked fish should look glossy
- Frozen fish should be solid
- Check sell-buy date

2. (a) **(Expect 5 guidelines @ 2 marks each)** **(10)**
(At least 2 should refer to preparation and 2 to storage and any one other)
- Handle food as little as possible during preparation
- Perishable foods should be stored in the fridge @ temps below 5°C
- Clean and disinfect surfaces often
- Cook food thoroughly to destroy bacteria
- Frozen foods should be thawed completely
- Never prepare cooked and raw foods on the same surface
- Certain foods should never be eaten raw e.g. eggs
- Left-overs should be cooled quickly and stored in fridge

- Store raw foods separate from cooked foods
- Keep food covered or in sealed containers
- Make sure storage areas are kept clean and well ventilated

(b) (Expect 3 points @ 4 marks each) (12)
- A HACCP system can identify potential hazards that could occur at certain points in the preparation of food.
- It could begin with e.g. the purchase of food, the delivery and storage of ingredients and the preparation, cooking storage and serving of food.
- Once the hazards have been identified they can then be controlled at certain stages called Control Points.
- These Controls can then be monitored and therefore prevent contamination.
- The system should be reviewed and evaluated.

(c) (Expect 2 explanations @ 4 marks each) (8)
<u>Infectious food poisoning:</u> Caused by the consumption of food that contains large amounts of pathogenic bacteria e.g. Salmonella
<u>Toxic food poisoning:</u> Ingesting food that is contaminated by a toxin produced by a bacterial cell

(d) (Name = 4 marks; 2 sources @ 2 marks each; 2 high risk foods @ 3 marks; 2 symptoms @ 3 marks each) (20)

3. **(a) (Expect 4 points @ 3 marks each)** (12)
- Base on net income
- Consider the ages of the family members
- Make a list of expenditure
- Plan for needs and essentials first
- Keep a record of what is spent in one month and make changes if necessary
- Allocate money for personal expenditure
- Allocate money for special occasions-Christmas, holidays etc.
- Plan savings for a rainy day

(b) (Expect 8 points @ 2 marks each) (16)
- <u>Total = €3,500</u>
- Mortgage = €600
- Household/Fuel 15% = €525
- Food 25% = €850
- Clothing 7% – 10% = €245
- Car 7% = €245
- Crèche 15% = €525
- Savings 5% = €175

- Health 5% = €175
- Leisure 5% = €175

(c) (Name = 3 marks; Details = 3 marks; 2 reasons @ 3 marks each)   (12)
Permanent Health Insurance/Salary Protection:
- protects if individual has to give up work due to illness
- individual receives a % of his/her salary
Voluntary Health Insurance:
- provides against the cost of medical treatment/consultants fees
- covers cost of hospital in-patient care
Critical Injury Policy:
- provides weekly income depending on amount of the premium
PRSI (Public Health Benefits):
- Entitles family to a range of benefits – medical, disability, dental etc.

(d) (Expect 2 points @ 5 marks each)   (10)
Family members who are working contribute to the financial success of the household purchasing food and necessities; Family provides accommodation for family members by purchasing a house or flat; Contribute taxes to the economy for the successful running of the country; Budget similar to Government budget; Spending creates new jobs; Savings accumulate money; Family depend on state in some circumstances etc.

4. (a) (Expect 3 factors @ 4 marks each)   (12)
- Amount of money available
- Time available to research
- Merchandising and Advertising
- Packaging
- Salespeople
- Peer pressure and influence of others
- Current trends
- Needs and wants

(b) (Name= 2 marks; advantage = 2 marks; disadvantage = 2 marks) x2 (12)
Retail Outlets: Small independent shops, Supermarkets, Department stores, Chain stores, Discount Stores, Markets.

(c)   (18)
(i) working principle (Expect 2 points @ 3 marks each) = 6
Electric energy is converted into heat energy in the element
(ii) guidelines for using the appliance (Expect 3 guidelines @ 3 marks each) = 9
(iii) energy efficiency. (Expect 1 point @ 3 marks each) = 3

(d) (Expect 2 points @ 4 marks each) (8)
- Retailer responsible for faulty goods so must sort out complaints
- Consumer entitled to refund, replacement or repair
- Manufacturer accepts responsibility for faults which occur in product within a reasonable period
- This can be upheld by the Small Claims Court

5. **(a) (Expect 4 functions @ 4 marks each)** (16)
   <u>Functions:</u> Physical; Economic; Emotional; Educational; Social

   (b) (Expect 3 points @ 4 marks each) (12)
   - Many are living independently on their own or in sheltered accommodation
   - Much to offer in terms of knowledge and life experience
   - Provide childminding for grand children
   - Provide financial support for their offspring
   - Take part in social activities and are less dependent on the family
   - Avail of support from voluntary services
   - Participate in voluntary services

   (c) (Expect 4 points @ 4 marks each) (16)

Past	Present
Extended family	Change in family structure — nuclear, blended
Mainly agricultural	
Mortality rate was high	Industry and Services
Strictly patriarchal	Life expectancy has improved
Large families	Egalitarian
Roles of men and women	Smaller families — Family planning
Education	
Standard of living	

   (d) (Expect 2 points @ 3 marks each) (6)
   Provides that one partner cannot sell, lease or mortgage the family home without the consent of the other. A spouse has to have written permission from the other.

Section C
Answer one elective question from this section.
Candidates who submitted Textiles, Fashion and Design coursework for
examination may <u>only</u> attempt Question 2.

Elective 1 — Home Design and Management (80 marks)
Candidates selecting this elective must answer 1 (a) and either 1 (b) <u>or</u> 1 (c).

1. (a) (i) (Expect 3 factors @ 5 marks each)   (15)
Economic factors e.g. Younger people earning more money, Buying as an
investment.
Social factor e.g. Family structure and sizes. Increase in population.
Government schemes: Planning laws- decrease in detached houses.
Apartments in urban areas. Terraced houses coming back into fashion.

  (ii) (Expect 3 points @ 5 marks each) one reference to each of (a),
    (b) and (c)   (15)
<u>Social</u> – Refer to: Personal preference, Occupation, Age, Social background,
Size of family, Life cycle of family etc.
<u>Cultural</u> – Refer to: Tradition, Historical influences, Aesthetic requirements etc.
<u>Environmental</u> – Refer to: Natural surroundings, Existing buildings, Green
living, Level of exposure etc.

  (iii) (Expect 4 points @ 3 marks each)   (12)
Full procedure expected for full marks
Notice of Planning permission published, Lodge application, Public inspection,
Site inspection, Permission granted.

  (iv) (Expect 2 points @ 4 marks each)   (8)
Registered builders. Certificate is issued when building is complete. Guarantees
against loss of deposit if builder goes bankrupt and against major structural
defects within ten years

and

1. (b)(i) (Expect 3 points @ 3 marks each)   (9)
  • Provides fresh air and removes impure air, Controls humidity, Controls
    temperature, Prevents condensation, Removes smells

  (ii) (Expect 3 points @ 3 marks each)   (9)
  • Natural methods – Fireplaces and flues, windows and doors, air bricks,
    vents/Coopers discs
  (iii) (Name = 4 marks; Principle – Expect 2 points @ 4 marks each)   (12)
<u>Extractor fan:</u> Propellers driven by Electricity, Draw out stale air, Shutters
close when not in use.
<u>Cooker hood:</u> Ducted–Air sucked out of room by fan, Ductless air can be
recycled. Filters remove fumes and absorb grease

or

1. (c) (i) (**Expect 3 inefficiencies @ 3marks each and 3 strategies @ 3 marks each**) (18)
   <u>Inefficiencies:</u> Old Appliances, Ordinary bulbs, Un-lagged cylinder, Baths, Draughts, dripping taps, Attic and wall insulation etc.
   <u>Strategies:</u> Buy energy efficient appliances, Replace bulbs with CFLs, Lag cylinder, Use showers, Draught proof or double glaze, Fix dripping taps etc.
   (ii) (**Expect 3 effects @ 4 marks each**) (12)
   Greenhouse effect/Climate change, Acid rain, Smog, Ozone.

Elective 2 – Textiles, Fashion and Design (40 marks)

2. (a) (i) (**Expect 5 marks for sketch and 4 marks for description**) (9)
   (ii) (a) (**Expect 2 principles of design @ 4 marks each**) = 8 marks (16)
   Balance, Proportion, Emphasis, Rhythm
   (b) (**Expect 2 points @ 4 marks each**) = 8 marks

and

2. (b) (15)
   <u>fibre composition</u> = 2 marks
   e.g. <u>Poly-cotton</u> – Polyethylene + Cellulose

   <u>yarn production</u> (**Expect 2 marks for each fibre, 1mark for blending**)= 5 marks
   <u>Cotton</u> – develops inside the boll of the cotton plant. The boll opens and the fibres are exposed. The fibre is removed and processed.
   <u>Polyester</u> – A viscous liquid is created from chemicals and extruded through the fine holes in a nozzle or spinneret. The hair-like strands are then cooled and stretched. The two fibres are then spun together to form poly-cotton.

   <u>fabric properties</u> (**Expect 2 @ 2 marks each**) = 4 marks
   Will dry faster than 100% cotton, Easier to iron, Can be set into pleats.

   <u>suitable uses of the fabric.</u> (**Expect 2 @ 2 marks each**) = 4 marks

or

2. (c) (i) (**Expect 3 points @ 3 marks each**) (9)
   Sybil Connolly and Irene Gilbert first started exporting clothing in the 1950s. The Grafton Academy trains some of our contemporary designers. John Rocca uses Irish made fabrics. Mary Robinson wore one of Louise Kennedy's creations for her inauguration. Phillip Tracey is world famous for his creative hats etc.

   (iii) (**Expect 2 points @ 3 marks each**) (6)
   Influence of Kilkenny Design, Knitted garments very fashionable-Lainey Keogh, Aran. Hand made jewellery, Newbridge jewellery, Carrickmacross lace. Irish leather goods etc.

Elective 3 – Social Studies (80 marks)

3. (a) (i) (Expect 3 points @ 4 marks each) (12)
Intelligence, Influence of family and home, Family size, Environment, the school attended etc.

 (ii) (Expect 2 @ 7 marks each) (14)
VTOS – Courses of up to 2 years for long term unemployed over 21. Personal development, business and computer skills. Training allowance paid.
Youthreach – Managed by VECs. Targets young people between 15 and 18 who have no formal education. Provides the knowledge, skills and attitudes to make transition to work and adult life.
FÁS – Provides community training work shops for adults.
PLC courses – Offer training with work experience. Means of getting into Further Education. Variety of courses. No fees paid. Exams under NCVA certification.
Distance learning – Open university and OSCAIL at DCU. Build up Degree through Credits. No entry requirements.
BTEA – Funded by Department of Social, Community and Family Affairs. Unemployed for 15 months and over 21. Many lone parents. Full time or part time. Receive social welfare payments and a small grant.
Special Initiatives for Disadvantaged Adults Scheme – Funds through VEC for books, materials etc.
Teagasc – Provides courses and certification in agriculture.
Community Education Schemes, Macra na Feirme, Adult Literacy Initiatives etc.

(iii) (Expect 4 points @ 6 marks each) (24)
self satisfaction, professional development, improve promotion chances, keeping skills up to date, the social aspect of life etc.

and

3. (b)(i) (a) (Expect 2 @ 2 marks each) = 4 (14)
 Crèches, Playgroups, Childminders, Nursery schools, Au-pairs
 (b) (Expect 5 points @ 2 marks each) =10 (14)
 Premises registered, Cost, Location, Materials age appropriate, Training of carers, Condition of premises, Ratio of carers to children, Safety, Insurance, Activities etc.

 (ii) (Expect 4 points @ 4 marks each) (16)
 Better educated, Economic reasons, Flexible hours, Job sharing, Maternity Leave, Working from home, Fewer children, Equal pay.

or

3. (c) (i) (Expect 4 factors @ 3 marks each)   (12)

Social factor, Age of children, Gender, Occupation, Class, Cost, Location.

(ii) (a) (Expect 2 @ 3 marks each) = 6.   (18)

(b) (Expect 2 @ 6 marks each) = 12

Must refer to Physical, Social and Emotional in each case.

LEAVING CERTIFICATE EXAMINATION 2005

HOME ECONOMICS – SCIENTIFIC AND SOCIAL

HIGHER LEVEL

FRIDAY, 10 JUNE — AFTERNOON, 2.00 to 4.30

280/320 MARKS

Instructions to Candidates

Section A   There are **twelve** questions in this section.
Candidates are required to answer any **ten** questions.
Each question carries **6** marks.

Section B   There are **five** questions in this section.
Candidates are required to answer **Question 1 and any other two questions**.
Question **1** is worth **80** marks.
Questions **2, 3, 4** and **5** are worth **50** marks each.

Section C   There are **three** questions in this section.
Candidates are required to answer **one** elective question to include
part **(a)** and either part **(b)** or part **(c)**.
**Candidates who submitted Textiles, Fashion and Design coursework
for examination may only attempt Question 2 from this section.**
Electives **1** and **3** are worth **80** marks each. Elective **2** is worth **40** marks.

Answer any <u>ten</u> questions from this section.
Each question is worth 6 marks.
Write your answers in the spaces provided.

1. Name <u>one</u> food source of <u>each</u> of the proteins listed below. (6)

Protein	Food Source
Albumin	
Caesinogen	
Collagen	
Actin	
Gluten	
Myosin	

2. (a) State <u>two</u> functions of lipids in the body. (2)

(i) _____

(ii) _____

(b) Complete the following table in relation to the digestion of lipids. (4)

Digestive Gland	Secretion	Enzyme	Change
Pancreas			

3. (a) State <u>two</u> biological functions of water. (4)

(i) _____

(ii) _____

(b) State <u>one</u> property of water. (2)

_____

4. (a) State <u>two</u> effects of Ultra-Heat Treatment (UHT) on milk. (4)

(i) _____

(ii) _____

(b) What is a fortified food? (2)

_____

_____

5. **(a)** Give <u>one</u> reason why a food manufacturer might use sensory analysis testing. (2)

_____

_____

(b) Name <u>two</u> categories of sensory analysis tests. List <u>one</u> test from each category. (4)

Category	Test

6. **(a)** State <u>two</u> uses of micro-organisms in food production. (4)

(i) _____

_____

(ii) _____

_____

(b) Suggest <u>one</u> method of controlling enzymic spoilage in foods. (2)

_____

7. **(a)** List <u>two</u> career opportunities in the food industry (2)

(i) _____

(ii) _____

(b) State <u>two</u> ways that the Food Safety Authority of Ireland (FSAI) supports the work of the food industry. (4)

(i) _____

_____

(ii) _____

_____

8. State <u>one</u> function of <u>each</u> of the food additives listed below. (6)

Food Additive	Function
Flavour Enhancer	
Emulsifier	
Antioxidant	

9. State the function of <u>each</u> of the following parts of a refrigerator: (6)

the thermostat _____

_____

_____

the refrigerant _____

_____

_____

10. In relation to the *management process* explain and give an example of <u>each</u> of the following: (6)

Input _____

_____

Example _____

Output _____

_____

Example _____

11. Name and explain the <u>two</u> compulsory deductions taken from a person's gross income. (6)

(i) _____

_____

_____

(ii) _____

_____

12. Identify <u>three</u> recent trends in housing developments in Ireland. (6)

(i) _____

_____

(ii) _____

_____

(iii) _____

_____

Section B

Answer Question 1 and any other two questions from this section.
Question 1 is worth 80 marks. Questions 2, 3, 4 and 5 are worth 50 marks each.

1. *A recent survey found the main sources of carbohydrate in the Irish diet are as illustrated below.*

Main Sources of Carbohydrate in the Irish Diet

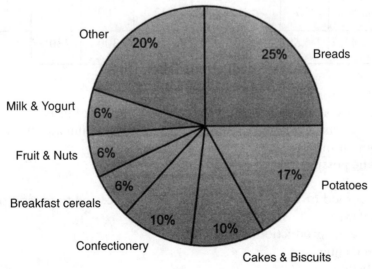

(North-South Food Consumption Survey, 2001)

(a) Using the information provided in the chart, and having regard to current healthy eating guidelines, suggest **three** ways that the food sources of carbohydrates in the diet should be adjusted.
Give a reason for **each** suggestion. (18)

(b) Describe the chemical structure of **each** of the following:
(i) monosaccharides
(ii) disaccharides
(iii) polysaccharides.
Give **one** example of each. (24)

(c) Name and explain **three** properties of carbohydrates that are useful in food preparation. (18)

(d) Evaluate the role of food labelling in assisting the consumer when selecting foods. (20)

2. *Preservation aims to ensure that the colour, flavour, texture and nutritive value of the preserved food is as near as possible to the fresh food.*

Nutritional Value of Fresh, Frozen and Canned Peas

Nutritional information per 100g	Energy (kcals)	Protein (g)	Carbohydrate (g)	Vitamin C (mg)	Vitamin A (µg)	Sodium (mg)	Iron (mg)	Thiamine (mg)
Fresh peas (raw)	67	5.8	10.6	25	300	1	1.9	32
Frozen peas (raw)	53	5.7	7.2	17	300	3	1.5	32
Canned peas	47	4.6	7	8	300	230	1.6	13

(a) Using the information in the table, comment on:
(i) the effects of freezing on the Vitamin C content of peas
(ii) the effects of canning on the Vitamin C, the Sodium and the Thiamine content of peas.
Give **one** possible reason in each case. (24)

(b) Profile a food of your choice that has been processed to extend the shelf life. Refer to:
(i) stages of production
(ii) packaging
(iii) labelling. (26)

3. *The microwave cooker has become an integral part of the kitchen in recent years.*

   (a) Set out details of a study you have carried out on a microwave cooker. Refer to:
   - (i) working principle
   - (ii) modern design features
   - (iii) guidelines for using the appliance. (30)

   (b) Evaluate the contribution of the microwave cooker to modern food preparation and cooking practices. (12)

   (c) Outline the protection provided to the consumer by the Hire Purchase Act 1960. (8)

4. *Studies show that impulse buying can account for 65% of purchases in supermarkets.*

   (Consumer Choice May 2001)

   (a) Describe **four** in-store techniques that supermarkets use to encourage consumer spending. (20)

   (b) Name **three** research methods used to gather information on the consumer. Explain how consumer research benefits (i) the retailer and (ii) the consumer. (19)

   (c) Name and outline the role of any **one** voluntary agency concerned with consumer protection. (11)

5. *Parents / legal guardians have the primary responsibility for the upbringing and development of their children. The State assists parents/legal guardians in this responsibility.*

   (Article 18, UN Convention on the Rights of Children)

   (a) Outline **four** rights of children within the family. (12)
   (b) Discuss how the state assists the family in the rearing of children. (18)
   (c) Analyse how (i) social factors and (ii) economic factors affect parenting roles within the family unit. (20)

Section C

Answer one elective question from this section.
Candidates who submitted Textiles, Fashion and Design coursework for examination may <u>only</u> attempt Question 2.

Elective 1 – Home Design and Management (80 marks)

Candidates selecting this elective must answer 1 (a) and either 1 (b) <u>or</u> 1 (c).

1. (a) *Colm and Ann Smyth have two children, Alan (16 months) and Aoife (3 yrs). They have recently moved into their new house. The back of the house is south-facing. To cut down on costs they have decided to carry out the interior design work themselves.*

    (i) Give an account of the factors that this couple should consider when planning the interior design of their home. (20)

    (ii) Design and sketch the layout of any <u>one</u> room in the house. In relation to the room describe <u>each</u> of the following:
       (a) the colour scheme
       (b) the lighting
       (c) the flooring. (20)

    (iii) Explain how any <u>two</u> principles of design have been applied when designing the layout of the room. (10)

and

1. (b) *The number of private rented dwellings almost doubled between 1991–2002.*

(Census, 2002)

    (i) Give an account of the comparative costs of buying a place to live and renting accommodation. (15)

    (ii) Comment on the adequacy of housing provision in Ireland to meet the variation in housing needs. (15)

or

1. (c) (i) Name the <u>two</u> main types of plastic used in the home. In relation to <u>each</u> list (a) its uses and (b) its properties. (20)

    (ii) Explain the underlying principle involved in double glazing as a method of reducing heat loss through windows. (10)

Elective 2 – Textiles, Fashion and Design (40 marks)
Candidates selecting this elective must answer 2 (a) and either 2 (b) <u>or</u> 2 (c).

2. (a) *Clothing design aims to produce a garment that is aesthetically pleasing and fit for its purpose.*
    (i) Sketch and describe a winter jacket suitable for a primary school student.
        (9)

    (ii) In relation to the fabric for the jacket, give details of:
        (a) type of fabric and reasons for choice
        (b) <u>one</u> fabric performance test that could be carried out to determine the suitability of the fabric
        (c) <u>one</u> functional finish that could be applied to the fabric.   (16)

and

2. (b) *Knitted fabrics are a popular choice for autumn and winter fashion collections.*
    (i) Explain how knitted fabric is constructed.   (9)
    (ii) List <u>two</u> desirable properties of knitted fabric.   (6)

or

2. (c) (i) Assess the impact of industrial influences on the clothing industry in Ireland.   (9)
    (ii) Discuss <u>one</u> career opportunity in the clothing industry.   (6)

Elective 3 – Social Studies (80 marks)
Candidates selecting this elective must answer 3 (a) and either 3 (b) <u>or</u> 3 (c).

3. (a) *Volunteering is the commitment of time and energy for the benefit of society and the local community. It can empower people to fulfil their potential while contributing to social and environmental change.*
        (Volunteering Ireland 2004)

    (i) Differentiate between (a) voluntary work and (b) unpaid work. (10)
    (ii) With reference to the above statement, discuss:
        (a) how voluntary work empowers a person to fulfil his/her potential
        (b) how voluntary work contributes to social and environmental change in the local community.   (24)
    (iii) Identify and explain the factors that affect attitudes to work.   (16)

and

3. (b) *Employment is expected to grow by 23,0000 while unemployment will average 5%.*

(Budget 2004)

    (i) Name and give details of one state initiative that encourages foreign investment thus creating employment. (10)

    (ii) Discuss the impact of developing technology on work and employment. (20)

or

3. (c) **Education provision should accommodate students with different needs.**

    (i) Give an account of the supports provided in second-level schools for students with special education needs. (18)

    (ii) Outline the benefits of pre-school education. (12)

LEAVING CERTIFICATE EXAMINATION, 2005

HOME ECONOMICS – SCIENTIFIC AND SOCIAL

ORDINARY LEVEL

FRIDAY, 10 JUNE – AFTERNOON, 2.00 to 4.30

280/320 MARKS

Instructions to Candidates

Section A   There are **twelve** questions in this section.
Candidates are required to answer any **ten** questions.
Each question carries **6** marks.

Section B   There are **five** questions in this section.
Candidates are required to answer **Question 1 and any other two questions.**
Question 1 is worth 80 marks.
Questions 2, 3, 4 and 5 are worth 50 marks each.

Section C   There are **three** questions in this section.
Candidates are required to answer **one** elective question to include
part (a) and either **part (b) or part (c).**
**Candidates who submitted Textiles, Fashion and Design coursework
for examination may <u>only</u> attempt Question 2 from this section.**
Electives 1 and 3 are worth 80 marks each. Elective 2 is worth 40
marks.

Section A

Answer any <u>ten</u> questions from this section.
Each question is worth 6 marks.
Write your answers in the spaces provided.

1. (a) List the *elements* found in protein. (4)

   _____

   (b) Explain what is meant by *primary* protein structure. (2)

   _____

   _____

2. (a) Name <u>two</u> types of fatty acids and list <u>one</u> food source of each type. (4)

Type of fatty acid	Food source

   (b) What is an essential fatty acid? (2)

   _____

   _____

3. (a) State <u>one</u> function of folate (folic acid). (2)

   _____

   (b) Name <u>two</u> good dietary sources of folate (folic acid). (4)

   (i) _____

   (ii) _____

4. (a) List <u>two</u> factors that influence the energy requirements of adults. (4)

   (i) _____

   (ii) _____

   (b) Explain the term *Energy Balance*. (2)

   _____

   _____

5. **(a)** Name __two__ water-soluble vitamins. (2)

(i) _____

(ii) _____

(b) List __two__ guidelines that should be followed when preparing vegetables in order to reduce vitamin loss. (4)

(i) _____

(ii) _____

6. **(a)** State __two__ reasons why food is processed. (4)

(i) _____

(ii) _____

(b) Name __two__ types of additives commonly used in processed food. (2)

(i) _____

(ii) _____

7. Classify fresh fish and give __one__ example of each class. (6)

Classification of fresh fish	Example

8. Explain __three__ effects of cooking on meat. (6)

(i) _____

_____

(ii) _____

_____

(iii) _____

_____

9. (a) State the purpose of family resource management. (2)

_____

_____

   (b) List **two** factors that affect the management of family resources. (4)

   (i) _____

   (ii) _____

10. Suggest a reason why **two** of the properties listed below are considered important when caring for fabrics. (6)

Property	Reason
Crease resistant	
Strong when wet	
Colour-fast	

11. (a) State **two** consumer responsibilities. (4)

   (i) _____

   (ii) _____

   (b) Name **one** voluntary agency concerned with consumer protection. (2)

12. Outline **three** factors that determine (influence) a person's choice of housing. (6)

   (i) _____

   (ii) _____

   (iii) _____

Section B

Answer Question 1 and any other two questions from this section.
Question 1 is worth 80 marks. Questions 2, 3, 4 and 5 are worth 50 marks each.

1. *A local restaurant has a choice of three meats to add to a pasta dish. The main nutrients present in each of the three meats are listed below.*

Nutritional Comparison of Ingredients per 100g

	Minced beef	Chicken fillet	Bacon
Energy (kcals)	221	116	428
Protein (g)	18.8	21.8	14.2
Lipids (g)	16.2	3.2	41.2
Carbohydrate (g)	0	0	0
Iron (mg)	2.7	0.5	1.0

(a) Using the information provided in the table and bearing in mind current healthy eating guidelines, recommend **one** meat for use in the pasta dish. Give **three** reasons for your choice. (16)

(b) Suggest a suitable accompaniment for the pasta dish referred to above. Give **two** reasons for your choice. (12)

(c) Give an account of lipids (fats) and refer to:
　(i) functions in the body
　(ii) sources in the diet
　(iii) properties
　(iv) energy value. (32)

(d) Summarise **five** factors that consumers should consider when buying meat and meat products. (20)

2. Sarah (16) attends her local post-primary school and gets the bus to school at 8.00 a.m. and returns home at 5.00 p.m. The table below shows the meals eaten by Sarah on a typical school day.

Breakfast	Nothing
Mid-morning	Chocolate bar Can of cola
Lunch	Sausage roll Packet of crisps Can of fizzy orange drink
Evening meal	Deep fried chicken and chips Ice cream Glass of water

(a) Identify and explain **four** possible diet-related problems that may arise if Sarah continues with this type of diet. (16)

(b) Suggest alternative (other) foods for Sarah's mid-morning snack and lunch. (10)

(c) State how the foods you have suggested meet the nutritional requirements of a teenager. (12)

(d) Discuss **three** factors that affect the food choices of teenagers. (12)

3. *The results of a food safety survey showed that only 22.5% of consumers identified 1°C to 5°C as the correct fridge temperature. Food poisoning bacteria were found in 40% of fridges tested.*

(*Consumer Choice*, June 2003)

(a) Give an account of the main causes of food spoilage. (16)

(b) Set out details of a study you have undertaken on a refrigeration appliance. Refer to:
   (i) the general criteria to be considered when selecting the appliance
   (ii) guidelines for use
   (iii) **two** modern design features. (34)

4. *John is 25 years old. His net weekly income is €370. He shares a house with three others and commutes to work each day by bus. He is a member of the local health and fitness club that has an annual membership charge of €350. He is planning to buy a car next year.*

(a) Using the information given above, plan and set out a weekly budget for John to ensure that he uses his money wisely. (24)

(b) Name and give details of **one** savings scheme that John could use in order to save for a car. Give **two** reasons for your choice. (16)

(c) Name **two** items of information, as required by the Consumer Credit Act (1995), that must be included in an advertisement for buying goods on credit. (10)

5. *The traditional family unit in Ireland is still the family based on marriage.*
(Consumer Choice, October 2003)

(a) Outline **four** conditions that are necessary to make a marriage legally valid in Ireland. (16)

(b) Identify and give an account of the options that are available to couples that are experiencing difficulties in their marriage. (24)

(c) Explain how marriage customs can vary between different cultures. (10)

Section C

Answer <u>one</u> question from this section.
Candidates who submitted Textiles, Fashion and Design coursework for examination may <u>only</u> attempt Question 2.

Elective 1 – Home Design and Management (80 marks)
Candidates selecting this elective must answer 1 (a) and either 1 (b) <u>or</u> 1 (c).

1. (a) The diagram below shows a floor plan for a three-bedroom bungalow.

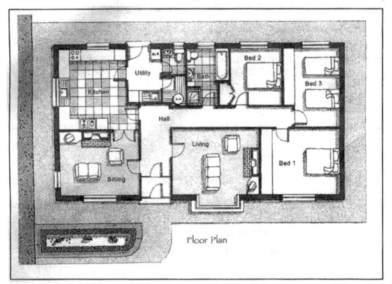

Publishers: Plan-A-Home, Lower Main St., Letterkenny, Co. Donegal

(i) Discuss the suitability of the house plan in the diagram above, for a couple with two teenage children. (15)

(ii) Give a brief account of **four** factors that should be considered when designing a family home. (16)

(iii) Outline the procedure (steps) involved in obtaining full planning permission. (10)

(iv) Suggest **three** actions that could be taken when building a house in order to improve energy efficiency. (9)

and

1. (b) (i) Give an account of the factors that should be considered when choosing floor coverings for the home. (16)

(ii) Recommend **one** type of floor covering for a kitchen. Give **two** reasons for your choice. (14)

or

1. (c) *Government policy aims to enable every household to have an affordable dwelling of good quality.*

 (Department of the Environment, Heritage and Local Government.
 Statement of Strategy 2001–2004)

 (i) Name and give details of any <u>one</u> house purchase scheme offered by local authorities to persons who are unable to finance a home of their own. (15)

 (ii) Comment on the provision of amenities for families in modern housing developments. (15)

Elective 2 – Textiles, Fashion and Design (40 marks)
Candidates selecting this elective must answer 2 (a) and either 2 (b) <u>or</u> 2 (c).

2. (a) *Leisure wear is essential in a teenager's wardrobe.*

 (i) Sketch and describe a tracksuit suitable for a teenager. (13)

 (ii) Explain how you have applied the following principles of design:
 • emphasis
 • balance (6)

 (iii) Name a fabric construction technique suitable for a sportswear fabric. Give <u>one</u> reason for your choice. (6)

and

2. (b) (i) Discuss <u>three</u> factors that influence clothing requirements. (9)

 (ii) Evaluate (assess) <u>two</u> accessories currently popular in teenage fashion. (6)

or

2. (c) *Developments in the textile industry has led to an increased range of man-made fabrics on the market.*

 (i) Write up a profile of a fabric made from manufactured fibres using the following headings:
 • fibre production
 • desirable properties
 • undesirable properties. (15)

Elective 3 – Social Studies (80 marks)
Candidates selecting this elective must answer 3 (a) and either 3 (b) or 3 (c).

3. (a) *The number of women in the labour force has increased significantly. In 2002 the female participation rate was 49%.*

(Census of Population, 2003).

    (i) Give an account of the reasons why the number of women in paid employment has increased in recent years. (20)

    (ii) Discuss how the increase in the number of dual-career women has impacted on (effects) (a) parental and (b) home-care responsibilities. (20)

    (iii) Name and give details of any **one** Government scheme that helps to reduce expenditure for low-income families. (10)

and

3. (b) *In today's society the need for leisure time is greater than ever.*
    (i) Discuss the reasons why leisure is important in today's society. (15)
    (ii) Give an account of **three** factors that influence family leisure patterns. (15)

or

3. (c) (i) Discuss the importance of community-based employment schemes for (a) the individual and (b) the local area. (20)

    (ii) Explain how the Protection of Young Persons (Employment) Act (1996) protects the interests of young people in the workplace. (10)